D1257986

THE SEACOAST READER

THE SEACOAST READER

Edited by John A. Murray

The Lyons Press

Printed in the United States of America
10 9 8 7 6 5 4 3 2 1

Library of Congress Cataloging-in-Publication Data

The seacoast reader / edited by John A. Murray.
     p. cm.— (A Nature conservancy book)
   ISBN 1-55821-781-9 (cl). — ISBN 1-55821-782-7 (pb)
   1. Coastal ecology. 2. Natural history. 3. Coasts.
I. Murray, John A., 1954– . II. Series.
QH541.5.C65S48 1999
577.5'1—dc21   99-12723
                                                      CIP

This book is dedicated to the memory of my mother, Patricia Hall Murray, who dearly loved the seacoasts, from Cape Cod to Cape Canaveral, and always made certain that her children spent a portion of every summer at "the shore."

Contents

Foreword   xi

Preface   xv

Introduction   xvii

1   BARRY LOPEZ
    A Presentation of Whales (from *Crossing
    Open Ground*)   1

2   HENRY DAVID THOREAU
    The Shipwreck (from *Cape Cod*)   21

3   JOHN MUIR
    The Discovery of Glacier Bay (from *Travels in
    Alaska*)   29

4   KENNETH BROWER
    On the Reef, Darkly   43

5   CHARLES DARWIN
    Galapagos Archipelago (from *Voyage of the
    Beagle*)   57

6   JAN DEBLIEU
    April Blow (from *Hatteras Journal*)   71

7   DANIEL DUANE
    Something Wicked This Way Comes   87

8   MARYBETH HOLLEMAN
    In This Light   95

Contents

9 WILLIAM W. WARNER
   The Bay (from *Beautiful Swimmers*) 105

10 GILBERT KLINGEL
   The Marvel of a Tide (from *Inagua*) 113

11 NANCY LORD
   A Day in the Life (from *Fishcamp*) 131

12 JOHN COLE
   from *Striper* 147

13 RICK BASS
   Hawaii 171

14 SUSAN ZWINGER
   Becoming Water 189

15 JEFF RIPPLE
   Where the Suwannee Meets the Sea 195

16 JENNIFER ACKERMAN
   Spindrift (from *Notes from the Shore*) 201

17 HENRY BESTON
   Orion Rises on the Dunes (from *The Outermost House*) 213

18 JOHN HAY
   Who Owns the Beach? (from *The Great Beach*) 217

19 MARK TWAIN
   The Hawaiian Coast (from *Roughing It*) 227

20 RACHEL CARSON
   The World of Reef Flats (from *The Edge of the Sea*) 241

Contents

21 JACK CONNOR
    from *Season at the Point*   245

22 JOHN A. MURRAY
    Island in the Stream   259

Notes on Contributors   283

Acknowledgments   289

About The Nature Conservancy and The
Coastal and Marine Program   291

$\mathcal{F}$OREWORD

$\mathcal{T}$hroughout the ages, people have been entranced, enchanted, and, at times, haunted by the seas. Melville wrote of them as vast open expanses "whose gently awful stirrings seem to speak of some human soul beneath." In our lifetime, the exploration of the seas has taken on new energy, thanks to an underwater technological revolution and the courage and vision of pioneering explorers such as Jacques Cousteau, Robert Ballard, and Silvia Earle. Furthermore, society as a whole is becoming increasingly aware of the importance of the oceans to our economic and environmental well-being.

In the five decades that The Nature Conservancy has worked to help preserve our common natural heritage, we have become well known for our work in terrestrial habitats. But in recent years the siren call of the seas has also beckoned.

We have sound reasons to heed this call. Shallow coastal ecoregions such as estuaries, coral reefs, kelp and mangrove forests, seagrass meadows, and tidepools are among the planet's most productive habitats. For example, the so-called margins of the ocean where land touches sea make up just 0.5 percent of the sea's volume, yet provide habitat for roughly 50 percent of harvested fish. Coral reefs, which are under great stress, are second only to rainforests in species diversity. In sheer economic terms, outdoor recreation and tourism, which depend on healthy coastal and marine ecosystems, account for more than half of ocean-related economic activity.

To protect these priceless biological resources, The Nature Conservancy has made coastal and marine conservation an organizational priority and will address the most serious threats to marine biodiversity, from cyanide fishing in the Asia-Pacific region to habitat destruction along the Gulf Coast to nutrification in the Caribbean. Currently, we are using promising new conservation strategies at a number of key sites in the United States, Latin America, the

Caribbean, and the Asia-Pacific region to address the most pressing near-shore environmental needs.

For example, to combat the deadly use of sodium cyanide to capture live reef fish for the restaurant and aquarium markets in the western Pacific, the Conservancy is helping Papua New Guinea develop and implement strict national fisheries plans. In Palau and many other places, we are working with government and business partners to install mooring buoys at popular dive sites to prevent anchor damage to coral reefs. To deter the unsustainable harvesting of fish in Belize's Port of Honduras, Conservancy field personnel are helping train fishermen to become catch-and-release sportfishing guides. Along the rich wetlands and lagoons of Upper Laguna Madre, Mexico, we are working with Mexican ranchers to conserve wetlands that provide critically important freshwater habitat for wintering waterfowl, shorebirds, and near-shore marine life. And here on American soil, we are helping the states of Florida, Georgia, and Alabama to develop a viable plan to protect natural water flows in the Apalachicola-Chatahoochee-Flint river basin, which feeds into Apalachicola Bay and the Gulf of Mexico.

We have assembled *The Seacoast Reader* to celebrate the beautiful and complex divide between land and sea and, we hope, to spur the imagination of lovers of seas and coasts everywhere. Perhaps you are not presently sitting on your favorite tropical beach, or walking on a rocky shore while listening to the mournful bellow of a lighthouse foghorn. But if you sit back and let your spirit of discovery and adventure soar, this treasury of essays from some of the most cherished names and brightest contemporary talents in American letters will take you on a memorable journey to twenty-two coastal and offshore places spanning three continents.

This is a truly impressive collection of writers. I hope you will share my pleasure in reading John Muir, Henry David Thoreau, and Mark Twain tackle subjects far afield from their traditional emphases on redwood forests, New England ponds, and heartland rivers. Or perhaps you will savor the graceful prose of Rachel Carson, which is as much a part of the Carson legacy as her prophetic work on pesticide pollution. Also, many of you will relish the opportunity to discover the tsunami-like power of such current writers as Rick Bass, Barry Lopez, and William Warner.

Because of The Nature Conservancy's unique role in preserving many of the planet's "Last Great Places," I am gratified that several of our long-term conservation projects are situated at locations highlighted in *The Seacoast Reader*. I hope you get the opportunity at some point to see and experience our community-oriented and science-based work at such coastal gems as the Peconic Bioreserve on Long Island, New York; New Jersey's Cape May Peninsula; Maryland's and Virginia's Chesapeake Bay; Georgia's Cumberland Island; the Florida Keys; the Galapagos Islands; and Palau, Micronesia. These projects reflect the seriousness with which we take the responsibility to ensure that the world's timeless coastal wonders do not forever vanish from our midst.

In assembling this collection, we received wonderful cooperation from the contributors and publishers who allowed us to reprint these works. I hope that in reading this book you will, like a child holding a seashell to her ear to listen for the roar of the ocean, experience a special link to the wonders of nearby and distant shores.

John C. Sawhill
President and Chief Executive Officer
The Nature Conservancy

$\mathcal{P}$REFACE

$\mathcal{J}$his series of nature anthologies, published in collaboration with The Nature Conservancy, is dedicated to bringing readers the finest nature writing from the past and present. Each book is devoted to a single environmental subject and alternates classic selections with contemporary writings. The first volume is dedicated to rivers. This second volume celebrates the beauty and majesty of the seacoasts. The third will focus on the literature of mountains. Future volumes in the series will explore writings about forests, endangered species, wetlands, lakes, deserts, grasslands, urban nature, and oceans.

As always, I am committed to featuring the work of undiscovered and emerging writers as well as the work of well-established and mature authors. If you have or know of superb writings on nature, please send them to me at: P.O. Box 102345, Denver, CO 80250. I am particularly interested in writing from the following groups: (1) writers known only locally or regionally but with potential for national acclaim, (2) writers from the Midwest, Northeast, and Deep South, (3) women writers and writers from ethnic groups offering alternative perspectives on nature, and (4) writers with experiences abroad. I promise to respond to each submission. Working together—readers and editor—we can build anthologies in the future that will hold both literary excellence and thematic and stylistic diversity as the standard.

I have many thanks to give. First, the writers and their publishers have been extremely cooperative and I thank them all; no anthology is possible without such quick and enthusiastic assistance. My editor, Lilly Golden, has been wonderfully helpful; all authors should be blessed with such warm, energetic, and perspicacious guidance. I must, too, thank my readers. Over the five years in which I edited the Sierra Club nature writing annuals, you constantly brightened my days with postcards, letters, and phone calls.

Finally, I must give thanks to the Murray family for their love and support, and especially my nine-year-old son, Naoki.

—J.A.M.
Denver, Colorado

$\mathcal{I}$NTRODUCTION

For two nights and two days, in the vastness of the sea,
he drifted, with death always near, until with rosy fingers
to the east on the third day the dawn began, opening
over a high and windless sea, and mounting
a rising wave he caught a glimpse of shore.
What a welcome thing life seems to children
whose mother, to everyone's surprise, suddenly recovers
from a long and desperate illness:
their pangs are gone, the gods have delivered them.
So dear and welcome to Odysseus
was the sight of land, of beaches and woods, on that
　　morning.

　　　　　　　　　　　　—The Odyssey (Book V)

i

Coasts. There are all manner of coasts. Every person born in this world has a coast, an edge, a boundary, a transitional zone between themselves and the world. Some present a rocky, dark aspect, while others are particularly sunny and as open as a beach. Still others offer the metaphorical version of a mangrove swamp, with deceptive channels and labyrinthine backwaters, or a trackless sea-front desert, or surging river delta, each an effective barrier in its own way. The people with whom I have formed the closest and longest unions in my life tend to keep—as a tropical coral reef bridges a quiet lagoon and the rolling sea—music, art, literature, science, public life between themselves and the deep. The astronomers tell us that on the moons of Jupiter there are rocky coasts, adjoining oceans of ice, and that even our galaxy has a coast—a meeting place where the last of our stars and nebulae mingle with the emptiness of the great gulf. Who knows but that our universe has a coast as well, a wild, remote place where the absence of an ordered, law-governed universe begins.

If we return to the origins of civilization we find that many of the first cities grew up along the shores of the Mediterranean Sea and Indian Ocean and South China Sea, coastal places where people could meet and trade, learn and love, invent and invest. Odysseus became acquainted with some of those coasts, as did the Vikings at a later time. King Lear ranted and raved on the Dover Cliffs. The Civil War began along the South Carolina coast with the Confederate bombardment of Fort Sumter. Winslow Homer devoted his life to painting the Atlantic Coast, from Gloucester to Nassau. In 1943 a young lieutenant from Boston lost his PT boat along the coast of Kolombangara Island. When I think of my life I think of it as a wave flowing toward a distant coast, born in the anonymity of the sea, destined to one day expend itself across the sand or against a rock, in gentleness or in violence, replaced in turn by another behind, as will ultimately occur to my generation, my country, my language, and even, one distant day, my species.

This is a book about coasts, about the places where two worlds—one solid and the other fluid, one dry and the other wet, one breathing the air and the other breathing the water—meet. It is a book about bays and bayous, estuaries and lagoons, coves and headlands, salt marshes and sandy beaches, mosquito-infested swamps and wind-swept cliffs. It is a book about places that initially appear strong, but are actually quite fragile; that may seem simple, but are surprisingly complex; that may impress the casual viewer as being changeless, but are in reality constantly changing. It is a book about the place our ancestors came from, a hundred million years ago, on pectoral fins and with bulging periscope eyes, the place toward which we migrate every summer, with snorkels and flippers, plastic buckets and beach towels, looking for grassy dunes of sand and green hollow waves and the flat distant horizon of what we once called home.

ii

At the equinox when the earth was veiled in a late rain,
wreathed with wet poppies, waiting spring,
The ocean swelled for a far storm, and beat its boundary,
the ground-swell shook the beds of granite.
　　　　　　　—Robinson Jeffers, from "Continent's End"

The selections in *The Seacoast Reader* range over three continents, four oceans, and a hundred and fifty years. They include essays by a pioneering natural scientist (Charles Darwin), a big wave surfer turned literary scholar (Dan Duane), an old-time riverboat pilot (Mark Twain), an art historian (Susan Zwinger), and quite a range of others. The selections take us from the familiar sandy beaches of Cape Hatteras to the exotic coral lagoons of the southwestern Pacific. They consider topics as diverse as the daily concerns of a sea urchin (Rachel Carson), the tragedy of a ship wrecked along the Cape Cod Coast (Henry David Thoreau), the effects of international tourism on an island paradise (Rick Bass), and a day in the life of a woman who makes her living from the sea (Nancy Lord). Despite their many variations, these essays all speak directly to the enduring beauty, power, and mystery of the world's seacoasts.

Three of the essays originate in western North America, a diverse coastline that ranges from the rugged rocky ramparts of the Olympic Peninsula in the far north to the sandy desert beaches of the Mexican Baja in the far south. Barry Lopez, who lives near the Oregon coast, writes of an incident that occurred in 1979, when forty-one sperm whales somehow became stranded on a remote section of beach: "They lay on the western shore of North America like forty-one derailed boxcars." What follows is both an inquiry into the biology of an extraordinary sea mammal and a study of the psychology of the land-bound creatures—human beings—who are suddenly confronted with the complexities and injustices of nature. The beach is aswarm with scientists and law enforcement officers, but, Lopez observes:

> As far as I know, no novelist, no historian, no moral philosopher, no scholar of Melville, no rabbi, no painter, no theologian had been on the beach. No one had thought to call them or fly them in. At the end they would not have been allowed past the barricades.

Susan Zwinger, who lives on an island near Seattle, in "Becoming Water," writes of a neighboring stretch of northern coastline in a literary style that could best be described as a prose version of the painting style of Vincent Van Gogh. With a rhythmic pattern and a lyrical flourish that evokes the freedom and powerful movement of water, Zwinger paints a magnificent word picture:

Flow in and out of a million tidal pools twice a day, gently surrounding the caves and crannies crammed with delicate hyroids and isopods and nudibranchs. The Sistine Chapels of pendulant chartreuse anemones, purple sea stars, and crimson dorises. Create a biological soup as the basis of all marine life. Fill up thousands of sleek fat salmon and follow them hundreds of miles into the interior of continents. Then disgorge your detritus as they litter the land with the nutrients of the sea.

It should come as little surprise to readers that, in addition to being a gifted prose writer, Zwinger is also an accomplished artist (her paintings sometimes depict fish swimming through churches) and former curator of the Santa Fe Museum of Art.

Dan Duane brings a different perspective to the collection and to interpretations of the western coast. Duane, who holds a Ph.D. in American Literature, is also a nationally known surfer. In his essay "Something Wicked This Way Comes" Duane considers the extraordinary Pacific surf that was generated in the winter of 1997–1998 by what has come to be known as the "El Niño effect."

In the end, you just have to trust that there's nothing else in the world like pushing your board off the edge of a heaving 30-foot wall of water, harnessing all that titanic impetus, and doing something beautiful and pointless with it. Far from a man-versus-nature showdown, it's an utterly wild kind of play. Timothy Leary once said that in the far future humans would attain a state of purely aesthetic existence; surfers, he felt, had already arrived.

One senses that for Duane these huge ocean-borne waves are symbolic of the creative act itself, which lifts the artist to exhilarating heights and offers a breathtaking ride.

Alaska has more coastline than the entire continental United States. Geographers estimate that the state (which is more of a subcontinent) has a general coastline of 10,686 kilometers and a tidal coastline of 54,564 kilometers. In places the Alaskan coast resembles Scandinavia and is deeply indented with glaciated fjords. In other areas marshlands and vast beaches predominate. Visiting the territory in the summer of 1879, John Muir was not the first Euroamerican to explore Glacier Bay (that honor belongs to the early Russians and to the later Vancouver expedition), but he was the first to write with literary eloquence about the spectacular region:

> Beneath the frosty shadows of the fjord we stood hushed and awe-stricken, gazing at the holy vision; and had we seen the heavens opened and God made manifest, our attention could not have been more tremendously strained . . . the treasures we had gained this glorious morning would enrich our lives forever.

Sadly, global warming brought on by post-industrial civilization has now melted the glaciers back as much as thirty miles from their original positions of even a century or two past. Where John Muir once walked child-like across glaciers of ice and snow, thick jungles of fireweed, alder, and prickly Devil's club now cover the ground.

Writing a century after Muir's expedition to Alaska, Nancy Lord's perspective is not that of a visiting naturalist, but of a resident with long tenure upon the coastal landscape. As a result, she has a correspondingly deep and intimate knowledge of the local life systems. Lord knows when the salmon return from the sea to spawn in the freshwater streams. She knows where to place her fishing nets, and where the perpetually hungry seals and otters live. She knows the bears and the eagles and the color of the sky and the sea when a storm is on the way. Similarly, Alaskan writer Marybeth Holleman has devoted her life to exploring the islands and bays of Prince William Sound. For both writers, coastal Alaska is not so much a frontier, a terra incognita, or a wilderness (and all the mythology those terms evoke) as it is home, a place where the glaciers and the peaks are as familiar as features on the horizon as the skyscrapers and distant urban skyline are to city folk.

Hawaii is, like Alaska, a realm of superlatives, particularly when it comes to beautiful coastlines. People from Paris to Pittsburgh recognize the Ne Pali Coast of Kuai, made famous by Steven Spielberg's dinosaur epic *Jurassic Park*. Waikiki Beach has long been synonymous with tropical superlatives. Long before statehood, a young man named Samuel Clemens visited the islands, and was thoroughly impressed by their beauty: "It was the sublimest spectacle I ever witnessed, and I think the memory of it will remain with me always." For contemporary writer and naturalist Rick Bass, Hawaii poses a unique literary and aesthetic challenge:

> I came determined not to view Hawaii as "paradise," to never, ever use that word, for it is a stereotype, and when a writer resorts to stereotypes, he or she—and the story—are sunk, like one of those old, westernmost islands . . . but then . . . I saw, while indeed that was true, there was also no other word—it *was* a paradise.

The eastern United States is represented by a diversity of selections, beginning with Thoreau's celebrated essay on Cape Cod, which opens with the 1849 shipwreck of the brig *St. John,* which had begun its voyage at Galway, Ireland. On coastlines around the world, such gruesome sights are unfortunately not uncommon:

> I saw many marble feet and matted heads as the cloths were raised, and one livid, swollen, and mangled body of a drowned girl, who probably had intended to go out to service in some American family,—to which some rags still adhered, with a string, half-concealed by the flesh, about its swollen neck; the coiled-up wreck of a human hulk, gashed by the rocks or fishes, so that the bone and muscle were exposed, but quite bloodless,—merely red and white,—with wide-open and staring eyes, yet lustreless, dead-lights; or like the cabin windows of a stranded vessel, filled with sand.

Thoreau's piece reminds us of the merciless fury of the sea (so often seen in the paintings of Winslow Homer), and of the vulnerability of the coasts to the raw power of nature.

Further down the coast, Jan DeBlieu, who lives on the North Carolina Outer Banks, describes the effects of an old-fashioned nor'easter. "In the continental United States," she writes,

> . . . no stretch of coastline except Florida is more vulnerable to hurricanes and northeast storms than the Outer Banks, the belly of the eastern seaboard that curls out just south of the Chesapeake Bay.

Up and down those legendary barrier islands are the wrecks of dozens of ships, most blown into the coast by the amazing power of ocean-borne storms.

Rachel Carson shows us a different side of the eastern coast, as she takes us for a tour of the reef flats found further down the coast of Florida. These shallow-water regions are rich and complex, inhabited by organisms as diverse and fascinating as the starfish and the sea urchin:

> All [of these organisms] are important in the economy of the marine world—as links in the living chains by which materials are taken from the sea, passed from one to another, returned to the sea, borrowed again. Some are important also in the geologic processes by which rock is worn away and ground to sand, by which the sediments that carpet the sea floor are accumulated, shifted, sorted, and distributed. And at their death their hard skeletons contribute calcium for the needs of other animals or for the building of the reefs.

Carson knew nature's great design was evident even in her humblest creations.

iii

> *Behold the much-desired ocean! Behold! All ye men,*
> *who have shared such efforts, behold the country of*
> *which the sons of Comogre and other natives have told*
> *us such wonders!*
>> —Vasco Núñez de Balboa
>> September 25, 1513

Balboa was right. There is nothing like spotting the ocean after a long passage across land. For Balboa, the pilgrimage took the form of a forced march through the jungles of Panama. Three hundred years later, on the same Pacific coast but further to the north, Captain William Clark, tanned by then as darkly as the elkskin around his journal, wrote excitedly, "Ocean in view!" He, too, had undertaken a long journey to see the great western sea, and was duly moved. Regardless of the place, or the time, the effect of the seacoast on the human spirit is nearly always the same—exhilaration. It can be measured in adjectives and adverbs, exclamation points and rhetorical flourishes.

The study of coasts has become more urgent in recent years, as growing world populations, from the Carolina coast to the islands of Indonesia, have brought increasing pressure to bear on these fragile regions. "As soon as we take one thing by itself," wrote John Muir, "we find that it is hitched to everything in the universe." So it is especially with seacoasts, which quietly perform a host of vital functions: protecting inland regions from hurricanes, providing vital habitat for valuable commercial species such as shrimp and salmon, and contributing to larger ecological processes in ways still only partially understood by science. Everywhere the seacoasts are beleaguered by growth, development, and pollution, and everywhere people like you and I and the authors in this book are fighting in ways both large and small, both private and public, for their preservation. I cannot help but think that posterity will be grateful to us for our efforts in this regard.

The writings in this book also remind us, if only through metaphor, that there are coasts and inlets within, coves and bays and rocky cliffs and marshy shorelines of the spirit, places that may not be on any map but are just as vital and as fragile, as much in need of care and protection, as any portion of the Atlantic, Gulf, or Pacific Coasts. In these places adjacent worlds meet—the past and present, the self and society, freedom and responsibility, instinct and reason, dream and reality. In each case we have two entities that are quite different, but mutually dependent on one another. In such places life and energy and imagination are concentrated. Here one can experience solitude, inspiration, and renewal as much as on any beach found in any atlas.

Let us turn the page now, and range out across the coasts of this world, from the far-famed coral reefs of Australia to the ice-cold, whale-haunted waters of Glacier Bay, from the Victorian flourishes of Mark Twain in Hawaii to the contemporary prose of a California surfer, from a violent hurricane on the Outer Banks of North Carolina to a quiet day on the sandy shores of the Pacific.

A *P*RESENTATION OF *W*HALES

Barry Lopez

*O*n that section of the central Oregon coast on the evening of June 16, 1979, gentle winds were blowing onshore from the southwest. It was fifty-eight degrees. Under partly cloudy skies the sea was running with four-foot swells at eight-second intervals. Moderately rough. State police cadets Jim Clark and Steve Bennett stood at the precipitous edge of a foredune a few miles south of the town of Florence, peering skeptically into the dimness over a flat, gently sloping beach. Near the water's edge they could make out a line of dark shapes, and what they had taken for a practical joke, the exaggeration a few moments before of a man and a woman in a brown Dodge van with a broken headlight, now sank in for the truth.

Clark made a hasty, inaccurate count and plunged with Bennett down the back of the dune to their four-wheel-drive. Minutes before, they had heard the voice of Corporal Terry Crawford over the radio; they knew he was patrolling in Florence. Rather than call him, they drove the six miles into town and parked across the street from where he was issuing a citation to someone for excessive noise. When Crawford had finished, Clark went over and told him what they had seen. Crawford drove straight to the Florence State Police office and phoned his superiors in Newport, forty-eight miles up the coast. At that point the news went out over police radios: thirty-six large whales, stranded and apparently still alive, were on the beach a mile south of the mouth of the Siuslaw River.

1

There were, in fact, forty-one whales—twenty-eight females and thirteen males, at least one of them dying or already dead. There had never been a stranding quite like it. It was first assumed that they were gray whales, common along the coast, but they were sperm whales: *Physeter catodon.* Deep-ocean dwellers. They ranged in age from ten to fifty-six and in length from thirty to thirty-eight feet. They were apparently headed north when they beached around 7:30 P.M. on an ebbing high tide.

The information shot inland by phone, crossing the Coast Range to radio and television stations in the more-populous interior of Oregon, in a highly charged form: giant whales stranded on a public beach accessible by paved road on a Saturday night, still alive. Radio announcers urged listeners to head for the coast to "save the whales." In Eugene and Portland, Greenpeace volunteers, already alerted by the police, were busy throwing sheets and blankets into their cars. They would soak them in the ocean, to cool the whales.

The news moved as quickly through private homes and taverns on the central Oregon coast, passed by people monitoring the police bands. In addition to phoning Greenpeace—an international organization with a special interest in protecting marine mammals—the police contacted the Oregon State University Marine Science Center in South Beach near Newport, and the Oregon Institute of Marine Biology in Charleston, fifty-eight miles south of Florence. Bruce Mate, a marine mammalogist at the OSU Center, phoned members of the Northwest Regional [Stranding] Alert Network and people in Washington, D.C.

By midnight, the curious and the awed were crowded on the beach, cutting the night with flashlights. Drunks, ignoring the whales' sudden thrashing, were trying to walk up and down on their backs. A collie barked incessantly; flash cubes burst at the huge, dark forms. Two men inquired about reserving some of the teeth, for scrimshaw. A federal agent asked police to move people back, and the first mention of disease was in the air. Scientists arrived with specimen bags and rubber gloves and fishing knives. Greenpeace members, one dressed in a bright orange flight suit, came with a large banner. A man burdened with a television camera labored over the foredune after them. They wished to tie a rope to one whale's flukes, to drag it back into the ocean. The police began to congregate with the scientists, looking for a rationale to control the incident.

In the intensifying confusion, as troopers motioned onlookers back (to "restrain the common herd of unqualified mankind," wrote one man later in an angry letter-to-the-editor), the thinking was that, somehow, the whales might be saved. Neal Langbehn, a federal protection officer with the National Marine Fisheries Service, denied permission to one scientist to begin removing teeth and taking blood samples. In his report later he would write: "It was my feeling that the whales should be given their best chance to survive."

This hope was soon deemed futile, as it had appeared to most of the scientists from the beginning—the animals were hemorrhaging under the crushing weight of their own flesh and were beginning to suffer irreversible damage from heat exhaustion. The scientific task became one of securing as much data as possible.

As dawn bloomed along the eastern sky, people who had driven recreational vehicles illegally over the dunes and onto the beach were issued citations and turned back. Troopers continued to warn people over bullhorns to please stand away from the whales. The Oregon Parks Department, whose responsibility the beach was, wanted no part of the growing confusion. The U.S. Forest Service, with jurisdiction over land in the Oregon Dunes National Recreation Area down to the foredune, was willing to help, but among all the agencies there was concern over limited budgets; there were questions, gently essayed, about the conflict of state and federal enforcement powers over the body parts of an endangered species. A belligerent few in the crowd shouted objections as the first syringes appeared, and yelled to scientists to produce permits that allowed them to interfere in the death of an endangered species.

Amid this chaos, the whales, sealed in their slick black neoprene skins, mewed and clicked. They slammed glistening flukes on the beach, jarring the muscles of human thighs like Jell-O at a distance of a hundred yards. They rolled their dark, purple-brown eyes at the scene and blinked.

They lay on the western shore of North America like forty-one derailed boxcars at dawn on a Sunday morning, and in the days that followed, the worst and the best of human behavior was shown among them.

The sperm whale, for many, is the most awesome creature of the open seas. Imagine a forty-five-year-old male fifty feet long, a slim, shiny black animal with a white jaw and marbled belly cutting the surface of green ocean water at twenty knots. Its flat forehead protects a sealed chamber of exceedingly fine oil; sunlight sparkles in rivulets running off folds in its corrugated back. At fifty tons it is the largest carnivore on earth. Its massive head, a third of its body length, is scarred with the beak, sucker, and claw marks of giant squid, snatched out of subterranean canyons a mile below, in a region without light, and brought writhing to the surface. Imagine a four-hundred-pound heart the size of a chest of drawers driving five gallons of blood at a stroke through its aorta: a meal of forty salmon moving slowly down twelve-hundred feet of intestine; the blinding, acrid fragrance of a two-hundred-pound wad of gray ambergris lodged somewhere along the way; producing sounds more shrill than we can hear—like children shouting on a distant playground—and able to sort a cacophony of noise: electric crackling of shrimp, groaning of undersea quakes, roar of upwellings, whining of porpoise, hum of oceanic cables. With skin as sensitive as the inside of your wrist.

What makes them awesome is not so much these things, which are discoverable, but the mysteries that shroud them. They live at a remarkable distance from us and we have no *Pioneer II* to penetrate their world. Virtually all we know of sperm whales we have learned on the slaughter decks of oceangoing whalers and on the ways at shore stations. We do not even know how many there are; in December 1978, the Scientific Committee of the International Whaling Commission said it could not set a quota for a worldwide sperm whale kill—so little was known that any number written down would be ridiculous.[1]

The sperm whale, in all its range of behaviors—from the enraged white bull called Mocha Dick that stove whaling ships off the coast of Peru in 1810, to a nameless female giving birth to a fourteen-foot, one-ton calf in equatorial waters in the Pacific—remains distant. The general mystery is enhanced by specific mysteries: the sperm whale's brain is larger than the brain of any other creature that ever lived. Beyond the storage of incomprehensible amounts of information, we do not know what purpose such size

[1] A quota of 5000 was nevertheless set. In June 1979, within days of the Florence stranding but apparently unrelated to it, the IWC dropped the 1980 world sperm whale quota to 2203 and set aside the Indian Ocean as a sanctuary. (By 1987 the quota was 0, though special exemptions permit some 200 sperm whales still to be taken worldwide.)

serves. And we do not know what to make of its most distinctive anatomical feature, the spermaceti organ. An article in *Scientific American,* published several months before the stranding, suggests that the whale can control the density of its spermaceti oil, thereby altering its specific gravity to assist it in diving. It is argued also that the huge organ, located in the head, serves as a means of generating and focusing sound, but there is not yet any agreement on these speculations.

Of the many sperm whale strandings in recorded history, only three have been larger than the one in Oregon. The most recent was of fifty-six on the eastern Baja coast near Playa San Rafael on January 6, 1979. But the Florence stranding is perhaps the most remarkable. Trained scientists arrived almost immediately; the site was easily accessible, with even an airstrip close by. It was within an hour's drive of two major West Coast marine-science centers. And the stranding seemed to be of a whole social unit. That the animals were still alive meant live blood specimens could be taken. And by an uncanny coincidence, a convention of the American Society of Mammalogists was scheduled to convene June 18 at Oregon State University in Corvallis, less than a two-hour drive away. Marine experts from all over the country would be there. (As it turned out, some of them would not bother to come over; others would secure access to the beach only to take photographs; still others would show up in sports clothes—all they had—and plunge into the gore that by the afternoon of June 18 littered the beach.)

The state police calls to Greenpeace on the night of June 16 were attempts to reach informed people to direct a rescue. Michael Piper of Greenpeace, in Eugene, was the first to arrive with a small group at about 1:30 A.M., just after a low tide at 12:59 A.M.

"I ran right out of my shoes," Piper says. The thought that they would still be alive—clicking and murmuring, their eyes tracking human movement, lifting their flukes, whooshing warm air from their blowholes—had not penetrated. But as he ran into the surf to fill a bucket to splash water over their heads, the proportions of the stranding and the impending tragedy overwhelmed him.

"I knew, almost from the beginning, that we were not going to get them out of there, and that even if we did, their chances of survival were a million to one," Piper said.

Just before dawn, a second contingent of Greenpeace volunteers arrived from Portland. A Canadian, Michael Bailey, took charge and announced there was a chance with the incoming tide that one of the smaller animals could be floated off the beach and towed to sea (weights ranged from an estimated three and a half to twenty-five tons). Bruce Mate, who would become both scientific and press coordinator on the beach (the latter to his regret), phoned the Port of Coos Bay to see if an oceangoing tug or fishing vessel would be available to anchor offshore and help—Bailey's crew would ferry lines through the surf with a Zodiac boat. No one in Coos Bay was interested. A commercial helicopter service with a Skycrane capable of lifting nine tons also begged off. A call to the Coast Guard produced a helicopter, but people there pronounced any attempt to sky-tow a whale too dangerous.

The refusal of help combined with the apparent futility of the effort precipitated a genuinely compassionate gesture: Bailey strode resolutely into the freezing water and, with twenty-five or thirty others, amid flailing flukes, got a rope around the tail of an animal that weighed perhaps three or four tons. The waves knocked them down and the whale yanked them over, but they came up sputtering, to pull again. With the buoyancy provided by the incoming tide they moved the animal about thirty feet. The effort was heroic and ludicrous. As the rope began to cut into the whale's flesh, as television cameramen and press photographers crowded in, Michael Piper gave up his place on the rope in frustration and waded ashore. Later he would remark that, for some, the whale was only the means to a political end—a dramatization of the plight of whales as a species. The distinction between the suffering individual, its internal organs hemorrhaging, its flukes sliced by the rope, and the larger issue, to save the species, confounded Piper.

A photograph of the Greenpeace volunteers pulling the whale showed up nationally in newspapers the next day. A week later, a marine mammalogist wondered if any more damaging picture could have been circulated. It would convince people something could have been done, when in fact, he said, the whales were doomed as soon as they came ashore.

For many, transfixed on the beach by their own helplessness, the value of the gesture transcended the fact.

By midmorning Piper was so disturbed, so embarrassed by the drunks and by people wrangling to get up on the whales or in front of photographers, that he left. As he drove off through the crowds (arriving now by the hundreds, many in campers and motor homes), gray whales were seen offshore, with several circling sperm whales. "The best thing we could have done," Piper said, alluding to this, "was offer our presence, to be with them while they were alive, to show some compassion."

Irritated by a callous (to him) press that seemed to have only one question—Why did they come ashore?—Piper had blurted out that the whales may have come ashore "because they were tired of running" from commercial whalers. Scientists scoffed at the remark, but Piper, recalling it a week later, would not take it back. He said it was as logical as any other explanation offered in those first few hours.

Uneasy philosophical disagreement divided people on the beach from the beginning. Those for whom the stranding was a numinous event were estranged by the clowning of those who regarded it as principally entertainment. A few scientists irritated everyone with their preemptive, self-important air. When they put chain saws to the lower jaws of dead sperm whales lying only a few feet from whales not yet dead, there were angry shouts of condemnation. When townspeople kept at bay—"This is history, dammit," one man screamed at a state trooper, "and I want my kids to see it!"—saw twenty reporters, each claiming an affiliation with the same weekly newspaper, gain the closeness to the whales denied them, there were shouts of cynical derision.

"The effect of all this," said Michael Gannon, director of a national group called Oregonians Cooperating to Protect Whales, of the undercurrent of elitism and outrage, "was that it interfered with the spiritual and emotional ability of people to deal with the phenomenon. It was like being at a funeral where you were not allowed to mourn."

Bob Warren, a patrolman with the U.S. Forest Service, said he was nearly brought to tears by what faced him Sunday morning. "I had no conception of what a whale beaching would be like. I was apprehensive about it, about all the tourists and the law-enforcement atmosphere. When I drove up, the whole thing hit me in the stomach: I saw these *numbers,* these damn orange numbers—41, 40, 39—spray-painted on these dying animals. The media were coming on like the marines, in taxicabs, helicopters, low-flying

7

aircraft. Biologists were saying, 'We've got to *euthanize* them.' It made me sick."

By this time Sunday morning, perhaps five hundred people had gathered; the crowd would swell to more than two thousand before evening, in spite of a drizzling rain. The state trooper who briefed Warren outlined the major problems: traffic was backing up on the South Jetty Road almost five miles to U.S. 101; the whales' teeth were "as valuable as gold" and individuals with hammers and saws had been warned away already; people were sticking their hands in the whales' mouths and were in danger of being killed by the pounding flukes; and there was a public-health problem—the whales might have come ashore with a communicable disease. (According to several experts, the danger to public health was minor, but in the early confusion it served as an excuse to keep the crowd back so scientists could work. Ironically, the threat would assume a life of its own two days later and scientists would find themselves working frantically ahead of single-minded state burial crews.)

One of the first things Warren and others did was to rope off the whales with orange ribbon and lath stakes, establishing a line beyond which the public was no longer permitted. Someone thoughtful among them ran the ribbon close enough to one whale to allow people to peer into the dark eyes, to see scars left by struggling squid, lamprey eels, and sharp boulders on the ocean floor, the patches of diatoms growing on the skin, the marbling streaking back symmetrically from the genital slit, the startlingly gentle white mouth ("What a really beautiful and chaste-looking mouth!" Melville wrote. "From floor to ceiling lined, or rather papered with a glistening white membrane, glossy as bridal satins"), to see the teeth, gleaming in the long, almost absurdly narrow jaw. In *The Year of the Whale,* Victor Scheffer describes the tooth as "creamy white, a cylinder lightly curved, a thing of art which fits delightfully in the palm of my hand."

The temptation to possess—a Polaroid of oneself standing over a whale, a plug of flesh removed with a penknife, a souvenir squid beak plucked deftly from an exposed intestine by a scientist—was almost palpable in the air.

"From the beginning," Warren continued, "I was operating on two levels: as a law-enforcement officer with a job, and as a person." He escorted people away from the whales, explaining as well as he could the threat of disease, wishing himself to reach out with them, to touch the animals. He recalls his rage watching people poke at a sensitive area under the whales' eyes to make them react, and calmly directing people to step back, to let the animals die in peace. Nothing could be done, he would say. How do you know? they would ask. He didn't.

Warren was awed by the sudden, whooshing breath that broke the silence around an animal perhaps once every fifteen minutes, and saddened by the pitiable way some of them were mired with their asymmetrical blowhole sanded in, dead. Near those still breathing he drove in lath stakes with the word live written on them. The hopelessness of it, he said, and the rarity of the event were rendered absurd by his having to yell into a bullhorn, by the blood on the beach, the whales' blinking, the taunters hoisting beer cans to the police.

One of the things about being human, Warren reflected, is learning to see beyond the vulgar. Along with the jocose in the crowd, he said, there were hundreds who whispered to each other, as if in a grove of enormous trees. And faces that looked as though they were awaiting word of relatives presumed dead in an air crash. He remembers in particular a man in his forties, "dressed in polyesters," who stood with his daughter in a tidal pool inside the barrier, splashing cool water on a whale. Warren asked them to please step back. "Why?" the man asked. Someone in the crowd yelled an obscenity at Warren. Warren thought to himself: Why is there no room for the decency of this gesture?

The least understood and perhaps most disruptive incident on the beach on that first day was the attempt of veterinarians to kill the whales, first by injecting M-99, a morphine-based drug, then by ramming pipes into their pleural cavities to collapse their lungs, and finally by severing major arteries and letting them bleed to death. The techniques were crude, but no one knew enough sperm whale anatomy or physiology to make a clean job of it, and no one wanted to try some of the alternatives—from curare to dynamite—that would have made the job quicker. The ineptitude of the veterinarians caused them a private embarrassment to which they gave little public expression. Their frustration at their own inability to do anything to "help" the whales was exacerbated by nonscientists demanding from the sidelines that the animals be "put out of their misery." (The reasons for attempting euthanasia were poorly understood, philosophically and medically, and the issue nagged people long after the beach bore not a trace of the incident itself.)

As events unfolded on the beach, the first whale died shortly after the stranding, the last almost thirty-six hours later; suffocation and overheating were the primary causes. By waiting as long as they did to try to kill some of the animals and by allowing others to die in their own time, pathologists, toxicologists, parasitologists, geneticists, and others got tissues of poor quality to work with.[2] The disappointment was all the deeper because never had so many scientists been in a position to gather so much information. (Even with this loss and an initial lack of suitable equipment—chemicals to preserve tissues, blood-analysis kits, bone saws, flensing knives—the small core of twenty or so scientists "increased human knowledge about sperm whales several hundred percent," according to Mate.)

The fact that almost anything learned was likely to be valuable was meager consolation to scientists hurt by charges that they were cold and brutal people, irreverently jerking fetuses from the dead. Among these scientists were people who sat alone in silence, who departed in anger, and who broke down and cried.

No one knows why whales strand. It is almost always toothed whales that do, rather than baleen whales, most commonly pilot whales, Atlantic white-sided dolphins, false killer whales, and sperm whales—none of which are ordinarily found close to shore. Frequently they strand on gently sloping beaches. Among the more tenable explanations: 1) extreme social cohesion, where one sick animal is relentlessly followed ashore by many healthy animals; 2) disease or parasitic infection that affects the animals' ability to navigate; 3) harassment, by predators and, deliberate or inadvertent, by humans; 4) a reversion to phylogentically primitive escape behavior—get out of the water—precipitated by stress.

---

[2] A subsequent report, presented at a marine-mammals conference in Seattle in October 1979, made it clear that the whales began to suffer the effects of heat stress almost immediately. The breakdown of protein structures in their tissues made discovery of a cause of death difficult; from the beginning, edema, capillary dilation, and hemorrhaging made their recovery unlikely. Ice, seawater pumps, and tents for shade rather than Zodiac boats and towlines were suggested if useful tissue was to be salvaged in the future from large whales.

At a public meeting in Florence—arranged by the local librarian to explain to a public kept off the beach what had happened, and to which invited scientists did not come—other explanations were offered. Someone had noticed whales splashing in apparent confusion near a river dredge and thought the sound of its engines might have driven the whales crazy. Local fishermen said there had been an unusual, near-shore warm current on June 16, with a concentration of plankton so thick they had trouble penetrating it with their depth finders. Another suggestion was that the whales might have been temporarily deranged by poisons in diatoms concentrated in fish they were eating.

The seventy-five or so people at the meeting seemed irritated that there was no answer, as did local reporters looking for an end to the story. Had scientists been there it is unlikely they could have suggested one. The beach was a gently sloping one, but the Florence whales showed no evidence of parasitism or disease, and modern research makes it clear that no single explanation will suffice. For those who would blame the machinations of modern man, scientists would have pointed out that strandings have been recorded since the time of Aristotle's *Historia animalium*.

The first marine biologist to arrive on the beach, at 3:30 A.M. Sunday, was Michael Graybill, a young instructor from the Oregon Institute of Marine Biology. He was not as perplexed as other scientists would be; a few months before he had dismantled the rotting carcass of a fifty-six-foot sperm whale that had washed ashore thirty miles south of Florence.

Graybill counted the animals, identified them as sperm whales, noted that, oddly, there were no nursing calves or obviously young animals, and that they all seemed "undersized." He examined their skin and eyes, smelled their breath, looked for signs of oral and anal discharge, and began the task of sexing and measuring the animals.

Driving to the site, Graybill worried most about someone "bashing their teeth out" before he got there. He wasn't worried about communicable disease; he was "willing to gamble" on that. He regarded efforts to save the whales, however, as unnatural interference in their death. Later, he cynically observed "how much 'science' took place at the heads of sperm whales" where people were removing teeth; and he complained that if they really cared about the worldwide fate of whales, Greenpeace volunteers would have stayed to help scientists with postmortems. (Some did. Others left because they could not stand to watch the animals die.)

Beginning Sunday morning, scientists had their first chance to draw blood from live, unwounded sperm whales (they used comparatively tiny one-and-a-half-inch, 18-gauge hypodermic needles stuck in vessels near the surface of the skin on the flukes). With the help of a blue, organic tracer they estimated blood volume at five hundred gallons. In subsequent stages, blubber, eyes, teeth, testicles, ovaries, stomach contents, and specific tissues were removed—the teeth for aging, the eyes for corneal cells to discover genetic relationships within the group. Postmortems were performed on ten females; three near-term fetuses were removed. An attempt was made to photograph the animals systematically.

The atmosphere on the beach shifted perceptibly over the next six days. On Sunday, a cool, cloudy day during which it rained, as many as three thousand people may have been on the beach. Police finally closed the access road to the area to discourage more from coming. Attempts to euthanize the animals continued, the jaws of the dead were being sawed off, and, in the words of one observer, "there was a television crew with a backdrop of stranded whales every twenty feet on the foredune."

By Monday the crowds were larger, but, in the estimation of a Forest Service employee, "of a higher quality. The type of people who show up at an automobile accident were gone; these were people who really wanted to see the whales. It was a four-and-a-half-mile walk in from the highway, and I talked with a woman who was seven months pregnant who made it and a man in a business suit and dress shoes who drove all the way down from Seattle."

Monday afternoon the crowds thinned. The beach had become a scene of postmortem gore sufficient to turn most people away. The outgoing tide had carried off gallons of blood and offal, drawing spiny dogfish sharks and smoothhound sharks into the breakers. As the animals died, scientists cut into them to relieve gaseous pressure—the resultant explosions could be heard half a mile away. A forty-pound chunk of liver whizzed by someone's back-turned shoulders; sixty feet of pearly-gray intestine unfurled with a snap against the sky. By evening the beach was covered with more than a hundred tons of intestines. Having to open the abdominal cavities so precipitately precluded, to the scientists' dismay, any chance of an uncontaminated examination.

By Tuesday the beach was closed to the public. The whale carcasses were being prepared for burning and burial, a task that would take four days, and reporters had given up asking why the stranding had happened, to comment on the stench.

The man responsible for coordinating scientific work at the stranding, thirty-three-year-old Bruce Mate, is well regarded by his colleagues. Deborah Duffield, a geneticist from Portland State University, reiterated the feelings of several when she said of him: "The most unusual thing was that he got all of us with our different, sometimes competing, interests to work together. You can't comprehend what an extraordinary achievement that is in a situation like this."

On the beach Mate was also the principal source of information for the press. Though he was courteous to interviewers and careful not to criticize a sometimes impatient approach, one suspected he was disturbed by the role and uncertain what, if anything, he owed the nonscientific community.

In his small, cramped office at the Marine Science Center in South Beach, Mate agreed that everyone involved—scientists, environmentalists, the police, the state agencies, the public—took views that were occasionally in opposition and that these views were often proprietary. He thought it was the business of science to obtain data and physical specimens on the beach, thereby acquiring rights of "ownership," and yet he acknowledged misgivings about this because he and others involved are to some extent publicly funded scientists.

The task that faced him was deceptively simple: get as much information as possible off the beach before the burning crews, nervous about a public-health hazard and eager to end the incident, destroyed the animals. But what about the way science dominated the scene, getting the police, for example, to keep the crowd away so science could exercise its proprietary interest? "I don't know how to cope with the public's desire to come and see. Letting those few people onto the beach would have precluded our getting that much more information to give to a much larger, national audience."

What about charges that science operated in a cold-blooded and, in the case of trying to collapse the whales' lungs, ignorant way? "Coming among these whales, watching them die and in some cases helping them to die—needless suffering is almost incomprehensible to me . . ." Mate paused, studied the papers on his desk, unsatisfied, it seemed, with his tack; ". . . there are moral and ethical questions here. It's like dealing with terminal cancer."

No one, he seemed to suggest, liked how fast it had all happened.

Had he been worried about anything on the beach? "Yes! I was appalled at the way professional people were going about [postmortems] without gloves. I was afraid for the Greenpeace people in a potentially life-threatening situation in the surf." He was also afraid that it would all get away from him because of the unknowns. What, in fact, *did* one save when faced with such an enormous amount of bone and tissue? But he came away happy. "This was the greatest scientific shot anyone ever had with large whales." After a moment he added, "If it happened tomorrow, we would be four times better."

Sitting at his desk, nursing a pinched nerve in his back, surrounded by phone messages from the press, he seemed seasoned.

Mate's twenty-seven-year-old graduate assistant, Jim Harvey, arrived on the beach at dawn on Sunday. At the first sight of the whales from the top of the dunes, strung out nose to flukes in a line five or six hundred yards long, the waves of a high tide breaking over them, Harvey simply sat down, awestruck at their size and number. He felt deeply sad, too, but as he drew near he felt "a rush of exhilaration, because there was so much information to be gathered." He could not get over the feeling, as he worked, of the size of them. (One afternoon a scientist stood confounded in a whale's abdomen, asking a colleague next to him, "Where's the liver?")

Deborah Duffield said of her experience on the beach: "It hurt me more than watching human beings die. I couldn't cope with the pain, the futility. . . . I just turned into myself. It brought out the scientist in me." Another scientist spoke of his hostility toward the sullen crowd, of directing that anger at himself, of becoming cold and going to work.

For Harvey and others, there was one incident that broke scientific concentration and brought with it a feeling of impropriety.

Several scientists had started to strip blubber from a dead whale. Suddenly the whale next to it began pounding the beach with its flukes. The pounding continued for fifteen minutes—lifting and slamming the flukes to the left, lifting and slamming the flukes to the right.

When the animal quieted, they resumed work.

"Scientists rarely get a chance to express their feelings," Harvey said. "I was interested in other people's views, and I wanted to share mine, which are biological. I noticed some people who sat quietly for a long time behind the barriers in religious stances. I very much wanted to know their views. So many of the people who came down here were so sympathetic and full of concern—I wished I had the time to talk to them all." Harvey remembered something vividly. On the first day he put his face near the blowhole of one of the whales: a cylinder of clean, warm, humid air almost a foot in diameter blew back his hair.

"My view on it," said Joe Davis of the Oregon Parks Department, "wasn't the scientific part. My thought on it now is how nice it would have been to have been somewhere else." His smile falls between wryness and regret.

When something remarkable happens and bureaucrats take it for only a nuisance, it is often stripped of whatever mystery it may hold. The awesome becomes common. Joe Davis, park manager at Honeyman Dunes State Park, adjacent to the stranding, was charged by the state with getting rid of the whales. He said he didn't take a moment to wonder at the mystery of it.

If ethical problems beset scientists, and mystical considerations occupied other onlookers, a set of concerns more prosaic confronted the police and the Oregon Parks Department. On Sunday night, June 17, police arrested a man in a camouflage suit caught breaking teeth out of a whale's jaw with a hammer and chisel. That night (and the next, and the next) people continued to play games with the police. The Parks Department, for its part, was faced with the disposal of five hundred tons of whale flesh that county environmental and health authorities said they couldn't burn—the solution to the problem at Playa San Rafael—and scientists said couldn't be buried. If buried, the carcasses would become hard envelopes of rotting flesh, the internal organs would liquefy and leach out onto the beach, and winter storms would uncover the whole mess.

This controversy, the public-health question, what to do about excessive numbers of press people, and concern over who was going to pay the bill (the Forest Service had donated tools, vehicles, and labor, but two bulldozers had had to be hired, at a hundred dollars and sixty dollars an hour) precipitated a meeting in Florence on Tuesday morning, June 19. A Forest Service employee, who asked not to be identified, thought the pressures that led to the meeting marked a difference between those who came to the beach out of compassion and genuine interest and those for whom it was "only a headache."

The principal issue, after an agreement was reached to burn the whales, then bury them, was who was going to pay. The state was reluctant; the scientists were impoverished. (It would be months before Mate would begin to recover $5,000 of his own money advanced to pay for equipment, transportation, and bulldozer time. "No one wants to fund work that's finished," Mate observed sardonically.) Commercial firms were averse to donating burning materials, or even transportation for them; G. P. Excavating of Florence did reduce rental fees on its bulldozers by about one-third and "broke even" after paying its operators.

The state finally took responsibility for the disposal and assumed the $25,000 cleanup bill, but it wanted to hear nothing about science's wish to salvage skeletons—it wanted the job finished.[3] Arrangements were made to bring in a crew of boys from the Young Adult Conservation Corps, and the Forest Service, always, it seemed, amenable, agreed to donate several barrels of Alumagel, a napalmlike substance.

It was further decided to ban the public from the beach during the burning, for health and safety reasons. Only the disposal crews, scientists, police, and selected press would be admitted. The criterion for press admittance was possession of "a legitimate press card."

The role of the press at such events is somewhat predictable. They will repeatedly ask the same, obvious questions; they will often know little of the science involved; occasionally they will intimi-

---

[3] Three months later on September 6, 1979, an eighty-five-foot female blue whale washed ashore in Northern California. Ensuing argument over responsibility for disposal prevented scientists from going near the whale until September 13, by which time it had been severely battered on the rocks and vandalized.

date and harass in order to ascertain (or assign) blame. An upper-level Forest Service employee accused the press of asking "the most uninteresting and intimidating kinds of questions." A State Parks employee felt the press fostered dissension over who was going to pay for the disposal. He was also angry with newspaper people for ignoring "the human side," the fact that many state police troopers worked long hours of overtime, and that Forest Service employees performed a number of menial tasks in an emotionally charged environment of rotting flesh. "After a week of sixteen-hour days, your nerves are raw, you stink, you just want to get away from these continual questions."

In the press's defense, the people who objected most were those worried about criticism of their own performance and those deeply frustrated by the trivialization of the event. The press—probing, perhaps inexpertly—made people feel no more than their own misgivings.

The publisher of the local *Siuslaw News,* Paul Holman, said before it was over that the whale stranding had become a nuisance. When police closed the road to the beach a man in a stateside truck began ferrying people the four and a half miles to the whales for a dollar each. And a dollar back. The local airport, as well as tourist centers offering seaplane rides, were doing a "land-office business" in flyovers. Gas station operators got tired of telling tourists how to get to the beach. The Florence City Hall was swamped with calls about the burning, one from a man who was afraid his horses would be killed by the fallout on his pasture. Dune-buggy enthusiasts were angry at whale people who for two days blocked access to their hill-climbing area.

Whatever its interest, the press was largely gone by Monday afternoon. As the burning and burying commenced, the number of interested scientists also thinned. By Wednesday there were only about thirty people left on the beach. Bob Adams, acting director of the Lane Regional Air Pollution Authority, was monitoring the smoke. Neal Langbehn of the National Marine Fisheries Service stood guard over a pile of plastic-wrapped sperm whale jaws. Michael Graybill led a team flensing out skulls. The state fretted over a way to keep the carcasses burning. (It would finally be done with thousands of automobile and truck tires, cordwood, diesel fuel, and Alumagel.) As Mate watched he considered the threshold of boredom in people, and mourned the loss, among other things, of forty-one sperm whale skeletons.

A journalist, one of the last two or three, asked somebody to take her picture while she stood with a small poodle in her arms in front of the burning pits.

As is often the case with such events, what is salvaged is as much due to goodwill as it is to expertise. The Forest Service was widely complimented for helping, and Stafford Owen, the acting area ranger at the agency's Oregon Dunes National Recreation Area during the incident, tried to say why: "Most of us aren't highly educated people. We have had to work at a variety of things all our lives—operating a chain saw, repairing a truck engine, running a farm. We had the skills these doctors and scientists needed."

A soft-spoken colleague, Gene Large, trying to elaborate but not to make too much of himself, said, "I don't think the scientists had as much knowledge [of large mammalian anatomy] as I did. When it came to it, I had to show some of them where the ribs were." After a moment, Large said, "Trying to cut those whales open with a chain saw was like trying to slaughter a beef with a pen knife. I didn't enjoy any part of it," Large said of the dismembering with chain saws and winches. "I think the older you get, the more sensitive you get. He mentioned an older friend who walked away from a dead, fifteen-foot, near-term fetus being lifted out of a gutted whale, and for a time wouldn't speak.

On Wednesday afternoon the whales were ignited in pits at the foot of the foredune. As they burned they were rendered, and when their oil caught fire they began to boil in it. The seething roar was muffled by a steady onshore breeze; the oily black smoke drifted southeast over the dunes, over English beach grass and pearly everlasting, sand verbena, and the purple flowers of beach pea, green leaves of sweet clover, and the bright yellow blooms of the monkey flower. It thinned until it disappeared against a weak-blue sky.

While fire cracked the blubber of one-eyed, jawless carcasses, a bulldozer the size of a two-car garage grunted in a trench being dug to the north for the last of them. These were still sprawled at the water's edge. Up close, the black, blistered skin, bearing scars of knives and gouging fingernails, looked like the shriveled surface of a pond evaporated beneath a summer sun. Their gray-blue

18

innards lay about on the sand like bags of discarded laundry. Their purple tongues were wedged in retreat in their throats. Spermaceti oil dripped from holes in their heads, solidifying in the wind to stand in translucent stalagmites twenty inches high. Around them were tidal pools opaque with coagulated blood and, beyond, a pink surf.

As far as I know, no novelist, no historian, no moral philosopher, no scholar of Melville, no rabbi, no painter, no theologian had been on the beach. No one had thought to call them or to fly them in. At the end they would not have been allowed past the barricades.

The whales made a sound, someone had said, like the sound a big fir makes breaking off the stump just as the saw is pulled away. A thin screech.

$\mathcal{T}$HE $\mathcal{S}$HIPWRECK

Henry David Thoreau

$\mathcal{W}$ishing to get a better view than I had yet had of the ocean, which, we are told, covers more than two thirds of the globe, but of which a man who lives a few miles inland may never see any trace, more than of another world, I made a visit to Cape Cod in October, 1849, another the succeeding June, and another to Truro in July, 1855; the first and last time with a single companion, the second time alone. I have spent, in all, about three weeks on the Cape; walked from Eastham to Provincetown twice on the Atlantic side, and once on the Bay side also, excepting four or five miles, and crossed the Cape half a dozen times on my way; but having come so fresh to the sea, I have got but little salted. My readers must expect only so much saltness as the land breeze acquires from blowing over an arm of the sea, or is tasted on the windows and the bark of trees twenty miles inland, after September gales. I have been accustomed to make excursions to the ponds within ten miles of Concord, but latterly I have extended my excursions to the seashore.

I did not see why I might not make a book on Cape Cod, as well as my neighbor on "Human Culture." It is but another name for the same thing, and hardly a sandier phase of it. As for my title, I suppose that the word Cape is from the French *cap;* which is from the Latin *caput,* a head; which is, perhaps, from the verb *capere,* to take,—that being the part of which we take hold of a thing: —Take Time by the forelock. It is also the safest part to take a serpent by. And as for Cod, that was derived directly from that "great store of cod-fish" which Captain Bartholomew Gosnold caught there in 1602; which fish appears to have been so called from the Saxon word *codde,* "a case in which seeds are lodged," either from the form of the fish, or the quantity of spawn it contains; whence also, perhaps, *codling ("pomum coctile"?)* and coddle,—to cook green like peas. (V. Dic.)

Cape Cod is the bared and bended arm of Massachusetts: the shoulder is at Buzzard's Bay; the elbow, or crazy-bone, at Cape Mallebarre; the wrist at Truro; and the sandy fist at Provincetown,— behind which the State stands on her guard, with her back to the Green Mountains, and her feet planted on the floor of the ocean, like an athlete protecting her Bay,—boxing with northeast storms, and, ever and anon, heaving up her Atlantic adversary from the lap of earth,—ready to thrust forward her other fist, which keeps guard the while upon her breast at Cape Ann.

On studying the map, I saw that there must be an uninter-rupted beach on the east or outside of the forearm of the Cape, more than thirty miles from the general line of the coast, which would afford a good sea view, but that, on account of an opening in the beach, forming the entrance to Nauset Harbor, in Orleans, I must strike it in Eastham, if I approached it by land, and probably I could walk thence straight to Race Point, about twenty-eight miles, and not meet with any obstruction.

We left Concord, Massachusetts, on Tuesday, October 9, 1849. On reaching Boston, we found that the Provincetown steamer, which should have got in the day before, had not yet arrived, on account of a violent storm; and, as we noticed in the streets a hand-bill headed, "Death! one hundred and forty-five lives lost at Cohas-set," we decided to go by way of Cohasset. We found many Irish in the cars, going to identify bodies and to sympathize with the sur-vivors, and also to attend the funeral which was to take place in the afternoon;—and when we arrived at Cohasset, it appeared that nearly all the passengers were bound for the beach, which was about a mile distant, and many other persons were flocking in from the neighboring country. There were several hundreds of them streaming off over Cohasset common in that direction, some on foot and some in wagons,—and among them were some sports-men in their hunting-jackets, with their guns, and game-bags, and dogs. As we passed the graveyard we saw a large hole, like a cel-lar, freshly dug there, and, just before reaching the shore, by a pleasantly winding and rocky road, we met several hay-riggings and farm-wagons coming away toward the meeting-house, each loaded with three large, rough deal boxes. We did not need to ask what was in them. The owners of the wagons were made the undertakers. Many horses in carriages were fastened to the fences near the shore, and, for a mile or more, up and down, the beach was covered with people looking out for bodies, and examining the fragments of the wreck. There was a small island called Brook Island, with a hut on it, lying just off the shore. This is said to be the rockiest shore in Massachusetts, from Nantasket to Scituate,— hard sienitic rocks, which the waves have laid bare, but have not been able to crumble. It has been the scene of many a shipwreck.

The brig *St. John,* from Galway, Ireland, laden with emigrants, was wrecked on Sunday morning; it was now Tuesday morning, and the sea was still breaking violently on the rocks. There were eighteen or twenty of the same large boxes that I have mentioned, lying on a green hillside, a few rods from the water, and surrounded by a crowd. The bodies which had been recovered, twenty-seven or eight in all, had been collected there. Some were rapidly nailing down the lids, others were carting the boxes away, and others were lifting the lids, which were yet loose, and peeping under the cloths, for each body, with such rags as still adhered to it, was covered loosely with a white sheet. I witnessed no signs of grief, but there was a sober dispatch of business which was affecting. One man was seeking to identify a particular body, and one undertaker or carpenter was calling to another to know in what box a certain child was put. I saw many marble feet and matted heads as the cloths were raised, and one livid, swollen, and mangled body of a drowned girl,—who probably had intended to go out to service in some American family,—to which some rags still adhered, with a string, half concealed by the flesh, about its swollen neck; the coiled-up wreck of a human hulk, gashed by the rocks or fishes, so that the bone and muscle were exposed, but quite bloodless,—merely red and white,—with wide-open and staring eyes, yet lustreless, dead-lights; or like the cabin windows of a stranded vessel, filled with sand. Sometimes there were two or more children, or a parent and child, in the same box, and on the lid would perhaps be written with red chalk, "Bridget such-a-one, and sister's child." The surrounding sward was covered with bits of sails and clothing. I have since heard, from one who lives by this beach, that a woman who had come over before, but had left her infant behind for her sister to bring, came and looked into these boxes, and saw in one—probably the same whose superscription I have quoted—her child in her sister's arms, as if the sister had meant to be found thus; and within three days after, the mother died from the effect of that sight.

We turned from this and walked along the rocky shore. In the first cove were strewn what seemed the fragments of a vessel, in small pieces mixed with sand and seaweed, and great quantities of feathers; but it looked so old and rusty, that I at first took it to be some old wreck which had lain there many years. I even thought of Captain Kidd, and that the feathers were those which sea-fowl had cast there; and perhaps there might be some tradition about it in the neighborhood. I asked a sailor if that was the *St. John.* He said it was. I asked him where she struck. He pointed to a rock in front of us, a mile from the shore, called the Grampus Rock, and added,—

"You can see a part of her now sticking up; it looks like a small boat."

I saw it. It was thought to be held by the chain-cables and the anchors. I asked if the bodies which I saw were all that were drowned.

"Not a quarter of them," said he.

"Where are the rest?"

"Most of them right underneath that piece you see."

It appeared to us that there was enough rubbish to make the wreck of a large vessel in this cove alone, and that it would take many days to cart it off. It was several feet deep, and here and there was a bonnet or a jacket on it. In the very midst of the crowd about this wreck, there were men with carts busily collecting the seaweed which the storm had cast up, and conveying it beyond the reach of the tide, though they were often obliged to separate fragments of clothing from it, and they might at any moment have found a human body under it. Drown who might, they did not forget that this weed was a valuable manure. This shipwreck had not produced a visible vibration in the fabric of society.

About a mile south we could see, rising above the rocks the masts of the British brig which the *St. John* had endeavored to follow, which had slipped her cables, and, by good luck, run into the mouth of Cohasset Harbor. A little further along the shore we saw a man's clothes on a rock; further, a woman's scarf, a gown, a straw bonnet, the brig's caboose, and one of her masts high and dry, broken into several pieces. In another rocky cove, several rods from the water, and behind rocks twenty feet high, lay a part of one side of the vessel, still hanging together. It was, perhaps, forty feet long, by fourteen wide. I was even more surprised at the power of the waves, exhibited on this shattered fragment, than I had been at the sight of the smaller fragments before. The largest timbers and iron braces were broken superfluously, and I saw that no material could withstand the power of the waves; that iron must go to pieces in such a case, and an iron vessel would be cracked up like an egg-shell on the rocks. Some of these timbers, however, were so rotten that I could almost thrust my umbrella through them. They told us that some were saved on this piece, and also showed where the sea had heaved it into this cove which was now dry. When I saw where it had come in, and in what condition, I wondered that any had been saved on it. A little further on a crowd of men was collected around the mate of the *St. John,* who was telling his story. He was a slim-looking youth, who spoke of the captain as the master, and seemed a little excited. He was saying that when they jumped into the boat, she filled, and, the vessel lurching, the weight of the water in the boat caused the painter to break, and so they were separated. Whereat one man came away, saying,—

"Well, I don't see but he tells a straight story enough. You see, the weight of the water in the boat broke the painter. A boat full of water is very heavy,"—and so on, in a loud and impertinently earnest tone, as if he had a bet depending on it, but had no humane interest in the matter.

Another, a large man, stood near by upon a rock, gazing into the sea, and chewing large quids of tobacco, as if that habit were forever confirmed with him.

"Come," says another to his companion, "let's be off. We've seen the whole of it. It's no use to stay to the funeral."

Further, we saw one standing upon a rock, who, we were told, was one that was saved. He was a sober-looking man, dressed in a jacket and gray pantaloons, with his hands in the pockets. I asked him a few questions, which he answered; but he seemed unwilling to talk about it, and soon walked away. By his side stood one of the life-boat men, in an oilcloth jacket, who told us how they went to the relief of the British brig, thinking that the boat of the *St. John,* which they passed on the way, held all her crew,—for the waves prevented their seeing those who were on the vessel, though they might have saved some had they known there were any there. A little further was the flag of the *St. John* spread on a rock to dry, and held down by stones at the corners. This frail, but essential and significant portion of the vessel, which had so long been the sport of the winds, was sure to reach the shore. There were one or two houses visible from these rocks, in which were some of the survivors recovering from the shock which their bodies and minds had sustained. One was not expected to live.

We kept on down the shore as far as a promontory called Whitehead, that we might see more of the Cohasset Rocks. In a little cove, within half a mile, there were an old man and his son collecting, with their team, the seaweed which that fatal storm had cast up, as serenely employed as if there had never been a wreck in the world, though they were within sight of the Grampus Rock, on which the *St. John* had struck. The old man had heard that there was a wreck and knew most of the particulars, but he said that he had not been up there since it happened. It was the wrecked weed that concerned him most, rock-weed, kelp, and seaweed, as he named them, which he carted to his barnyard; and those bodies were to him but other weeds which the tide cast up, but which were of no use to him. We afterwards came to the life-boat in its harbor, waiting for another emergency,—and in the afternoon we saw the funeral procession at a distance, at the head of which walked the captain with the other survivors.

On the whole, it was not so impressive a scene as I might have expected. If I had found one body cast upon the beach in some lonely place, it would have affected me more. I sympathized rather with the winds and waves, as if to toss and mangle these poor human bodies was the order of the day. If this was the law of Nature, why waste any time in awe or pity? If the last day were come, we should not think so much about the separation of friends or the blighted prospects of individuals. I saw that corpses might be multiplied, as on the field of battle, till they no longer affected us in any degree, as exceptions to the common lot of humanity. Take all the graveyards together, they are always the majority. It is the individual and private that demands our sympathy. A man can attend but one funeral in the course of his life, can behold but one corpse. Yet I saw that the inhabitants of the shore would be not a little affected by this event. They would watch there many days and nights for the sea to give up its dead, and their imaginations and sympathies would supply the place of mourners far away, who as yet knew not of the wreck. Many days after this, something white was seen floating on the water by one who was sauntering on the beach. It was approached in a boat, and found to be the body of a woman, which had risen in an upright position, whose white cap was blown back with the wind. I saw that the beauty of the shore itself was wrecked for many a lonely walker there, until he could perceive, at last, how its beauty was enhanced by wrecks like this, and it acquired thus a rarer and sublimer beauty still.

Why care for these dead bodies? They really have no friends but the worms or fishes. Their owners were coming to the New World, as Columbus and the Pilgrims did,—they were within a mile of its shores; but, before they could reach it, they emigrated to a newer world than ever Columbus dreamed of, yet one of whose existence we believe that there is far more universal and convincing evidence—though it has not yet been discovered by science—than Columbus had of this: not merely mariners' tales and some paltry drift-wood and seaweed, but a continual drift and instinct to all our shores. I saw their empty hulks that came to land; but they themselves, meanwhile, were cast upon some shore yet further west, toward which we are all tending, and which we shall reach at last, it may be through storm and darkness, as they did. No doubt, we have reason to thank God that they have not been "shipwrecked into life again." The mariner who makes the safest port in Heaven, perchance, seems to his friends on earth to be shipwrecked, for they deem Boston Harbor the better place; though perhaps invisible to them, a skillful pilot comes to meet him, and the fairest and balmiest gales blow off that coast, his good ship makes the land in halcyon days, and he kisses the shore in rapture there, while his old hulk tosses in the surf here. It is hard to part with one's body, but, no doubt, it is easy enough to do without it when once it is gone. All their plans and hopes burst like a bubble! Infants by the score dashed on the rocks by the enraged Atlantic Ocean! No, no! If the *St. John* did not make her port here, she has been telegraphed there. The strongest wind cannot stagger a Spirit; it is a Spirit's breath. A just man's purpose cannot be split on any Grampus or material rock, but itself will split rocks till it succeeds.

$\mathscr{T}$HE $\mathscr{D}$ISCOVERY
OF $\mathscr{G}$LACIER $\mathscr{B}$AY

John Muir

$\mathscr{F}$rom here, on October 24, we set sail for Guide Charley's ice-mountains. The handle of our heaviest axe was cracked, and as Charley declared that there was no firewood to be had in the big ice-mountain bay, we would have to load the canoe with a store for cooking at an island out in the Strait a few miles from the village. We were therefore anxious to buy or trade for a good sound axe in exchange for our broken one. Good axes are rare in rocky Alaska. Soon or late an unlucky stroke on a stone concealed in moss spoils the edge. Finally one in almost perfect condition was offered by a young Hoona for our broken-handled one and a half-dollar to boot; but when the broken axe and money were given he promptly demanded an additional twenty-five cents' worth of tobacco. The tobacco was given him, then he required a half-dollar's worth more of tobacco, which was also given; but when he still demanded something more, Charley's patience gave way and we sailed in the same condition as to axes as when we arrived. This was the only contemptible commercial affair we encountered among these Alaskan Indians.

We reached the wooded island about one o'clock, made coffee, took on a store of wood, and set sail direct for the icy country, finding it very hard indeed to believe the woodless part of Charley's description of the Icy Bay, so heavily and uniformly are all the shores forested wherever we had been. In this view we were joined by John, Kadachan, and Toyatte, none of them on all their lifelong canoe travels having ever seen a woodless country.

We held a northwesterly course until long after dark, when we reached a small inlet that sets in near the mouth of Glacier Bay, on the west side. Here we made a cold camp on a desolate snow-covered beach in stormy sleet and darkness. At daybreak I looked eagerly in every direction to learn what kind of place we were in; but gloomy rain-clouds covered the mountains, and I could see nothing that would give me a clue, while Vancouver's chart, hitherto a faithful guide, here failed us altogether. Nevertheless, we made haste to be off; and fortunately, for just as we were leaving the shore, a faint smoke was seen across the inlet, toward which Charley, who now seemed lost, gladly steered. Our sudden appearance so early that gray morning had evidently alarmed our neighbors, for as soon as we were within hailing distance an Indian with his face blackened fired a shot over our heads, and in a blunt, bellowing voice roared, "Who are you?"

Our interpreter shouted, "Friends and the Fort Wrangell missionary."

Then men, women, and children swarmed out of the hut, and awaited our approach on the beach. One of the hunters having brought his gun with him, Kadachan sternly rebuked him, asking with superb indignation whether he was not ashamed to meet a missionary with a gun in his hands. Friendly relations, however, were speedily established, and as a cold rain was falling, they invited us to enter their hut. It seemed very small and was jammed full of oily boxes and bundles; nevertheless, twenty-one persons managed to find shelter in it about a smoky fire. Our hosts proved to be Hoona seal-hunters laying in their winter stores of meat and skins. The packed hut was passably well ventilated, but its heavy, meaty smells were not the same to our noses as those we were accustomed to in the sprucy nooks of the evergreen woods. The circle of black eyes peering at us through a fog of reek and smoke made a novel picture. We were glad, however, to get within reach of information, and of course asked many questions concerning the ice-mountains and the strange bay, to most of which our inquisitive Hoona friends replied with counter-questions as to our object in coming to such a place, especially so late in the year. They had heard of Mr. Young and his work at Fort Wrangell, but could not understand what a missionary could be doing in such a place as this. Was he going to preach to the seals and gulls, they asked, or to the ice-mountains? And could they take his word? Then John explained that only the friend of the missionary was seeking ice-mountains, that Mr. Young had already preached many good words in the villages we had visited, their own among the others, that our hearts were good and every Indian was our friend. Then we gave them a little rice, sugar, tea, and tobacco, after which they began to gain confidence and to speak freely. They told us that the big bay was called by them Sit-a-da-kay, or Ice Bay; that there were many large ice-mountains in it, but no gold-mines; and that the ice-mountain they knew best was at the head of the bay, where most of the seals were found.

Notwithstanding the rain, I was anxious to push on and grope our way beneath the clouds as best we could, in case worse weather should come; but Charley was ill at ease, and wanted one of the seal-hunters to go with us, for the place was much changed. I promised to pay well for a guide, and in order to lighten the canoe proposed to leave most of our heavy stores in the hut until our return. After a long consultation one of them consented to go. His wife got ready his blanket and a piece of cedar matting for his bed, and some provisions—mostly dried salmon, and seal sausage made of strips of lean meat plaited around a core of fat. She followed us to the beach, and just as we were pushing off said with a pretty smile, "It is my husband that you are taking away. See that you bring him back."

We got under way about 10 A.M. The wind was in our favor, but a cold rain pelted us, and we could see but little of the dreary, treeless wilderness which we had now fairly entered. The bitter blast, however, gave us good speed; our bedraggled canoe rose and fell on the waves as solemnly as a big ship. Our course was northwestward, up the southwest side of the bay, near the shore of what seemed to be the mainland, smooth marble islands being on our right. About noon we discovered the first of the great glaciers, the one I afterward named for James Geikie, the noted Scotch geologist. Its lofty blue cliffs, looming through the draggled skirts of the clouds, gave a tremendous impression of savage power, while the roar of the new-born icebergs thickened and emphasized the general roar of the storm. An hour and a half beyond the Geikie Glacier we ran into a slight harbor where the shore is low, dragged the canoe beyond the reach of drifting icebergs, and, much against my desire to push ahead, encamped, the guide insisting that the big ice-mountain at the head of the bay could not be reached before dark, that the landing there was dangerous even in daylight, and that this was the only safe harbor on the way to it. While camp was being made, I strolled along the shore to examine the rocks and the fossil timber that abounds here. All the rocks are freshly glaciated, even below the sea-level, nor have the waves as yet worn off the surface polish, much less the heavy scratches and grooves and lines of glacial contour.

The next day being Sunday, the minister wished to stay in camp; and so, on account of the weather, did the Indians. I therefore set out on an excursion, and spent the day alone on the mountain-slopes above the camp, and northward, to see what I might learn. Pushing on through rain and mud and sludgy snow, crossing many brown, boulder-choked torrents, wading, jumping, and wallowing in snow up to my shoulders was mountaineering of the most trying kind. After crouching cramped and benumbed in the canoe, poulticed in wet or damp clothing night and day, my limbs had been asleep. This day they were awakened and in the hour of trial proved that they had not lost the cunning learned on many a mountain peak of the High Sierra. I reached a height of fifteen hundred feet, on the ridge that bounds the second of the great glaciers. All the landscape was smothered in clouds and I began to fear that as far as wide views were concerned I had climbed in vain. But at length the clouds lifted a little, and beneath their gray fringes I saw the berg-filled expanse of the bay, and the feet of the mountains that stand about it, and the imposing fronts of five huge glaciers, the nearest being immediately beneath me. This was my first general view of Glacier Bay, a solitude of ice and snow and newborn rocks, dim, dreary, mysterious. I held the ground I had so dearly won for an hour or two, sheltering myself from the blast as best I could, while with benumbed fingers I sketched what I could see of the landscape, and wrote a few lines in my notebook. Then, breasting the snow again, crossing the shifting avalanche slopes and torrents, I reached camp about dark, wet and weary and glad.

While I was getting some coffee and hardtack, Mr. Young told me that the Indians were discouraged, and had been talking about turning back, fearing that I would be lost, the canoe broken, or in some other mysterious way the expedition would come to grief if I persisted in going farther. They had been asking him what possible motive I could have in climbing mountains when storms were blowing; and when he replied that I was only seeking knowledge,

Toyatte said, "Muir must be a witch to seek knowledge in such a place as this and in such miserable weather."

After supper, crouching about a dull fire of fossil wood, they became still more doleful, and talked in tones that accorded well with the wind and waters and growling torrents about us, telling sad old stories of crushed canoes, drowned Indians, and hunters frozen in snowstorms. Even brave old Toyatte, dreading the tree-less, forlorn appearance of the region, said that his heart was not strong, and that he feared his canoe, on the safety of which our lives depended, might be entering a skookum-house (jail) of ice, from which there might be no escape; while the Hoona guide said bluntly that if I was so fond of danger, and meant to go close up to the noses of the ice-mountains, he would not consent to go any farther; for we should all be lost, as many of his tribe had been, by the sudden rising of bergs from the bottom. They seemed to be losing heart with every howl of the wind, and, fearing that they might fail me now that I was in the midst of so grand a congregation of glaciers, I made haste to reassure them, telling them that for ten years I had wandered alone among mountains and storms, and good luck always followed me; that with me, therefore, they need fear nothing. The storm would soon cease and the sun would shine to show us the way we should go, for God cares for us and guides us as long as we are trustful and brave, therefore all childish fear must be put away. This little speech did good. Kadachan, with some show of enthusiasm, said he liked to travel with good-luck people; and dignified old Toy-atte declared that now his heart was strong again, and he would venture on with me as far as I liked for my "wawa" was "delait" (my talk was very good). The old warrior even became a little sentimental, and said that even if the canoe was broken he would not greatly care, because on the way to the other world he would have good companions.

Next morning it was still raining and snowing, but the south wind swept us bravely forward and swept the bergs from our course. In about an hour we reached the second of the big gla-ciers, which I afterwards named for Hugh Miller. We rowed up its fiord and landed to make a slight examination of its grand frontal wall. The berg-producing portion we found to be about a mile and a half wide, and broken into an imposing array of jagged spires and pyramids, and flat-topped towers and battlements, of many shades of blue, from pale, shimmering, limpid tones in the crevasses and hollows, to the most startling, chilling, almost shrieking vitriol blue on the plain mural spaces from which bergs had just been discharged. Back from the front for a few miles the glacier rises in a series of wide steps, as if this portion of the glacier had sunk in successive sections as it reached deep water, and the sea had found its way beneath it. Beyond this it extends indefinitely in a gently rising prairie-like expanse, and branches along the slopes and cañons of the Fairweather Range.

From here a run of two hours brought us to the head of the bay, and to the mouth of the northwest fiord, at the head of which lie the Hoona sealing-grounds, and the great glacier now called the Pacific, and another called the Hoona. The fiord is about five miles long, and two miles wide at the mouth. Here our Hoona guide had a store of dry wood, which we took aboard. Then, setting sail, we were driven wildly up the fiord, as if the storm-wind were saying, "Go, then, if you will, into my icy chamber; but you shall stay in until I am ready to let you out." All this time sleety rain was falling on the bay, and snow on the mountains; but soon after we landed the sky began to open. The camp was made on a rocky beach near the front of the Pacific Glacier, and the canoe was carried beyond the reach of the bergs and berg-waves. The bergs were now crowded in a dense pack against the discharging front, as if the storm-wind had determined to make the glacier take back her crystal offspring and keep them at home.

While camp affairs were being attended to, I set out to climb a mountain for comprehensive views; and before I had reached a height of a thousand feet the rain ceased, and the clouds began to rise from the lower altitudes, slowly lifting their white skirts, and lingering in majestic, wing-shaped masses about the mountains that rise out of the broad, icy sea, the highest of all the white mountains, and the greatest of all the glaciers I had yet seen. Climbing higher for a still broader outlook, I made notes and sketched, improving the precious time while sunshine streamed through the luminous fringes of the clouds and fell on the green waters of the fiord, the glittering bergs, the crystal bluffs of the vast glacier, the intensely white, far-spreading fields of ice, and the ineffably chaste and spiritual heights of the Fairweather Range, which were now hidden, now partly revealed, the whole making a picture of icy wildness unspeakably pure and sublime.

Looking southward, a broad ice-sheet was seen extending in a gently undulating plain from the Pacific Fiord in the foreground to the horizon, dotted and ridged here and there with mountains which were as white as the snow-covered ice in which they were half, or more than half, submerged. Several of the great glaciers of the bay flow from this one grand fountain. It is an instructive example of a general glacier covering the hills and dales of a country that is not yet ready to be brought to the light of day—not only covering but creating a landscape with the features it is destined to have when, in the fullness of time, the fashioning ice-sheet shall be lifted by the sun, and the land become warm and fruitful. The view to the westward is bounded and almost filled by the glorious Fairweather Mountains, the highest among them springing aloft in sublime beauty to a height of nearly sixteen thousand feet, while from base to summit every peak and spire and dividing ridge of all the mighty host was spotless white, as if painted. It would seem that snow could never be made to lie on the steepest slopes and precipices unless plastered on when wet, and then frozen. But this snow could not have been wet. It must have been fixed by being driven and set in small particles like the storm-dust of drifts, which, when in this condition, is fixed not only on sheer cliffs, but in massive, overcurling cornices. Along the base of this majestic range sweeps the Pacific Glacier, fed by innumerable cascading tributaries, and discharging into the head of its fiord by two mouths only partly separated by the brow of an island rock about one thousand feet high, each nearly a mile wide.

Dancing down the mountain to camp, my mind glowing like the sunbeaten glaciers, I found the Indians seated around a good fire, entirely happy now that the farthest point of the journey was safely reached and the long, dark storm was cleared away. How hopefully, peacefully bright that night were the stars in the frosty sky, and how impressive was the thunder of the icebergs, rolling, swelling, reverberating through the solemn stillness! I was too happy to sleep.

About daylight next morning we crossed the fiord and landed on the south side of the rock that divides the wall of the great glacier. The whiskered faces of seals dotted the open spaces between the bergs, and I could not prevent John and Charley and Kadachan from shooting at them. Fortunately, few, if any, were hurt. Leaving the Indians in charge of the canoe, I managed to climb to the top of the wall by a good deal of step-cutting between the ice and dividing rock, and gained a good general view of the glacier. At one favorable place I descended about fifty feet below the side of the glacier, where its denuding, fashioning action was clearly shown. Pushing back from here, I found the surface crevassed and sunken in steps, like the Hugh Miller Glacier, as if it were being undermined by the action of tide-waters. For a distance of fifteen or twenty miles the river-like ice-flood is nearly level, and when it recedes, the ocean water will follow it, and thus form a long extension of the fiord, with features essentially the same as those now extending into the continent farther south, where many great glaciers once poured into the sea, though scarce a vestige of them now exists. Thus the domain of the sea has been, and is being, extended in these ice-sculptured lands, and the scenery of their shores enriched. The brow of the dividing rock is about a thousand feet high, and is hard beset by the glacier. A short time ago it was at least two thousand feet below the surface of the over-sweeping ice; and under present climatic conditions it will soon take its place as a glacier-polished island in the middle of the fiord, like a thousand others in the magnificent archipelago. Emerging from its icy sepulchre, it gives a most telling illustration of the birth of a marked feature of a landscape. In this instance it is not the mountain, but the glacier, that is in labor, and the mountain itself is being brought forth.

The Hoona Glacier enters the fiord on the south side, a short distance below the Pacific, displaying a broad and far-reaching expanse, over which many lofty peaks are seen; but the front wall, thrust into the fiord, is not nearly so interesting as that of the Pacific, and I did not observe any bergs discharged from it.

In the evening, after witnessing the unveiling of the majestic peaks and glaciers and their baptism in the down-pouring sunbeams, it seemed inconceivable that nature could have anything finer to show us. Nevertheless, compared with what was to come the next morning, all that was as nothing. The calm dawn gave no promise of anything uncommon. Its most impressive features were the frosty clearness of the sky and a deep, brooding stillness made all the more striking by the thunder of the newborn bergs. The sunrise we did not see at all, for we were beneath the shadows of the fiord cliffs; but in the midst of our studies, while the Indians were getting ready to sail, we were startled by the sudden appearance of a red light burning with a strange unearthly splendor on the topmost peak of the Fairweather Mountains. Instead of vanishing as suddenly as it had appeared, it spread and spread until the whole range down to the level of the glaciers was filled with the celestial fire. In color it was at first a vivid crimson, with a thick, furred appearance, as fine as the alpenglow, yet indescribably rich and deep—not in the least like a garment or mere external flush or bloom through which one might expect to see the rocks or snow, but every mountain apparently was glowing from the heart like molten metal fresh from a furnace. Beneath the frosty shadows of the fiord we stood hushed and awe-stricken, gazing at the holy vision; and had we seen the heavens opened and God made manifest, our attention could not have been more tremendously strained. When the highest peak began to burn, it did not seem to be steeped in sunshine, however glorious, but rather as if it had been thrust into the body of the sun itself. Then the supernal fire slowly descended, with a sharp line of demarkation separating it from the cold, shaded region beneath; peak after peak, with their spires and ridges and cascading glaciers, caught the heavenly glow, until all the mighty host stood transfigured, hushed, and thoughtful, as if awaiting the coming of the Lord. The white, rayless light of morning, seen when I was alone amid the peaks of the California Sierra, had always seemed to me the most telling of all the terrestrial manifestations of God. But here the mountains themselves were made divine, and declared His glory in terms still more impressive. How long we gazed I never knew. The glorious vision passed away in a gradual, fading change through a thousand tones of color to pale yellow and white, and then the work of the ice-world went on again in everyday beauty. The green waters of the fiord were filled with sun-spangles; the fleet of icebergs set forth on their voyages with the upspringing breeze; and on the innumerable mirrors and prisms of these bergs, and on those of the shattered crystal walls of the glaciers, common white light and rainbow light began to burn, while the mountains shone in their frosty jewelry, and loomed again in the thin azure in serene terrestrial majesty. We turned and sailed away, joining the outgoing bergs, while "Gloria in excelsis" still seemed to be sounding over all the white landscape, and our burning hearts were ready for any fate, feeling that, whatever the future might have in store, the treasures we had gained this glorious morning would enrich our lives forever.

When we arrived at the mouth of the fiord, and rounded the massive granite headland that stands guard at the entrance on the north side, another large glacier, now named the Reid, was discovered at the head of one of the northern branches of the bay. Pushing ahead into this new fiord, we found that it was not only packed with bergs, but that the spaces between the bergs were crusted with new ice, compelling us to turn back while we were yet several miles from the discharging frontal wall. But though we were not then allowed to set foot on this magnificent glacier, we obtained a fine view of it, and I made the Indians cease rowing while I sketched its principal features. Thence, after steering northeastward a few miles, we discovered still another large glacier, now named the Carroll. But the fiord into which this glacier flows was, like the last, utterly inaccessible on account of ice, and we had to be content with a general view and sketch of it, gained as we rowed slowly past at a distance of three or four miles. The mountains back of it and on each side of its inlet are sculptured in a singularly rich and striking style of architecture, in which subordinate peaks and gables appear in wonderful profusion, and an imposing conical mountain with a wide, smooth base stand out in the main current of the glacier, a mile or two back from the discharging ice-wall.

We now turned southward down the eastern shore of the bay, and in an hour or two discovered a glacier of the second class, at the head of a comparatively short fiord that winter had not yet closed. Here we landed, and climbed across a mile or so of rough boulder-beds, and back upon the wildly broken, receding front of the glacier, which, though it descends to the level of the sea, no longer sends off bergs. Many large masses, detached from the wasting front by irregular melting, were partly buried beneath mud, sand, gravel, and boulders of the terminal moraine. Thus protected, these fossil icebergs remain unmelted for many years, some of them for a century or more, as shown by the age of trees growing above them, though there are no trees here as yet. At length melting, a pit with sloping sides is formed by the falling in of the overlying moraine material into the space at first occupied by the buried ice. In this way are formed the curious depressions in drift-covered regions called kettles or sinks. On these decaying glaciers we may also find many interesting lessons on the formation of boulders and boulder-beds, which in all glaciated countries exert a marked influence on scenery, health, and fruitfulness.

Three or four miles farther down the bay, we came to another fiord, up which we sailed in quest of more glaciers, discovering one in each of the two branches into which the fiord divides. Neither of these glaciers quite reaches tide-water. Notwithstanding the apparent fruitfulness of their fountains, they are in the first stage of decadence, the waste from melting and evaporation being greater now than the supply of new ice from their snowy fountains. We reached the one in the north branch, climbed over its wrinkled brow, and gained a good view of the trunk and some of the tributaries, and also of the sublime gray cliffs of its channel.

Then we sailed up the south branch of the inlet, but failed to reach the glacier there, on account of a thin sheet of new ice. With the tent-poles we broke a lane for the canoe for a little distance; but it was slow work, and we soon saw that we could not reach the glacier before dark. Nevertheless, we gained a fair view of it as it came sweeping down through its gigantic gateway of massive Yosemite rocks three or four thousand feet high. Here we lingered until sundown, gazing and sketching; then turned back, and encamped on a bed of cobblestones between the forks of the fiord.

We gathered a lot of fossil wood and after supper made a big fire, and as we sat around it the brightness of the sky brought on a long talk with the Indians about the stars; and their eager, child-like attention was refreshing to see as compared with the deathlike apathy of weary town-dwellers, in whom natural curiosity has been quenched in toil and care and poor shallow comfort.

After sleeping a few hours, I stole quietly out of the camp, and climbed the mountain that stands between the two glaciers. The ground was frozen, making the climbing difficult in the steepest places; but the views over the icy bay, sparkling beneath the stars, were enchanting. It seemed then a sad thing that any part of so precious a night had been lost in sleep. The starlight was so full that I distinctly saw not only the berg-filled bay, but most of the lower portions of the glaciers, lying pale and spirit-like amid the mountains. The nearest glacier in particular was so distinct that it seemed to be glowing with light that came from within itself. Not even in dark nights have I ever found any difficulty in seeing large glaciers; but on this mountain-top, amid so much ice, in the heart of so clear and frosty a night, everything was more or less luminous, and I seemed to be poised in a vast hollow between two skies of almost equal brightness. This exhilarating scramble made me glad and strong and I rejoiced that my studies called me before the glorious night succeeding so glorious a morning had been spent!

I got back to camp in time for an early breakfast, and by daylight we had everything packed and were again under way. The fiord was frozen nearly to its mouth, and though the ice was so thin it gave us but little trouble in breaking a way for the canoe, yet it showed us that the season for exploration in these waters was wellnigh over. We were in danger of being imprisoned in a jam of icebergs, for the water-spaces between them freeze rapidly, binding the floes into one mass. Across such floes it would be almost impossible to drag a canoe, however industriously we might ply the axe, as our Hoona guide took great pains to warn us. I would have kept straight down the bay from here, but the guide had to be taken home, and the provisions we left at the bark hut had to be got on board. We therefore crossed over to our Sunday storm-camp, cautiously boring a way through the bergs. We found the shore lavishly adorned with a fresh arrival of assorted bergs that had been left stranded at high tide. They were arranged in a curving row, looking intensely clear and pure on the gray sand, and, with the sunbeams pouring through them, suggested the jewel-paved streets of the New Jerusalem.

On our way down the coast, after examining the front of the beautiful Geikie Glacier, we obtained our first broad view of the great glacier afterwards named the Muir, the last of all the grand company to be seen, the stormy weather having hidden it when we first entered the bay. It was now perfectly clear, and the spacious prairie-like glacier, with its many tributaries extending far back into the snowy recesses of its fountains, made a magnificent display of its wealth, and I was strongly tempted to go and explore it at all hazards. But winter had come, and the freezing of its fiords was an insurmountable obstacle. I had, therefore, to be content for the present with sketching and studying its main features at a distance.

When we arrived at the Hoona hunting-camp, men, women, and children came swarming out to welcome us. In the neighborhood of this camp I carefully noted the lines of demarkation between the forested and deforested regions. Several mountains here are only in part deforested, and the lines separating the bare and the forested portions are well defined. The soil, as well as the trees, had slid off the steep slopes, leaving the edge of the woods raw-looking and rugged.

At the mouth of the bay a series of moraine islands show that the trunk glacier that occupied the bay halted here for some time and deposited this island material as a terminal moraine; that more of the bay was not filled in shows that, after lingering here, it receded comparatively fast. All the level portions of trunks of glaciers occupying ocean fiords, instead of melting back gradually in times of general shrinking and recession, as inland glaciers with sloping channels do, melt almost uniformly over all the surface until they become thin enough to float. Then, of course, with each rise and fall of the tide, the sea water, with a temperature usually considerably above the freezing-point, rushes in and out beneath them, causing rapid waste of the nether surface, while the upper is being wasted by the weather, until at length the fiord portions of these great glaciers become comparatively thin and weak and are broken up and vanish almost simultaneously.

Glacier Bay is undoubtedly young as yet. Vancouver's chart, made only a century ago, shows no trace of it, though found admirably faithful in general. It seems probable, therefore, that even then the entire bay was occupied by a glacier of which all those described above, great though they are, were only tributaries. Nearly as great a change has taken place in Sum Dum Bay since Vancouver's visit, the main trunk glacier there having receded from eighteen to twenty-five miles from the line marked on his chart. Charley, who was here when a boy, said that the place had so changed that he hardly recognized it, so many new islands had been born in the mean time and so much ice had vanished. As we have seen, this Icy Bay is being still farther extended by the recession of the glaciers. That this whole system of fiords and channels was added to the domain of the sea by glacial action is to my mind certain.

We reached the island from which we had obtained our store of fuel about half-past six and camped here for the night, having spent only five days in Sitadaka, sailing round it, visiting and sketching all the six glaciers excepting the largest, though I landed only on three of them,—the Geikie, Hugh Miller, and Grand Pacific,—the freezing of the fiords in front of the others rendering them inaccessible at this late season.

$\mathcal{O}$N THE $\mathcal{R}$EEF, $\mathcal{D}$ARKLY

Kenneth Brower

$\mathcal{G}$eerat Vermeij sat in a spare, termite-ridden apartment built above a small biology laboratory in the Palau Archipelago of Micronesia, seven degrees north of the equator. The room was littered with shells of all descriptions, some loose on the tabletops like spare change, others wet and drying on the sink, still more wrapped in toilet paper and jammed by the dozen into plastic bags. Vermeij found two snails to demonstrate the problems in distinguishing species. He held up the first.

"Here's a shell that superficially, to me, looks very much like a young morula," he said. "In fact, when I picked it up the first time, I thought it *was* a young morula. But I know that it isn't. It's a nassarius. It's a young *Nassarius graniferus*. It has very, very similar sculpture on top to a young morula."

The morula in Vermeij's palm was black. The nassarius was white.

"Of course someone with eyesight would know right away," I suggested.

"Of course," he agreed. "The morula is dark, and the nassarius is white."

Vermeij is twenty-eight years old. He is lean and in a fragile way handsome. His face in thought is ascetic. It's a Dutch face, and in Palau, not far from the old Netherlands New Guinea, it seemed to have a historical rightness. It was a face from Joseph Conrad. It looked correct under coconut palms and trade-wind cumuli.

Vermeij's goatee is sparse and boyish, his features youthful in their enthusiasms. He moves with a trace of the brittleness of the blind, forever anticipating a bump. He has a questing stride with just a hint of reserve to it. He will gladly show you how far he can broad-jump, if you point him in a safe direction. The legs are full of spring and they take him an amazing distance.

Vermeij's was the first juvenile case of glaucoma in his province of the Netherlands. He was born blind, or nearly so. He could see colors and vague outlines until he was three, then the light went out. It will never come back; his present set of eyes are plastic. The last color he saw was yellow.

The Vermeij family left the Netherlands when Geerat was eight, partly for his sake. "At that time," he says, "Holland did not have particularly good education for the blind. They made you go to one of these hideous institutions. The discipline was awful. I spent three years in such places. I think if I stayed I would have gone nuts."

In Holland Vermeij did have one teacher, a Miss Mooy, whom he remembers as extraordinary. She took Geerat and his classmates into the heath and showed them things. He began collecting acorns, shells, leaves, and such, with the approval of his father, an avid amateur naturalist. When the Vermeijs moved to New Jersey, one of the three states then known for enlightened programs for the blind, Miss Mooy's place was taken by Mrs. Caroline Colberg. Geerat was a ten-year-old in Mrs. Colberg's fourth-grade class when she brought in some shells from Florida. They were semitropical, like nothing he had felt before. His fingers traced the extravagant sculpture, the glassy involutions, and encountered there the first intimations of their genius.

"I got to see helmet shells," he says. "Helmet shells are very different from anything you see in Holland. The *smoothness*. It's nice smooth stuff with good, even sculpture on it. I thought it was gorgeous. Most shells in Holland are kind of rough and calcareous. All northern shells are that way."

The sensation was epochal. Vermeij's consuming interest, since the helmet shells, has been the tropics.

The town of Koror, Palau's capital, woke at six-thirty to the siren on top of the police station. Geerat Vermeij was up forty minutes before that to take his morning shower, because at six o'clock the public works shuts the water off. The shower was cold, a fine way to start the tropical day. Afterward Vermeij sat and waited for breakfast, listening to the town waking. There was no glass in the windows, and the morning sounds entered through the screens easily.

Somewhere below a child asked a question. Sleepy, rising inflection. A woman answered irritably. A rooster crowed. Conversation began to stir, a question here, a declaration there. A pig squealed, then subsided. Tires crunched on the crushed-coral road surface. They rolled over the tips of staghorn corals, the tubes of pipe-organ corals, the convolutions of a brain coral, half-buried, a *memento mori* of the reef. Alas, poor brain coral. They rolled too over mollusks that came up with the corals in the dredge. Cone shells are imbedded in Koror's roads, *Conus magus* and *imperialis* and *tessulatus* and *textile,* their patterns long since faded. The fluted shells of *Tridacna,* the giant clam, curve above the earth like the tips of buried boulders. The tires rolled over trochus, thais, murexes, mitrids. The car slowed to take the corner, then the coralline-molluscan mumble of the tires diminished. Another rooster crowed. A shorebird skimmed the laboratory lawn, braked, and gave a cry as it landed. A group of children were on the move, the locus of their voices traveling downhill. Several dogs got very excited about something. The siren sounded. "Breakfast!" said Dr. Edith Vermeij, and Dr. Geerat Vermeij bounded up from his chair.

Vermeij earned his B.S. in three years and his Ph.D. in three. He is now an associate professor at the University of Maryland. In recent years he has collected shells in Jamaica, Puerto Rico, Netherlands Antilles, Guadeloupe, Panama, Costa Rica, Ecuador, Peru, Chile, Brazil, Senegal, Ivory Coast, Ghana, Sierra Leone, Kenya, Madagascar, Singapore, Philippines, Hawaii, Guam, Saipan, and Palau. He has become a biogeographer. The patterns that interest him are global.

When he refers, shell in hand, to his mental globe, his journey there is tactile and auditory. In Vermeij's geography, all continents are dark. When he thinks of Senegal, he remembers the dryness, the sounds and smells of the city of Dakar, and a couple of large limpets. When he thinks of Israel he remembers the dry heat, the friendliness, and a couple of species of *Drupa.* The features that leap at Vermeij from his mental globe are not land masses but shorelines. His world is littoral.

"How do you do it?" I asked Vermeij one morning. "Show me exactly how you tell them apart."

He agreed to try, and picked up two unwrapped shells at random from the table. They were reasonably similar. One was *Thais armigera,* the other *Vasum turbinellus.* He held up the thais.

"Okay," he said. "The first thing you notice about *Thais armigera* is that it's knobby." He hesitated. "But so is *Vasum.* What *do* I do when I pick up a shell? I sort of know right away. For one thing, the thais has a widish aperture." He began again. This time he lifted the vasum.

"Okay. *Vasum* and *Thais.* They're similar. They both have big knobs. *Thais* has a wide aperture, *Vasum* has a narrow aperture. They both have short spines, they both have knobs. But with the knobs on the vasums, at least the Palauan vasums, by far the largest knobs are closer to the suture between adjacent whorls."

He picked up the thais again.

"Whereas on this shell it's . . . it's true also, but much less so. Somewhat less so. This second row of spines is still pretty strong, I'll admit."

He began again.

"*Vasum turbinellus* has the posteriormost row of knobs much the strongest. And they gradually become smaller as you go anterior, except for this very anterior set of knobs, which is again longer. Whereas on the thais it's . . . it's a little different. The description actually would be the same, because here again the anterior knobs get continually shorter. But there's a difference. The large spines on the thais point move backward, a little bit." He lifted the vasum. "On this one. . . on this one they. . . they point backward too. So that doesn't work either. It's just a . . ."

He paused, perplexed.

"You seemed to know them right away. . . as soon as you touched them," I offered. "What was the first clue?"

"It was probably the more triangular nature of this vasum. As opposed to the somewhat more expanded aperture of the thais."

I waited, but Vermeij didn't seem to want to say more on the subject. "I'm amazed that they're in different genera," I said.

"Families," he answered. "In fact, I think they're in different suborders."

I decided, then, not to ask him about subspecies. On Ilha Fernando de Noronha, off the coast of Brazil, he had discovered a new subspecies of nerite, distinguishing it from the subspecies that were its cousins. I was doubtful now that he could tell me how.

The smell of dead mollusks was strongest outside Vermeij's kitchen door. It was there, in a deep outdoor sink, that he gave his shells their first washing. The larger shells never came inside. They remained by the back door, propped against the walls. Vermeij spent hours each day removing the inhabitants with pins and washing out their houses. As he handled the shells, he thought about them. "There's a lot of drudgery," he admitted once, "but there's also a lot of learning. I get to see the shells in detail again."

Dr. Vermeij had spent so much time at the splashing sink, up to his elbows in the phylum Mollusca, that he smelled of it. He was redolent of dying gastropods. And of fish stomachs, which he opened regularly for evidence of fish predation of mollusks. The apartment's aroma of molluscan death reached its apogee not in the scattered piles of mollusks, but in the malacologist.

When a shell falls into Geerat Vermeij's hand, at the sink or elsewhere, it is caught up in a kind of dance. It revolves, flips, cants one way or another as his fingertips count whorls, gauge thicknesses, measure spires.

Most mollusks are identifiable by shape, according to Vermeij. Cone shells present problems for him, because color pattern distinguishes them more than their forms, which are all very similar. But cones are hard for everyone, he says. Their designs are often obscured by growths. Vermeij has trouble, too, with shells smaller than five millimeters. With shells approaching that limit he uses his thumbnail instead of his fingertips. His chitinous nail, sending up a private Morse code of clicks from the minute landscape of calcium carbonate, tells him what he's holding.

"I've been handling shells for twenty years, and I've never gotten tired of it," Vermeij mused as he handled still another. Through the intermediaries of his fingers, he rolled and rolled the shell with his mind, wondering what the shape meant. What, Vermeij asks himself continually, is the adaptive significance?

"This is *Fragum fragum,* a sand-dwelling bivalve," he told me. "Run your hand from the umbo—which is this thing on top— down to this edge here, and then back again. You'll notice it's sharper one way." I did as he advised. In one direction the shell was rough, like a cat's tongue; in the other it was smooth. "When it burrows," said Vermeij, "and it's a very fast burrower, its foot goes down and forward. It is exactly in that direction that the spines are least resistant. The most resistance is when you try to pull them out. It's a wonderful adaptation that an awful lot of sand animals have."

This was, of course, a Dick and Jane exercise in shell contemplation. Vermeij's more serious thoughts run to the geometry of shell shape and the adaptive function of that. He considers himself foremost a shell geometrician. *The angle of elevation of the coiling axis relative to the plane of the aperture* and a host of other angles and figures preoccupy him.

Vermeij applies the word "geometry" broadly. ("Organ music is the only loud music I like. It has a whole different geometrical effect for me. You sit in a room and you're entirely surrounded by music.") For Vermeij geometry has become more than a science.

One day he set a shell down on the apartment table and leaned back proudly.

"Logarithmic spiral," he said. "This is the figure that is generated when shape does not change with size. It's the most beautiful shape in nature, I think."

The nearly perpetual splashing of the outdoor sink, then, though it sounded tedious to me, for Vermeij was not. For him it was drowned out by organ music. At the sink he was lost in his digital ruminations. The shapes of shells were his sunsets.

Quietly, so quietly that I suspected Vermeij had not heard, one, then two, then three small Palauan boys began pulling themselves in slow motion up onto the ledge outside his window. They pressed black faces to the screen—seven of them, finally—and they watched Vermeij from three feet away.

"You have some spectators," I informed him.

"I know," he said.

The room had suddenly become dark. The boys, jammed as they were in the window, shut out the light. That made no difference to Vermeij, of course. Expressionless, the boys watched him work. There wasn't a clue on their faces as to what they made of him. After five minutes they began conferring among themselves, exchanging short sentences in the Palauan tongue, a polysyllabic and often guttural language. Their voices had the pleasant huskiness common to Palauan children. The Palauan language is full of changes in pitch, and Vermeij likes it. Monotonous languages and voices irritate him.

"What's this?" asked one boy finally, in English.

"It's writing. It's braille," said Vermeij, eager at the chance to communicate. He held up the heavy brown braille paper, the stylus, and the braille slate, and he showed the boys how he wrote from right to left. The boys watched him gravely and said nothing more.

Vermeij worked on for five minutes. Then the boys' silence at last got to him, and he began to feel like something in a zoo. Decisively he set his writing things aside. "All right, that's all," he said. "I'm done. All finished. Why don't you go play somewhere else." The boys did not get the idea at first, but when they did, they departed as silently as they had come.

Vermeij moved to the kitchen sink and began washing shells. An electronic noise made by some insect came, as usual, from a tree outside the kitchen window. The tree hummed as if a transformer were hidden in the epiphytes that bearded its branches. Below the hilltop a girls' softball game was in progress, and the shrieks of the players and of the audience carried up. The shrieks came regularly, like breathing. It sounded like the most exciting softball game in history, but in truth Palauan girls scream at the softest grounder, the shallowest fly, the most routine play at first.

The tree hummed, the girls screamed, Vermeij's sink splashed, the noon siren sounded.

To date, Vermeij's principal contribution to his science has been, he believes, his discovery of certain differences between Pacific and Atlantic shells. He has found that Pacific shells are more heavily armored than Atlantic. They show a higher incidence of antipredatory devices—obstructed apertures, inflexible opercula, low spires, and strong external shell sculpture. The reason, Vermeij believes, is that the Pacific has had a longer history without major geological perturbation. Predator–prey relationships have evolved without as much interruption in the Pacific and have become more complex. Survival for mollusks there has become a neater trick.

Vermeij does not want to spend the rest of his career developing this theory, as he probably should. He is leery of specialization. Until his final year of graduate school, his preoccupation with mollusks was total, but in that last year he broadened his reading. He is now a student of all invertebrates, and of biochemistry. He has written a paper on vines. He is interested in slow muscle and fast muscle in the claws of crabs.

In Palau one evening we watched him root through the garbage and come up with a fish head that Edith, his wife, had boiled for soup. He knows little about fish, but he was fascinated by the teeth. He kept running his fingers over the strange, rounded molars, indulging in pure, uninformed speculation. Though he remains most knowledgeable about mollusks, especially snails and nerites, he likes to think it may not always be so. He is one of those scientists who want to be free—as Newton was, and as Newton put it—to pick up "a smoother pebble or prettier shell than ordinary, whilst the great ocean of truth lay all undiscovered before me."

The reef curved away to either side of where we stood. Long white combers broke on it, marking it as far as I could see. On the arc to the south was a distant wreck. The tide was low. Our shins were awash.

Vermeij turned and started north along the slight ridge of coral stones that made the spine of the reef. He stepped carefully among the reef's irregular vertebrae, hunting the line that divides lagoon from ocean. The surf broke forty yards offshore, and the Pacific, its energy spent, lapped the rocks in a gentle current and rippled past our ankles. The sun was radiant on our shoulders, though a cool wind allowed us to believe it wasn't. The sea smell was strong.

Vermeij soon tired of the higher rocks, left the reef's spine, and walked toward the ocean. The reef shelved very gradually under sea, in that direction. He collected for a time in knee-deep water, turning stones and searching their bottom surfaces. When his fingers encountered a snail, they pulled it off and dropped it in the bucket. They rolled the snail in transit, identifying it somewhere along its parabola to the pail.

"A new species of *Thais,*" he said, bucketing a specimen. "New for this trip, anyway."

He crouched in the water and began collecting on his haunches, so that his arms could sweep a wider area. His loins were in the Pacific. He heard the incoming waves and avoided them with a water-ouzel motion, straightening his knees but dipping his torso, so that the work of his hands could go on uninterrupted. He moved in nice synchrony with the waves, rising just in time, with a shorebird's sense of the sea's rhythm.

He brought up a cobalt-blue, slender-armed starfish. He tucked his pail between his knees to free his hands, and he patted down the undersides of the animal's rays, two at a time, from base to tip, feeling for any molluscan parasites. The starfish was clean, and he tossed it away. "Blue starfish," he said, and he gave the Latin name.

He moved on. For a time he worked in silence. Then I saw him smile tightly. "Fire coral here," he said.

"Sting you?" I asked.

"A little, on the knuckle."

The hydroid corals, called fire corals or stinging corals, are common on Indo-Pacific reefs. They are protean, forming saucers, blades, and branches. They encrust other corals, taking their shape, or grow over old bottles and wrecks, rendering these rich and strange, but disguising themselves in the process. For this reason, and because they vary in color, they are hard to recognize, but Vermeij knows instantly when he has found one.

The pressure of his knuckle had tripped the triggers of thousands of nematocysts, or stinging cells, on the coral's surface. Within the capsule of each nematocyst was a coiled tube armed with folded barbs. The opercula of the capsules sprang open, the tubes uncoiled, their barbs unfolded and stabbed Vermeij. The poison-filled hollow in which each tube had reposed emptied its contents into him. The poison contained 5-hydroxytryptamine, a potent pain-producer and histamine-releaser, which worked directly on pain receptors in his skin. Vermeij made the identification even faster than with the gastropods he knows so well. The problem was never presented formally to his brain; it was intercepted by his sympathetic nervous system, which mindlessly gave its readout. "FIRE CORAL," it said.

Vermeij is stung regularly by fire corals, and he accepts their nettlesomeness casually, as a mild reprimand. There are worse things around. The seas Vermeij has chosen for his work are the most venomous in the world. He has been stung by fire-worms, hydroids, sea urchins, Portuguese men-of-war.

"See this coral here?" Vermeij asked. "Jesus! Lovely!"

He didn't linger at the lovely coral, but left it and moved on. He found something he could not identify. It was under a rock, and he was unable to scrape it off. He smelled his fingers, making use of another sense.

"What is it?" I asked.

"I don't know. But it has a very peculiar smell, like iodine."

He moved on again, without having resolved the problem. The sun was hot on our shoulders and I shifted the shirt that I had draped across mine. I realized that I was a little sunsick. Vermeij worked on, dark, like Samson, amid the blaze of noon. He turned rocks and shifted them. If a rock did not move easily, he abandoned it for the next.

"I never look in the sand underneath the rocks, after turning them over," he said. "There are a lot of dangerous things down there. Cones. Some very dangerous fish."

Despite his precaution, Vermeij occasionally does pick up a cone shell. He knows instantly what he has found, and the knowledge is electric, but he does not drop his catch. He quickly shifts his fingers to the apex, where the cone's proboscis cannot immediately find them, and he deposits the animal in his bucket.

The teeth of a cone are long, fine, chitinous, and hollow. In the species *Conus striatus* they are designed exactly like Eskimo harpoons, but are perfectly transparent, and as lovely as harpoons by Steuben. Cone teeth are miniatures on a scale that no glass-carver could achieve. Their barbs are as sharp as ice crystals, and for the tropical worms, snails, small fish, and shell collectors that they strike, the teeth do have an arctic chill. An early symptom of their venom is numbness.

One night in Palau Vermeij dreamed he was stung by a cone he had collected. The numbness spread from his hand to his arm and shoulder, and then he woke up. Symptoms are, as in Vermeij's dream, first a stinging sensation, then numbness, then a spreading paralysis. The victim loses sensation in his limbs and has difficulty speaking and swallowing. If he is to live, his recovery begins after about six hours. Otherwise his sight is affected, his respiratory muscles begin to fail, he loses consciousness, and he dies.

I put on my face mask, lay in the water, and watched Vermeij's fingers work. They were ghostly underwater and they moved ceaselessly, meandering, then marching over the coral stones, pausing in crannies, moving on. They completed their scans so quickly that I found them hard to follow. When fingers met something animate, they retracted for a cautious instant, then returned, and in a flurry of touches they felt the thing out. Sometimes, after heavy collecting, Vermeij's fingers are so roughened that they slow his reading to a crawl. Scanning braille notes with fingers full of sponge spicules and coral cuts is like reading by moonlight through a bad prescription.

Vermeij turned over rocks for fifteen minutes without either of us speaking. For all he knew, he was alone on the reef. He did not care.

"Nice coral here. Pretty," he said at last. He directed his words to the reef at large, for he no longer knew where I stood.

Lying in perfect camouflage along Palau's reefs, in places just like this, was *Synanceja horrida,* the stonefish. Sluggish, big-mouthed, bug-eyed, covered with warts and debris, abysmally ugly, the stonefish is armed with spines that produce probably the most excruciating pain known to man. Swimming slowly among the same corals, all lace and frills and bands of color, wildly beautiful, is *Pterois volitans,* the lionfish. A victim of the lionfish, like that of the stonefish, thrashes, screams, and loses consciousness. His skin reddens, swells, and sloughs away. "Cardiac failure," writes Bruce Halstead, a student of marine venoms, "delirium, convulsions, various nervous disturbances, nausea, vomiting, lymphangitis, lymphadenitis, joint aches, fever, respiratory distress and convulsions may be present, and death may occur."

Yellow sea snakes, yellow-lipped sea kraits, annulated sea snakes, reef sea snakes, banded small-headed sea snakes, graceful small-headed sea snakes, elegant sea snakes, wandering sea snakes, beaked sea snakes, Darwin's, Gray's, Grey's, blue-banded, broad-banded sea snakes, and thirty-odd other species hunt the tropical waters where Vermeij collects. The sea snakes have the most toxic venom in the snake kingdom. Their poison works with an odd gentleness. The fangs are painless, or nearly so. If the victim realizes at all that he has been bitten, it is in a slight stinging sensation. There is no swelling or unusual bleeding. The affected part may become sensitive to touch briefly, then a local anesthesia sets in. There is a latent period of an hour or two. Then the victim begins to feel sluggish. He has increasing difficulty moving his limbs and special trouble opening his mouth. His urine turns red. His tendon reflexes diminish, then disappear. The muscles of his eyelids become paralyzed. He feels a kind of false drowsiness, then a real drowsiness. Soon he is motionless, eyes closed, and he appears to be sleeping. He is not. Survivors report that they remained conscious but unable to move, or to open their eyes or mouths. For many victims, of course, the false sleep becomes real and final.

On the sandy patches of reef where Vermeij probes for the long-spired snails that live buried in sand, stingrays, too, lie buried. when stepped upon or handled, stingrays whip their tails across their backs and strike with the retro-barbed sawblades of their stings. The venom works directly on the heart and vascular system.

"Look at all this *Caulerpa*," Vermeij said.

He was running his fingers through a green patch of the edible algae that Palauans sometimes come to the reef to gather. *Caulerpa* sways in the current like soft coral, but it is not. It's a real plant in a realm of animals that masquerade as such. In the midst of the reef's sharp edges it felt soft and wonderful. But Vermeij moved on.

He worked his way steadily deeper, toward the breaking surf. He was thigh-deep now, heading southwest. In that direction there was nothing but ocean, and, five hundred miles away, New Guinea. He continued still deeper, until he was collecting with his cheek beside the swells, his arm extended full length, his fingers exploring. The secondary waves rolled in bigger here, and Vermeij, warned by the sound they made as they began to break, straightened just ahead of them, with his shorebird's distaste for wasted motion. He left off his hunting not a moment too soon.

The wave that finally hit him was arrhythmic. It did not break, and followed closely a wave that did. It hid from him in the noise of its predecessor and socked him in the chest. He regained his balance with a small smile of surprise.

The ocean threw several more sneak punches at him in the course of the day. The collecting pail never went under, I noticed. He bore it like a standard, and the ocean never trod on it.

Night was coming on, the tree frogs were warming up their instruments, the rice was cooking on the stove. Edith Vermeij went to the cupboard and poured rum and Coke for everyone. Vermeij broke off his work. He washed up, left the sink, and crossed to his chair, his arms held slightly out before him. When he had located the chair with a shin, he turned and fell back into it with abandon, as was his habit. He sat with his heels on the edge of the seat, knees under chin, and he began to smile oddly.

The malacologist's mind, when it is not in gear professionally, keeps itself idling in plays on words. When he has nothing to do, as on airplane trips—an especially deadly time for him—he does simple anagrams, "top" becoming "opt" and so on, or he plays similar games of his own invention. He was playing some such game tonight, or working on a pun. Vermeij puns compulsively and with a crazy delight.

Outside the frogs sang like strident battalions of telegraphers all sending the same message. A toad soloed against it. The rapid mellow drumming was a jungle-movie sound, like someone beating a tattoo on a long slender log. The first toad stopped and another began. The toads sometimes seemed to respect each other's songs and not interrupt, but now two toads started drumming together, making a single noise with a resonating pulse.

A gecko on the screen made its scolding noise, as if with a mechanical birdcall. Three of the high-pitched barks, Palauans say, mean that someone is to visit. Tonight the geckos all made long speeches, and no one called on us. Now and again the squeak of a bat came down from the dark, slipping to a pitch that our human ears could register. The high note was a reminder that we were hearing only a slice of the night. Hundreds of bats were hunting the air above the laboratory hilltop. In full spectrum the night must have truly roared.

A squall approached, sending ahead of it a gust that buffeted the screen. Vermeij had moved already to the window, sensing some sort of insensible gust before the gust, and he stood ready for the wind's cool benediction. I had seen him do that several times before. The gust rattled the screen, bringing with it for a moment, in its coolness and its smell of distance, the recollection of another latitude. The first scattered drops hit, then the sky dumped and the tin roof thundered.

Vermeij nodded upward at the violence on the roof.

"I've been in the tropics for years now, and I've never got used to it," he said.

The nine o'clock siren sounded. The rain fell harder and soon it seemed to beat a circular pattern on the tin. The toads, wet and happy, all began to drum together, their percussion pulsing, and the whole night swirled and eddied with sound.

The sun of a new day was directly overhead. It was not yet ten, but the white ball had raced already to zenith, where it would hang until late afternoon, then plunge precipitously. I studied Vermeij in the perfect saturation of its light.

He crouched chest-deep in the lagoon, his back to me. He was perfectly still and listed slightly to one side, like a statue undermined by the sea. I knew from experience that underwater he was moving, working tirelessly, scanning the sand and corals at his sides, then circling behind to scan what lay at his heels. I had watched it often enough to see without watching. His fingers now were walking palely through the most lavish colors in nature. There are no hues on earth like those of a tropical coral reef. A school of opalescent fusiliers turned away in perfect unison, deflected by the motion of his hand. An angelfish outlined in electric blue, as if struck just now by lightning, studied his forearm and moved on. Feather worms buried in coral heads snapped their circular fans shut as his fingers drew near. A clown fish, painted for the circus, ran from him to its anemone and did its dance among the tentacles. Cleanerfish with blue-green stripes that glowed like neon, bold with the privilege of their office, hunted his toes for parasites. They gave him tiny, insensible, fishy kisses, were disappointed, and moved on. A Spanish mackerel circled in from deeper water, then out again, and as it turned the light scattered prismatically from its sides.

Vermeij moved sideways to a new spot and became a statue again. In front of him the shallows were turquoise, the deeper passages dark blue and serpentine. Across the channel, the adjacent island rose mountainous and green. Against the green two white terns, blinding in the sun, spiraled upward, then dropped a little, but above the island's summit a great tropical cumulus continued their ascent, climbing up and up, as tropical clouds do, all banners and battlements, with the albedo nearly of the birds, into a blue sky.

"Here's a coral I've never seen before," Vermeij said, to his wife, or to himself, or to the great ocean of truth that lay all undiscovered before him.

$\mathcal{G}$ALAPAGOS $\mathcal{A}$RCHIPELAGO

Charles Darwin

$\mathcal{T}$he natural history of these islands is eminently curious, and well deserves attention. Most of the organic productions are aboriginal creations, found nowhere else; there is even a difference between the inhabitants of the different islands; yet all show a marked relationship with those of America, though separated from that continent by an open space of ocean, between 500 and 600 miles in width. The archipelago is a little world within itself, or rather a satellite attached to America, whence it has derived a few stray colonists, and has received the general character of its indigenous productions. Considering the small size of these islands, we feel the more astonished at the number of their aboriginal beings, and at their confined range. Seeing every height crowned with its crater, and the boundaries of most of the lava-streams still distinct, we are led to believe that within a period, geologically recent, the unbroken ocean was here spread out. Hence, both in space and time, we seem to be brought somewhat near to that great fact—that mystery of mysteries—the first appearance of new beings on this earth.

Of terrestrial mammals, there is only one which must be considered as indigenous, namely, a mouse (Mus Galapagoensis), and this is confined, as far as I could ascertain, to Chatham island, the most easterly island of the group. It belongs, as I am informed by Mr. Waterhouse, to a division of the family of mice characteristic of America. At James island, there is a rat sufficiently distinct from the common kind to have been named and described by Mr. Waterhouse; but as it belongs to the old-world division of the family, and as this island has been frequented by ships for the last hundred and fifty years, I can hardly doubt that this rat is merely a variety, produced by the new and peculiar climate, food, and soil, to which it has been subjected. Although no one has a right to speculate without distinct facts, yet even with respect to the Chatham island mouse, it should be borne in mind, that it may possibly be an American species imported here; for I have seen, in a most unfrequented part of the Pampas, a native mouse living in the roof of a newly-built hovel, and therefore its transportation in a vessel is not improbable; analogous facts have been observed by Dr. Richardson in North America.

Of land-birds I obtained twenty-six kinds, all peculiar to the group and found nowhere else, with the exception of one lark-like finch from North America (Dolichonyx oryzivorus), which ranges on that continent as far north as 54°, and generally frequents marshes. The other twenty-five birds consist, firstly, of a hawk, curiously intermediate in structure between a Buzzard and the American group of carrion-feeding Polybori; and with these latter birds it agrees most closely in every habit and even tone of voice. Secondly, there are two owls, representing the short-eared and white barn-owls of Europe. Thirdly, a wren, three tyrant fly-catchers (two of them species of Pyrocephalus, one or both of which would be ranked by some ornithologists as only varieties), and a dove—all analogous to, but distinct from, American species. Fourthly, a swallow, which though differing from the Progne purpurea of both Americas, only in being rather duller coloured, smaller, and slenderer, is considered by Mr. Gould as specifically distinct. Fifthly, there are three species of mocking-thrush—a form highly characteristic of America. The remaining land-birds form a most singular group of finches, related to each other in the structure of their beaks, short tails, form of body, and plumage: there are thirteen species, which Mr. Gould has divided into four sub-groups. All these species are peculiar to this archipelago; and so is the whole group, with the exception of one species of the sub-group Cactornis, lately brought from Bow island, in the Low Archipelago. Of Cactornis, the two species may be often seen climbing about the flowers of the great cactus-trees; but all the other species of this group of finches, mingled together in flocks, feed on the dry and sterile ground of the lower districts. The males of all, or certainly of the greater number, are jet black; and the females (with perhaps one or two exceptions) are brown. The most curious fact is the perfect gradation in the size of the beaks in the different species of Geospiza, from one as large as that of a hawfinch to that of a chaffinch, and (if Mr. Gould is right in including his sub-group, Certhidea, in the main group), even to that of a warbler. There are no less than six species with insensibly graduated beaks. The beak of Cactornis is somewhat like that of a starling; and that of the fourth sub-group, Camarhynchus, is slightly parrot-shaped. Seeing this gradation and diversity of structure in one small, intimately related group of birds, one might really fancy that from an original paucity of birds in this archipelago, one species had been taken and modified for different ends. In a like manner it might be fancied that a bird originally a buzzard, had been induced here to undertake the office of the carrion-feeding Polybori of the American continent.

Of waders and water-birds I was able to get only eleven kinds, and of these only three (including a rail confined to the damp summits of the islands) are new species. Considering the wandering habits of the gulls, I was surprised to find that the species inhabiting these islands is peculiar, but allied to one from the southern parts of South America. The far greater peculiarity of the land-birds, namely, twenty-five out of twenty-six being new species or at least new races, compared with the waders and web-footed birds, is in accordance with the greater range which these latter orders have in all parts of the world. We shall hereafter see this law of aquatic forms, whether marine or fresh-water, being less peculiar at any given point of the earth's surface than the terrestrial forms of the same classes, strikingly illustrated in the shells, and in a lesser degree in the insects of this archipelago.

Two of the waders are rather smaller than the same species brought from other places: the swallow is also smaller, though it is doubtful whether or not it is distinct from its analogue. The two owls, the two tyrant fly-catchers (Pyrocephalus) and the dove, are also smaller than the analogous but distinct species, to which they are most nearly related; on the other hand, the gull is rather larger. The two owls, the swallow, all three species of mocking-thrush, the dove in its separate colours though not in its whole plumage, the Totanus, and the gull, are likewise duskier coloured than their analogous species; and in the case of the mocking-thrush and Totanus, than any other species of the two genera. With the exception of a wren with a fine yellow breast, and of a tyrant fly-catcher with a scarlet tuft and breast, none of the birds are brilliantly coloured, as might have been expected in an equatorial district. Hence it would appear probable, that the same causes which here make the immigrants of some species smaller, make most of the peculiar Galapageian species also smaller, as well as very generally more dusky coloured. All the plants have a wretched, weedy appearance, and I did not see one beautiful flower. The insects, again, are small sized and dull coloured, and, as Mr. Waterhouse informs me, there is nothing in their general appearance which would have led him to imagine that they had come from under the equator. The birds, plants, and insects have a desert character, and are not more brilliantly coloured than those from southern Patagonia; we may, therefore, conclude that the usual gaudy colouring of the intertropical productions, is not related either to the heat or light of those zones, but to some other cause, perhaps to the conditions of existence being generally favourable to life.

We will now turn to the order of reptiles, which gives the most striking character to the zoology of these islands. The species are not numerous, but the numbers of individuals of each species are extraordinarily great. There is one small lizard belonging to a South American genus, and two species (and probably more) of the Amblyrhynchus—a genus confined to the Galapagos islands. There is one snake which is numerous; it is identical, as I am informed by M. Bibron, with the Psammophis Temminckii from Chile. Of sea-turtle I believe there is more than one species; and of tortoises there are, as we shall presently show, two or three species or races. Of toads and frogs there are none: I was surprised at this, considering how well suited for them the temperate and damp upper woods appeared to be. It recalled to my mind the remark made by Bory St. Vincent,[1] namely, that none of this family are found on any

---

[1] Voyage Aux Quatre Iles d'Afrique. With respect to the Sandwich Islands, see Tyerman and Bennett's Journal, vol. i. p. 434. For Mauritius, see Voyage par un Officier, &c., Part i, p. 170. There are no frogs in the Canary Islands (Webb et Berthelot, Hist. Nat. des Iles Canaries). I saw none at St. Jago in the Cape de Verds. There are none at St. Helena.

of the volcanic islands in the great oceans. As far as I can ascertain from various works, this seems to hold good throughout the Pacific, and even in the large islands of the Sandwich archipelago. Mauritius offers an apparent exception, where I saw the Rana Mascariensis in abundance: this frog is said now to inhabit the Seychelles, Madagascar, and Bourbon; but on the other hand, Du Bois, in his voyage of 1669, states that there were no reptiles in Bourbon except tortoises; and the Officier du Roi asserts that before 1768 it had been attempted, without success, to introduce frogs into Mauritius—I presume, for the purpose of eating: hence it may be well doubted whether this frog is an aboriginal of these islands. The absence of the frog family in the oceanic islands is the more remarkable, when contrasted with the case of lizards, which swarm on most of the smallest islands. May this difference not be caused, by the greater facility with which the eggs of lizards, protected by calcareous shells, might be transported through salt-water, than could the slimy spawn of frogs?

I will first describe the habits of the tortoise (Testudo nigra, formerly called Indica), which has been so frequently alluded to. These animals are found, I believe, on all the islands of the Archipelago; certainly on the greater number. They frequent in preference the high damp parts, but they likewise live in the lower and arid districts. I have already shown, from the numbers which have been caught in a single day, how very numerous they must be. Some grow to an immense size: Mr. Lawson, an Englishman, and vice-governor of the colony, told us that he had seen several so large, that it required six or eight men to lift them from the ground; and that some had afforded as much as two hundred pounds of meat. The old males are the largest, the females rarely growing to so great a size: the male can readily be distinguished from the female by the greater length of its tail. The tortoises which live on those islands where there is no water, or in the lower and arid parts of the others, feed chiefly on the succulent cactus. Those which frequent the higher and damp regions, eat the leaves of various trees, a kind of berry (called guayavita) which is acid and austere, and likewise a pale green filamentous lichen (Usnera plicata), that hangs in tresses from the boughs of the trees.

The tortoise is very fond of water, drinking large quantities, and wallowing in the mud. The larger islands alone possess springs, and these are always situated towards the central parts, and at a considerable height. The tortoises, therefore, which frequent the lower districts, when thirsty, are obliged to travel from a long distance. Hence broad and well-beaten paths branch off in every direction from the wells down to the sea-coast; and the Spaniards by following them up, first discovered the watering places. When I landed at Chatham Island, I could not imagine what animal travelled so methodically along well-chosen tracks. Near the springs it was a curious spectacle to behold many of these huge creatures, one set eagerly travelling onwards with outstretched necks, and another set returning, after having drunk their fill. When the tortoise arrives at the spring, quite regardless of any spectator, he buries his head in the water above his eyes, and greedily swallows great mouthfuls, at the rate of about ten in a minute. The inhabitants say each animal stays three or four days in the neighbourhood of the water, and then returns to the lower country; but they differed respecting the frequency of these visits. The animal probably regulates them according to the nature of the food on which it has lived. It is, however, certain, that tortoises can subsist even on those islands, where there is no other water than what falls during a few rainy days in the year.

I believe it is well ascertained, that the bladder of the frog acts as a reservoir for the moisture necessary to its existence: such seems to be the case with the tortoise. For some time after a visit to the springs, their urinary bladders are distended with fluid, which is said gradually to decrease in volume, and to become less pure. The inhabitants, when walking in the lower district, and overcome with thirst, often take advantage of this circumstance, and drink the contents of the bladder if full: in one I saw killed, the fluid was quite limpid, and had only a very slightly bitter taste. The inhabitants, however, always first drink the water in the pericardium, which is described as being best.

The tortoises, when purposely moving towards any point, travel by night and day, and arrive at their journey's end much sooner than would be expected. The inhabitants, from observing marked individuals, consider that they travel a distance of about eight miles in two or three days. One large tortoise, which I watched, walked at the rate of sixty yards in ten minutes, that is 360 yards in the hour, or four miles a day,—allowing a little time for it to eat on the road. During the breeding season, when the male and female are together, the male utters a hoarse roar or bellowing, which, it is said, can be heard at the distance of more than a hundred yards. The female never uses her voice, and the male only at these times; so that when the people hear this noise, they know that the two are together. They were at this time (October) laying their eggs. The female, where the soil is sandy, deposits them together, and covers them up with sand; but where the ground is rocky she drops them indiscriminately in any hole: Mr. Bynoe found seven placed in a fissure. The egg is white and spherical; one which I measured was seven inches and three-eighths in circumference, and therefore larger than a hen's egg. The young tortoises, as soon as they are hatched, fall a prey in great numbers to the carrion-feeding buzzard. The old ones seem generally to die from accidents, as from falling down precipices: at least, several of the inhabitants told me, that they had never found one dead without some evident cause.

The inhabitants believe that these animals are absolutely deaf; certainly they do not overhear a person walking close behind them. I was always amused when overtaking one of these great monsters, as it was quietly pacing along, to see how suddenly, the instant I passed, it would draw in its head and legs, and uttering a deep hiss fall to the ground with a heavy sound, as if struck dead. I frequently got on their backs, and then giving a few raps on the hinder part of their shells, they would rise up and walk away;—but I found it very difficult to keep my balance. The flesh of this animal is largely employed, both fresh and salted; and a beautifully clear oil is prepared from the fat. When a tortoise is caught, the man makes a slit in the skin near its tail, so as to see inside its body, whether the fat under the dorsal plate is thick. If it is not, the animal is liberated; and it is said to recover soon from this strange operation. In order to secure the tortoises, it is not sufficient to turn them like turtles, for they are often able to get on their legs again.

There can be little doubt that this tortoise is an aboriginal inhabitant of the Galapagos; for it is found on all, or nearly all, the islands, even on some of the smaller ones where there is no water; had it been an imported species, this would hardly have been the case in a group which has been so little frequented. Moreover, the old Bucaniers found this tortoise in greater numbers even than at present: Wood and Rogers also, in 1708, say that it is the opinion of the Spaniards, that it is found nowhere else in this quarter of the world. It is now widely distributed; but it may be questioned whether it is in any other place an aboriginal. The bones of a tortoise at Mauritius, associated with those of the extinct Dodo, have generally been considered as belonging to this tortoise: if this had been so, undoubtedly it must have been there indigenous; but M. Bibron informs me that he believes that it was distinct, as the species now living there certainly is.

The Amblyrhynchus, a remarkable genus of lizards, is confined to this archipelago: there are two species, resembling each other in general form, one being terrestrial and the other aquatic. This latter species (A. cristatus) was first characterized by Mr. Bell, who well foresaw, from its short, broad head, and strong claws of equal length, that its habits of life would turn out very peculiar, and different from those of its nearest ally, the Iguana. It is extremely common on all the islands throughout the group, and lives exclusively on the rocky sea-beaches, being never found, at least I never saw one, even ten yards in-shore. It is a hideous-looking creature, of a dirty black colour, stupid, and sluggish in its movements. The usual length of a full-grown one is about a yard, but there are some even four feet long; a large one weighed twenty pounds: on the island of Albemarle they seem to grow to a greater size than elsewhere. Their tails are flattened sideways, and all four feet partially webbed. They are occasionally seen some hundred yards from the shore, swimming about; and Captain Collnett, in his Voyage, says, "They go to sea in herds a-fishing, and sun themselves on the rocks; and may be called alligators in miniature." It must not, however, be supposed that they live on fish. When in the water this lizard swims with perfect ease and quickness, by a serpentine movement of its body and flattened tail—the legs being motionless and closely collapsed on its sides. A seaman on board sank one, with a heavy weight attached to it, thinking thus to kill it directly; but when, an hour afterwards, he drew up the line, it was quite active. Their limbs and strong claws are admirably adapted for crawling over the rugged and fissured masses of lava, which everywhere form the coast. In such situations, a group of six or seven of these hideous reptiles may oftentimes be seen on the black rocks, a few feet above the surf, basking in the sun with outstretched legs.

I opened the stomachs of several, and found them largely distended with minced sea-weed (Ulvæ), which grows in thin foliaceous expansions of a bright green or a dull red colour. I do not recollect having observed this sea-weed in any quantity on the tidal rocks; and I have reason to believe it grows at the bottom of the sea, at some little distance from the coast. If such be the case, the object of these animals occasionally going out to sea is explained. The stomach contained nothing but the sea-weed. Mr. Bynoe, however, found a piece of a crab in one; but this might have got in accidentally, in the same manner as I have seen a caterpillar, in the midst of some lichen, in the paunch of a tortoise. The intestines were large, as in other herbivorous animals. The nature of this lizard's food, as well as the structure of its tail and feet, and the fact of its having been seen voluntarily swimming out at sea, absolutely prove its aquatic habits; yet there is in this respect one strange anomaly, namely, that when frightened it will not enter the water. Hence it is easy to drive these lizards down to any little point overhanging the sea, where they will sooner allow a person to catch hold of their tails than jump into the water. They do not seem to have any notion of biting; but when much frightened they squirt a drop of fluid from each nostril. I threw one several times as far as I could, into a deep pool left by the retiring tide; but it invariably returned in a direct line to the spot where I stood. It swam near the bottom, with a very graceful and rapid movement, and occasionally aided itself over the uneven ground with its feet. As soon as it arrived near the edge, but still being under water, it tried to conceal itself in the tufts of sea-weed, or it entered some crevice. As soon as it thought the danger was past, it crawled out on the dry rocks, and shuffled away as quickly as it could. I several times caught this same lizard, by driving it down to a point, and though possessed of such perfect powers of diving and swimming, nothing would induce it to enter the water; and as often as I threw it in, it returned in the manner above described. Perhaps this singular piece of apparent stupidity may be accounted for by the circumstance, that this reptile has no enemy whatever on shore, whereas at sea it must often fall a prey to the numerous sharks. Hence, probably, urged by a fixed and hereditary instinct that the shore is its place of safety, whatever the emergency may be, it there takes refuge.

During our visit (in October), I saw extremely few small individuals of this species, and none I should think under a year old. From this circumstance it seems probable that the breeding season had not then commenced. I asked several of the inhabitants if they knew where it laid its eggs: they said that they knew nothing of its propagation, although well acquainted with the eggs of the land kind—a fact, considering how very common this lizard is, not a little extraordinary.

We will now turn to the terrestrial species (A. Demarlii), with a round tail, and toes without webs. This lizard, instead of being found like the other on all the islands, is confined to the central part of the archipelago, namely to Albemarle, James, Barrington, and Indefatigable islands. To the southward, in Charles, Hood, and Chatham islands, and to the northward, in Towers, Bindloes, and Abingdon, I neither saw nor heard of any. It would appear as if it had been created in the centre of the archipelago, and thence had been dispersed only to a certain distance. Some of these lizards inhabit the high and damp parts of the islands, but they are much more numerous in the lower and sterile districts near the coast. I cannot give a more forcible proof of their numbers, than by stating that when we were left at James Island, we could not for some time find a spot free from their burrows on which to pitch our single tent. Like their brothers the sea-kind, they are ugly animals, of a yellowish orange beneath, and of a brownish red colour above: from their low facial angle they have a singularly stupid appearance. They are, perhaps, of a rather less size than the marine species; but several of them weighed between ten and fifteen pounds. In their movements they are lazy and half torpid. When not frightened, they slowly crawl along with their tails and bellies dragging on the ground. They often stop, and doze for a minute or two, with closed eyes and hind legs spread out on the parched soil.

They inhabit burrows, which they sometimes make between fragments of lava, but more generally on level patches of the soft sandstone-like tuff. The holes do not appear to be very deep, and they enter the ground at a small angle: so that when walking over these lizard-warrens, the soil is constantly giving way, much to the annoyance of the tired walker. This animal, when making its burrow, works alternately the opposite sides of its body. One front leg for a short time scratches up the soil, and throws it towards the hind foot, which is well placed so as to heave it beyond the mouth of the hole. That side of the body being tired, the other takes up the task, and so on alternately. I watched one for a long time, till half its body was buried; I then walked up and pulled it by the tail; at this it was greatly astonished, and soon shuffled up to see what was the matter; and then stared me in the face, as much as to say, "What made you pull my tail?"

They feed by day, and do not wander far from their burrows; if frightened, they rush to them with a most awkward gait. Except when running down hill, they cannot move very fast, apparently from the lateral position of their legs. They are not at all timorous: when attentively watching any one, they curl their tails, and, rais-ing themselves on their front legs, nod their heads vertically, with a quick movement, and try to look very fierce: but in reality they are not at all so; if one just stamps on the ground, down go their tails, and off they shuffle as quickly as they can. I have frequently observed small fly-eating lizards, when watching anything, nod their heads in precisely the same manner; but I do not at all know for what purpose. If this Amblyrhynchus is held and plagued with a stick, it will bite it very severely; but I caught many by the tail, and they never tried to bite me. If two are placed on the ground and held together, they will fight, and bite each other till blood is drawn.

The individuals, and they are the greater number, which inhabit the lower country, can scarcely taste a drop of water throughout the year; but they consume much of the succulent cac-tus, the branches of which are occasionally broken off by the wind. I several times threw a piece to two or three of them when together; and it was amusing enough to see them trying to seize and carry it away in their mouths, like so many hungry dogs with a bone. They eat very deliberately, but do not chew their food. The little birds are aware how harmless these creatures are: I have seen one of the thick-billed finches picking at one end of a piece of cactus (which is much relished by all the animals of the lower region), whilst a lizard was eating at the other end and afterwards the little bird with the utmost indifference hopped on the back of the reptile.

I opened the stomachs of several, and found them full of veg-etable fibres and leaves of different trees, especially of an acacia. In the upper region they live chiefly on the acid and astringent berries of the guayavita, under which trees I have seen these lizards and huge tortoises feeding together. To obtain the acacia-leaves they crawl up the low stunted trees; and it is not uncommon to see a pair quietly browsing, whilst seated on a branch several feet above the ground. These lizards, when cooked, yield a white meat, which is liked by those whose stomachs soar above all prejudices. Humboldt has remarked that in intertropical South America, all lizards which inhabit dry regions are esteemed delicacies for the table. The inhabitants state that those which inhabit the upper damp parts drink water, but that the others do not, like the tortoises, travel up for it from the lower sterile country. At the time of our visit, the females had within their bodies numerous large, elongated eggs, which they lay in their burrows: the inhabitants seek them for food.

These two species of Amblyrhynchus agree, as I have already stated, in their general structure, and in many of their habits. Neither have that rapid movement, so characteristic of the genera Lacerta and Iguana. They are both herbivorous, although the kind of vegetation on which they feed is so very different. Mr. Bell has given the name to the genus from the shortness of the snout; indeed, the form of the mouth may almost be compared to that of the tortoise: one is led to suppose that this is an adaptation to their herbivorous appetites. It is very interesting thus to find a well-characterized genus, having its marine and terrestrial species, belonging to so confined a portion of the world. The aquatic species is by far the most remarkable, because it is the only existing lizard which lives on marine vegetable productions. As I at first observed, these islands are not so remarkable for the number of the species of reptiles, as for that of the individuals; when we remember the well-beaten paths made by the thousands of huge tortoises—the many turtles—the great warrens of the terrestrial Amblyrhynchus—and the groups of the marine species basking on the coast-rocks of every island—we must admit that there is no other quarter of the world where this Order replaces the herbivorous mammalia in so extraordinary a manner. The geologist on hearing this will probably refer back in his mind to the Secondary epochs, when lizards, some herbivorous, some carnivorous, and of dimensions comparable only with our existing whales, swarmed on the land and in the sea. It is, therefore, worthy of his observation, that this archipelago, instead of possessing a humid climate and rank vegetation, cannot be considered otherwise than extremely arid, and, for an equatorial region, remarkably temperate.

To finish with the zoology: the fifteen kinds of sea-fish which I procured here are all new species; they belong to twelve genera, all widely distributed, with the exception of Prionotus, of which the four previously known species live on the eastern side of America. Of land-shells I collected sixteen kinds (and two marked varieties), of which, with the exception of one Helix found at Tahiti, all are peculiar to this archipelago: a single fresh-water shell (Paludina) is common to Tahiti and Van Diemen's Land. Mr. Cuming, before our voyage, procured here ninety species of sea-shells, and this does not include several species not yet specifically examined, of Trochus, Turbo, Monodonta, and Nassa. He has been kind enough to give me the following interesting results: of the ninety shells, no less than forty-seven are unknown elsewhere—a wonderful fact, considering how widely distributed sea-shells generally are. Of the forty-three shells found in other parts of the world, twenty-five inhabit the western coast of America, and of these eight are distinguishable as varieties; the remaining eighteen (including one variety) were found by Mr. Cuming in the Low archipelago, and some of them also at the Philippines. This fact of shells from islands in the central part of the Pacific occurring here, deserves notice, for not one single sea-shell is known to be common to the islands of that ocean and to the west coast of America. The space of open sea running north and south off the west coast, separates two quite distinct conchological provinces; but at the Galapagos Archipelago we have a halting-place, where many new forms have been created, and whither these two great conchological provinces have each sent several colonists. The American province has also sent here representative species; for there is a Galapageian species of Monoceros, a genus only found on the west coast of America; and there are Galapageian species of Fissurella and Cancellaria, genera common on the west coast, but not found (as I am informed by Mr. Cuming) in the central islands of the Pacific. On the other hand, there are Galapageian species of Oniscia and Stylifer, genera common to the West Indies and to the Chinese and Indian seas, but not found either on the west coast of America or in the central Pacific. I may here add, that after the comparison by Messrs. Cuming and Hinds of about 2000 shells from the eastern and western coasts of America, only one single shell was found in common, namely, the Purpura patula, which inhabits the West Indies, the coast of

Panama, and the Galapagos. We have, therefore, in this quarter of the world, three great conchological sea-provinces, quite distinct, though surprisingly near each other, being separated by long north and south spaces either of land or of open sea.

$\mathcal{A}$ PRIL $\mathcal{B}$ LOW

Jan DeBlieu

$\mathcal{F}$or nine hours last night a northeast wind railed against the Hatteras coast, stripping pants and socks from clotheslines and hurtling buckets across fields of flattened reeds. At the time the gale hit I happened to be at home nursing a pair of sunburned shoulders, but I might as easily have been on the beach, so completely did the squall take me by surprise. Certainly nothing about the water or sky that day had hinted at the bad weather to come. For more than a week the incessant Hatteras breezes had been pleasantly light, and during afternoon lulls the island had seemed like a sliver of land suspended between two layers of lucent and fathomless blue. A big blow was the last thing on my mind when, at 7 o'clock, I watched the sun slide behind the wax myrtle bushes in back of the house in a sky still tranquil and dotted with rosy swabs of clouds. A half-hour later the stepladder on the porch was knocked flat by a strong gust, and the lid to the barbecue grill flew upside-down into the neighbor's yard. I ventured out long enough to retrieve the grill cover and weight it down with bricks. Then I shut the door and planted myself in the kitchen with a book.

Through the windows I could see the feathery tips of cedar keeling to the southwest in the last minutes of foggy, blue light. Wind seeped through the wood-slatted walls of my old house, rippling the leaves of houseplants and rustling a stack of newspapers I had left in a living room chair. Where an hour before the house had been quiet, it was now full of clamor. The metal damper to the oil furnace squeaked on its hinges as downgusts pulled it open and shut. Panes of glass rattled, and outside the kitchen window a dis-connected telephone wire slapped erratically against the side of the house. The slaps were just frequent enough to be irritating, and the rush of the wind just loud enough to set goosebumps on my arms beneath a heavy wool sweater.

This was the first storm of any consequence since I moved six weeks ago to the Outer Banks, a chain of barrier islands that juts more than twenty miles into the Atlantic Ocean off North Carolina. In early March I settled into a sixty-year-old frame house in the vil-lage of Rodanthe, a small but spreading town on Hatteras Island. From the attic in the back of the house I can see the shallow, briny waters of Pamlico Sound, and two hundred yards from my front door the chilly waves of the Atlantic Ocean wash a steeply sloped beach that is separated from the village by a single five-foot dune. The houses closest to the ocean are built on stilts. Mine is not. Last night, as the tea kettle boiled and the first drops of rain washed the front porch, it seemed that the crash of the surf grew louder and closer. The house creaked and sighed on its foundation, like a ship straining against its anchor. A beach ball rolled through my yard and lodged among the stubby, waving branches of a myrtle bush. At 8:30 the power went out.

In the continental United States no stretch of coastline except Florida is more vulnerable to hurricanes and northeast storms than the Outer Banks, the belly of the eastern seaboard that curls out just south of the Chesapeake Bay. The banks include two long capes: the unpopulated Cape Lookout and the more famous Cape Hatteras, comprised of Hatteras and Ocracoke islands and the southern tip of Bodie Island. Known to mariners for three hundred years as the Graveyard of the Atlantic, the Hatteras coast bears scars from storms that have flattened dunes and gouged new inlets in a single day. Floods occasionally wash out streets and lift houses off their foundations; in fact, local legend has it that several of the houses surrounding mine floated to their present locations during a spring storm in 1944. To weatherworn Hatteras natives, a puny northeaster like last night's was of no great concern. To me, a new-comer to the coast, the storm was exhilarating, bracing, good mate-rial for stories—but only as long as I kept a grip on my imagination.

My thoughts on the potential danger of this particular blow might not have been so vivid had it come at a different time. For the previous week and a half, though, I had spent most of my time reading articles and talking to naturalists from the Cape Hatteras National Seashore about the unusually severe erosion on the Outer Banks, especially on Hatteras Island just north of Rodanthe. Several evenings before, I had read a series of articles that had concluded it is a waste of time and money to attempt to stabilize the beaches of the cape as long as sea level continues to rise and storms continue to ravage the coast. To my surprise, the authors had agreed that it is not hurricanes that pose the greatest threat to the safety of island residents but the more frequent and long-lived northeasters that can develop in as little as twelve hours and churn up waves large enough to overwash State Highway 12, the only road to the mainland. Chances are that a major storm will one day demolish the settlements on the cape. And the possibility exists that the storm could flood the highway before residents realize the danger and have time to drive to safety.

As I sat in my darkened house and listened to the wind, it was difficult not to think of those dire predictions. Yet realistically I could conjure up no cause for great alarm. Despite the draftiness of my house, it has withstood enough storms to acquire an atmosphere of assorted personal histories; it is the kind of old, musty dwelling that would serve as a good home for ghosts. Its very longevity was testimony to its sturdiness, I decided, as the squeak from the damper again sent prickles up my spine. I briefly considered walking out to the beach to peek over the dunes at the surf, but settled instead on passing the hours before bedtime by baking a cake.

In the amber light thrown off by two kerosene lamps, I leafed through a dog-eared cookbook to a pecan upside-down cake that could easily be mixed by hand. Grabbing some unshelled pecans from a plastic bag under the sink, I began cracking them open, feeling cozy and snug. A particularly strong gust shook the house, and I thought of the shorebirds I had seen feeding on the beach a few days before, the earliest of the flocks that would soon come migrating through. In this kind of weather they would be huddled back in the marsh. The ghost crabs that had only begun to dig out of their winter burrows would have ducked back underground. Some animals were bound to die tonight, and if the ocean jumped the primary dune, most of the shrubs to the east of the highway would no doubt be choked by salt. I turned on the gas oven—for warmth as much as for the cake—and poured a yellow batter into a pan on top of a frothing mixture of butter, brown sugar, and nuts.

By 10:30, when I bit into the first moist piece of cake, my eyes had grown strained from the diffused, flickering light, and I was jumpy from the racket of the wind. Giving up on the evening, I made my way through dark rooms to bed, still acutely aware of the force of the gusts just on the other side of the walls. My last thought was of a series of tall, peaked dunes that line the road north of town. I wondered if they would still be standing by the storm's end. Probably, I thought. I'm probably making too much of this one brief blow.

The dunes I thought about as I drifted toward sleep are a favorite sight of mine on the straight and often tiresome road to Nags Head and Manteo, the nearest towns to Rodanthe on the drive north toward the mainland. In a landscape dominated by horizontal lines, the dunes rise steeply from the sandy hollows just east of Highway 12 and drop fifteen feet to the tideline in a nearly perpendicular descent. They are a tribute to the National Park Service's long struggle to limit the damage inflicted by storms on the Outer Banks. Covered with the shaggy stems of *Spartina patens*—a saltmeadow grass that resembles hay—they remind me more of camel humps than of dunes. In some areas, low, salt-tolerant shrubs such as wax myrtle creep up their backsides like soldiers overrunning a hill. The shrubs are in fact invading foreign terrain, for under natural conditions woody plants could not survive so close to the swash of high tides.

Sixty years ago the profile of the dunes resembled the more gradually sloped ridge of sand that fronts the beach at Rodanthe. Periodically, waves churned up by storms and pushed by northeast winds would spill over them, moving vast amounts of sediment into marshes on the western edge of the island and thwarting efforts to maintain a permanent highway from north to south. The immersion in ocean water killed all but the marsh grasses and left the island's profile even flatter than it is today. Compared to other barrier islands on the North American Atlantic seaboard, the Outer Banks were anomalies—unusually thin and unusually low, little more, really, than well-developed shoals colonized by a few hardy species of plants.

Coping with occasional overwashes had been a part of life on Hatteras Island for as long as anyone could remember. Nevertheless, there was strong belief among local residents that flooding had been less of a problem before English colonists cleared the island of large stands of cedar and oak in the eighteenth and early nineteenth centuries. Although no one knew for certain where the forests had stood, it was widely believed that they had covered most of the island, and a few large stumps remained as evidence of their existence. By the late 1920s, however, the only sizable woods left on Hatteras Island were near the town of Buxton, where the cape widens and arcs sharply to the southwest. Moreover, much of the island had been denuded by stock animals that ranged freely, grazing on saltmeadow hay. Gradually, people became concerned that without large areas of vegetation to trap and hold sand, the soil on which they had built their homes would eventually be washed into Pamlico Sound.

Studies of barrier island movement and sand transport only began to gain acceptance in the early 1930s, when the state of North Carolina organized a public works project to build three parallel lines of ocean-front dunes from the North Carolina-Virginia border to Ocracoke Inlet, the inlet that separates Cape Hatteras from Cape Lookout to the south. Few people were naive enough to hope the dunes would protect the islands from the most extreme storms, but many believed they would reduce the rate of erosion, help stabilize the beaches, and protect private property. The dunes were also expected to foster a favorable habitat at the center of the islands for woody trees and shrubs that would anchor sand and attract a greater variety of animal life—that would, in other words, make the islands of Cape Hatteras resemble wider, more stable barrier islands. After geologists conducted a survey to determine the optimum location for a dune line in relation to the tides and the slope of the beach, low fences were erected to trap blowing sand. As the sand began to mount, the new dunes were planted with cordgrass, sea oats, American beach grass, and wire grass, all of which propagate through rhizomes—creeping stems that grow underground and anchor themselves in loose, shifting soil.

The grasses thrived, and within two years a series of low but discernible dunes had developed along enough of the shoreline to encourage additional work. In 1936 the federal government established the Cape Hatteras National Seashore and turned over the dune-building project to the Civilian Conservation Corps and the Work Projects Administration. Despite the hopes of federal officials, it was not until 1952, when private foundations donated $618,000, that the government appropriated funds to purchase land to operate the national seashore as a public park. Extending from the southern boundary of Nags Head to Ocracoke Inlet, the seashore encompassed seventy miles of ocean beach, the vast majority of which was undeveloped. Eight villages lay within its bounds, and the government agreed that the villagers' property would remain privately owned.

In the intervening years the seedlings had spread prolifically, transforming expanses of blowing sand into meadows of shaggy grass. The ridge of dunes had continued to build despite erosion by severe storms, including one in 1936 and another in 1944 that flooded entire sections of the cape. By the 1950s it was generally assumed that the dune-building projects would continue indefinitely and that the expense would be borne by the park service. That assumption was strengthened in 1952, when park service director Conrad L. Wirth wrote an open "Letter to the People of the Outer Banks" in which he proclaimed that his agency would "protect and control the sand dunes, . . . reestablish them when necessary, and hold them to protect the communities from the intrusion of the ocean." It was a tall order to fill, and one that would greatly exceed the amount of labor and financial support the park service director anticipated.

By augmenting the work that had been done during the preceding twenty years, Wirth believed the park service could establish a formidable system of dunes that would require little effort to maintain. During his administration the park service bulldozed sand into low ridges and planted millions of grass seedlings. The dunes on Hatteras Island rose gradually but consistently, some to the unprecedented height of fifteen feet. Majestic in stature and festooned in midsummer with the tawny tassels of sea oats, they seemed a triumph of modern technology; but as they grew, the shoreline receded. The gently sloped beaches, once 150 yards wide, had steepened and narrowed to 75 yards. Undaunted, Wirth assured a congressional subcommittee in 1963 that additional work would stabilize the dune system and enable the beaches to build back out to the east. The cost of the work would probably exceed $5 million, he said, and would require another decade of concerted effort.

For the next three years the park service continued extensive plantings, concentrating on the shoreline of Ocracoke Island but also repairing breaches that opened in the dunes on Hatteras Island. Yet the beaches steadily receded. Finally, in 1966, the park service began pumping sand into severely eroded areas, and in 1968 George B. Hartzog, the new park service director, told the same congressional subcommittee he expected such beach nourishment projects to become common measures, despite enormous costs. (Fifteen years later a North Carolina Coastal Resources Commission task force would estimate the cost of beach nourishment at $1,000 per linear foot of shoreline. To be effective, the procedure would have to be repeated every five years.) By 1971 the park service was spending up to $500,000 annually to replenish sand in areas where ten feet of shoreline was being lost every year. And by 1973 construction had begun on a pipeline designed to carry sand from Cape Point to a badly eroded stretch north of Buxton.

Hartzog believed the federal government had a responsibility to slow the rate of erosion on national seashores as much as possible, even though geologists had shown that the barrier islands of the Atlantic were migrating rapidly to the west and that longshore currents tended to erode sand from the north ends of islands and push it to the south. Under the prevailing wisdom of the day—a wisdom that placed great faith in the ability of engineers to shape and mold the beaches—it sounded like wise and practical policy. But during the early 1970s, studies by Robert Dolan, a coastal geologist at the University of Virginia, and Paul J. Godfrey, a botanist at the University of Massachusetts, suggested what park service officials at Cape Hatteras had long before come to suspect. In a series of papers published in respected scientific journals, Dolan and Godfrey argued that by eliminating overwash on the narrow islands of the cape, the park service had destroyed the mechanism by which sand is normally transported onto the shore and into the marshes. By trapping large amounts of sand, the carefully constructed dunes had hastened the narrowing of the beaches.

Dolan and Godfrey supported their argument with observations taken at Cape Lookout, the southernmost segment of the Outer Banks and the only area not included in the dune-building programs. In a paper written with University of Virginia marine biologist William Odum, the scientists noted that the beaches of Cape Lookout were still 125 to 200 yards wide, while some of those on Hatteras Island had receded to 30 yards. The beaches of

Ocracoke Island, where dunes had been built only fifteen years before, had narrowed to about 75 yards.

How could the larger dunes have so drastically affected the profile of the shore? The scientists argued that they prevented the waves from spreading their force over a large area, which would have allowed sand to settle out on the beach and occasionally spill into the low runnels behind the primary dunes. Now, instead of dissipating on a smooth, gradual plane, storm surges traveled up a steep beach and jammed into a vertical sand wall. During the most severe storms, heavy surf bit into the sides of the dunes, scarping cliffs and carrying out to sea sand that would normally be transported to the marshes. At the same time, the protected valleys in back of the dunes had been colonized by shrubs and trees that were not adapted to immersion in salt water and that would certainly not survive a major flood.

The scientists said they had found no evidence to support the theory that large forests had once covered most of the Outer Banks. Instead, their work suggested that the islands had been inhabited primarily by plants that could survive occasional tidal floods. Finally, they pointed out that hurricanes drifting north up the coast can force water to pile up in Pamlico Sound, flooding the islands from the west. Before construction of the dunes, the waters would simply flow off to the east without causing much harm. Now the surges would leave the marshes under several feet of water, drowning plants and contributing to soil loss on the sand-starved western shores. Large dunes, they concluded, are ecologically unsuitable for the Outer Banks as long as sea level continues to rise and the barrier islands tend to migrate to the west. "Man has attempted to draw a line and prevent the sea from passing. The results have been unexpected and negative."

Park service administrators took note of the study and of several additional papers published by Godfrey and Dolan. In July 1973 they quietly decided to suspend a $4.5 million beach-nourishment project that had been authorized after a northeaster had overwashed the highway just north of Buxton. They planned to ask Congress to allocate the remaining $1.4 million from the project to study alternative measures for erosion control. Had the decision escaped wide publicity, it might have precipitated no more than a flurry of protest among Cape Hatteras residents. But in August a coastal geologist from Duke University named Orrin H.

Pilkey, Jr., gave a presentation to journalists at a seminar on coastal geology and barrier island movement. An outspoken opponent of beach-erosion control measures, Pilkey said the federal government had finally realized the futility of trying to stabilize barrier beaches. "The park service hasn't announced it yet," he said, "but their new policy is to let Buxton fall into the sea." Despite the flippancy of the comment, its essence was true. Shortly after the suspension of the Buxton project, park service officials agreed they could do no more to protect private holdings within the national seashore.

Local reaction was swift and vehement. Business owners and politicians boisterously criticized the park service for reneging on the promise made by Wirth, and two North Carolina congressmen suggested that responsibility for beach-erosion control be given to the United States Army Corps of Engineers. Many Hatteras residents had been reluctant to surrender their land to the national seashore for fear that they would be giving up a source of substantial income and, inevitably, control over their way of life. Now it seemed their worst fears were being realized. Even people who agreed with the decision to discontinue erosion control criticized the manner in which it had been implemented. William W. Woodhouse, Jr., a North Carolina State University soil scientist, complained that "the Dolan-Godfrey theorizing has been seized upon as a convenient smoke screen to protect from view the cruel-sounding withdrawal of protection from private development. . . . Why not admit that the forecast of protection was an error? The cost has been excessive, it hasn't worked, and it's wrong anyway."

In a matter of weeks the issue gained national attention and was featured in the *Washington Post* and the *New York Times* and on national television networks. The park service decision affected not only Cape Hatteras but every national seashore, including Cape Cod, Fire Island, and Point Reyes. Surprisingly to the people of the Outer Banks, public sentiment came down strongly in the park service's favor. Consumer groups declared it a waste of money to continue fighting the forces of nature, and editorials upbraided landowners on the cape for expecting taxpayers to protect their interests. In the face of such criticism, local protest sputtered and eventually died. In its place grew a rift between park service officials and families whose residence on the cape predated the establishment of the national seashore. The schism has partially healed with time, but local sentiment is still dominated by a stubborn isolationism and by the belief that fair weather residents will never understand the hardships associated with living under the constant threat of a hostile sea.

More than a decade later many coastal scientists have begun to question whether ocean overwash is as important a factor in shaping barrier islands as Dolan and Godfrey believed. With the combined factors of sea level rise, sand movement, and storm frequency, geologists have found it difficult to predict how quickly a shoreline will erode. The equation has been complicated by a dramatic shift in storm and hurricane patterns, which seem to run in cycles of a decade or more. Ocean overwash is still considered an important geologic process, but in the past decade the Hatteras coast has been hit by few major storms. The ocean flooding common in the 1950s and 1960s has not occurred. Ironically, the beaches of Cape Lookout have steepened, and ten-foot dunes have replaced the sandy flats that first caused Dolan and Godfrey to question the wisdom of trying to stabilize a storm-battered coast.

Most scientists now believe that overwash has a much less profound effect on barrier islands than the constant opening of inlets, which tend to catch south-flowing sand and form wide deltas on an island's western edge. Eventually, as the beaches retreat to the west and the inlets shoal over, the deltas drain off and salt marshes form—a natural western extension of the island's shifting terrain.

Whether or not Dolan and Godfrey overestimated the importance of overwash, their work touched the lives of every resident on Cape Hatteras. Since September 1973 the park service has done nothing to stabilize the dunes or beaches, except for emergency plantings to prevent a section of Highway 12 on Ocracoke Island from being covered with sand, and a separate project undertaken in hopes of preserving the famous black-and-white-spiraled Cape Hatteras lighthouse. When the structure was built in 1870 it stood fifteen hundred feet from the sea, but in recent years storm surges have brought water within seventy feet of its base. Plans have been made not to curb erosion around the lighthouse but to shape the pattern of loss so the structure will be left standing on an island all its own.

But the landscape of Hatteras will be left to its own devices. The rolling stretches of empty sand have disappeared beneath mats of sea oats and beach grass that resprout after floods and resume their laborious accrual of sand. Each year gnarls of myrtle and cedar creep farther into the marshes, displacing the *Spartina* grasses so well adapted to living in salty swash. And on certain stretches of Hatteras Island the fifteen- and twenty-foot dunes have succumbed to frequent batterings, leaving in their place wider beaches and ridges five feet high. As I slept, the dunes north of Rodanthe would be absorbing the shock of storm-whipped breakers that chopped at their bases, speeding their demise.

All night I remained dully aware of the wind rushing past the house in ferocious bursts. Near midnight the gale reached its greatest force—a mere forty-seven miles per hour—and a loud bang somewhere off the back of the house woke me from a light and nervous sleep. I responded by pulling the quilt closer to my chin. Whatever it was would have to wait at least until dawn. At 3 o'clock the lights flickered on and roused me again. Squinting and grumbling at myself for forgetting to turn off the bedroom ceiling lamp, I got out of bed long enough to walk to the kitchen and peer out the window at the motley collection of boards, bottles, and boxes of tools on my back porch. A piece of plywood had toppled on its side; that would account for the midnight crash. I turned out the lamp in the kitchen and started for the bedroom. Before I reached the doorway the bedroom light pulsed once and died.

I stumbled to a chair in the living room, rubbed my eyes, and looked across the road at the dark shape of the Chicamacomico lifesaving station, a landmark in Rodanthe and the most completely preserved of the seven stations established in 1874 on the Outer Banks by the U.S. Lifesaving Service—the forerunner of the Coast Guard. For eighty winters the stations were staffed by men who patrolled the shores around the clock to watch for foundering ships. Lifesaving surfmen rescued sailors from the sound as well as the ocean; many fishermen even consider the sound to be the more dangerous of the two. The sound can grow too choppy for safe navigation within an hour, and despite its shallowness—five feet or less in most places—heavy winds can force enough tide against the islands to raise the water level to ten feet.

Neither the sound nor the ocean could be treated as anything but a dangerous foe in this kind of weather. The thought made me cringe. For a moment I badly wanted contact with a neighbor, a weatherman, anyone who might be able to tell me if the road would flood and if the wind would blow all night and into the day. I resisted an urge to call the Coast Guard station at Oregon Inlet and wandered instead to the kitchen, feeling for the flashlight I had left on the table. In the feeble beam I could see dribbles of cake batter on the rim of the mixing bowl. There had been no electricity to pump water from the well, so I had left the dishes unwashed.

Near the mixing bowl were a notebook with some information on Hatteras weather and a park service pamphlet on the *Altoona,* a 102-foot schooner wrecked at the tip of the cape in 1878. The pamphlet explained that shipping channels off the cape are constantly reshaped by the juncture of the north-flowing Gulf Stream and a southbound countercurrent known as the Virginia Coastal Drift. Collision of the currents causes sand to settle out of the water and replenish the treacherous shoals that have beached hundreds of ships since 1565. The pamphlet did not mention what meteorologists call Hatteras-style lows, the weather systems that develop because of the unusual circulation patterns caused by the conversion of the currents.

A few days before, I had visited the federal marine weather station in Buxton to ask about weather systems around the cape and to find out what I could about the ceaseless wind that had chafed at my nerves all spring. It has been the presence of the wind more than any other factor—more even than the sulfurous water in my well and the ubiquitous salt and sand—that I have had difficulty adjusting to here. "You have to remember that we're out in the middle of the ocean," Wally DeMaurice, a meteorologist, told me. "There's nothing to knock the wind down, no mountains or tall buildings or trees. Any breeze that develops is going to have miles of open water to build up speed."

DeMaurice also explained that Cape Hatteras's unusually violent weather patterns are unlike any in the world except those off the east coast of Australia. In addition to the circulatory effects caused by offshore currents, the low-pressure troughs that develop here interact with cold-air masses that build up on the eastern side of the Appalachian Mountains. When conditions are right, the collision of the warm and cold air quickly spawns thunderheads and waterspouts, which can cause tremendous damage if they come ashore. "The bottom line is that even our not-so-violent storms can produce some extremely violent weather," DeMaurice said.

On one page of the notebook I jotted down several of DeMaurice's comments about the potential damage to the cape from hurricanes and northeasters. The previous fall, in October 1984, Hurricane Josephine had hovered two hundred miles east of Hatteras Island and had created an eight-foot storm surge that flooded Nags Head, severely eroded the tip of Ocracoke Island, and devastated a stretch of tall dunes only a half-mile north of Rodanthe. In the process Highway 12 had been buried under eight feet of sand. "It was a surfer's dream, because there were waves but no wind," he said. "But it did great damage all up and down the cape. The erosion was severe. Even a moderate storm can now create problems, and if we have a major storm—well, I'll leave it to your imagination.

"We've had more than fifteen years of unusually mild weather here, and people have gotten careless. They assume that they'll be able to ride out a hurricane or a storm like the Ash Wednesday storm of nineteen sixty-two. That one cut an inlet just north of Buxton. There's been nothing to equal it since. Seems to me it's only a matter of time before nature gets the best of us. I can't say exactly when it will happen; it may be years. I will say, though, that I expect us to have major problems with overwashes on Highway Twelve within the next five years. The island is just too badly eroded."

The warning was the last thing I had written. I tossed the notebook back on the table and picked up a fragment of shell that had been chipped and polished in its tumblings against the sand. Nothing the meteorologist had said particularly surprised me. Predictions of doom are commonplace on barrier islands, and most of the people I had met on Hatteras had grown inured to them. Some residents frankly consider the transient nature of the island to be part of its allure. Enjoy it now; tomorrow it may be gone.

I looked more closely at the shell. It was a thick clam, and its edges were tinted with a rusty shade common in many shells on the Rodanthe beach. Chances are it originally had been buried in the mud of Pamlico Sound and that hundreds of years later Hatteras Island had literally rolled over it, like a bulldozer, and unearthed it. The same would be true of the oyster shells strewn across the beach. The quartz gravel so abundant along the shoreline in the spring would have been dredged from riverbeds that existed eighteen thousand years ago, when a four-hundred-foot drop in sea level exposed the continental shelf and the rivers extended miles beyond their present mouths.

When it got down to it, anyone who looked would have a difficult time missing evidence of the island's movement to the west and south. A mile up the beach near a curve in the highway—the point where the dunes had been destroyed by Josephine—I had found the beach strewn with chunks of peat that centuries ago had formed the substrate of a salt marsh. Later I had chatted with a cottage owner who told me that in 1974 he dug twenty or more cedar and oak stumps from a quarter-mile stretch of ocean beach near his house. The stumps were the sole remains of a woody section that once fronted Pamlico Sound and had been smothered in sand as the island moved west. During a trip to Nags Head one day, I had detoured down a dead-end road at the northern tip of Hatteras Island. Photographs taken in the mid-1970s show the road extending another half-mile to the north. Now its terminus sits on a cliff that drops into Oregon Inlet.

For a moment I stopped thinking and listened hard to the wind. It seemed to be abating slightly, although it was possible that I had just grown used to the roar. The storm had blown long enough and hard enough to move some amount of sand to the marshes, but whether it would be significant I had no way of knowing.

Two weeks after I moved to Rodanthe a park service naturalist had told me that the layer of sand at the northern end of Hatteras Island is unusually thin. I had found the statement difficult to believe; how could sand "thin" like a receding hairline? Yet Stanley Riggs, an eminent geologist, had confirmed it. Seismic readings have indicated that Rodanthe sits near the edge of the Pleistocene rock that forms the foundation of Cape Hatteras and the shoals offshore. Because the rock is unusually close to the surface here, the layer of sand and peat that covers it is unusually thin. As a result of this and other factors, the beach at Rodanthe is migrating more quickly than other portions of the cape, and the rate of erosion is unusually high. Some geologists believe that at one time Hatteras Island may have turned sharply inland here, much like the tip of land near Buxton known locally as Cape Point.

The Croatoan Indians of Hatteras might have called it Cape Chicamacomico, but if it ever existed it is long gone. In my hazy predawn cognizance, I found it intriguing to be sitting on a rock topped with a thin cap of sand rippling briskly to the west. My house and yard very likely would be submerged in a century, perhaps a good deal sooner. An interesting thought—more interesting to me that night than the thought of living on a sedentary mound of clay. To reside here for any length of time would require constant accommodation to change; the alternatives, in comparison, seemed rather dull. Maybe it was the lateness of the hour or my hunch that the storm's wildness was near an end, but my nervousness had disappeared. At the moment I had no desire to be anywhere but in a candlelit kitchen on an ephemeral finger of sand.

By 6:30 this morning the wind had stilled, leaving the island in a white light baffled by moisture and fog. I woke at the sound of a passing car, then realized I heard nothing except the plaintive notes of a meadowlark that has taken to calling for its mate from a perch across the street. The damper had stopped creaking, and the telephone wire no longer slapped the side of the house. After a night of much noise and little sleep, the peacefulness of the morning carried the force of an intoxicant. Pausing only long enough to groan over the dirty dishes and the streaks of flour across the kitchen floor, I stepped outside and walked the two hundred yards to the beach.

Before I was halfway there I could see a line of oily foam where water had lapped over the truncated dune. The textured surface of the foam shimmered with pinks, purples, and blues, and it wriggled as I climbed toward it, a gelatinous roll laced with tunnels of air. Beyond, the beach was strewn with hundreds of frothy skeins, some pure white, some yellow from age. Most still curled to the west in the shape of the waves that had tossed them onto land.

Spray from the surf had turned the air milky and thick. I walked out to the water, picking my way around piles of foam as high as my knees. This must be what it is like, I thought, to be surrounded by corpses, the only survivor of a war. In the surf the battle still raged: bone-chilling breakers thrashed against shore, tossing up suds. But the tide had receded and the waves reflected the colorless sky. The stillness had caught me as completely by surprise as the beginning of the blow had twelve hours before. I might have been standing in the Arctic, so white and foreign was the scene before me.

Near the water three black-headed gulls poked at the sand, searching for small crustaceans. For them it was business as usual. An older couple I had seen before on the beach strolled toward me, and the woman waved. "Isn't it spectacular?" she cried. No one else was out. I turned south toward the dunes that border the Chicamacomico station. Weaving between foam and broken shells, I walked to a slough where heaps of froth drifted toward the sea in steady procession until an incoming wave knocked them back toward the dunes. Yesterday afternoon the slough had been nothing more than a thin runnel cut by the month's highest tide, and the beach and offshore waters had seemed familiar and warm, a collage of green, blue, and buff. Now the colorless tide washed through an unfamiliar creek. Everything moved—the breakers, the seabound froth, the shimmers of color in the stranded heaps of foam. Everything but the milky air.

I remained on the beach only a short while, thinking that I would return after breakfast and the luxury of a shower. But by mid-morning when I ventured out again, the sky had deepened to blue and the mounds of foam had scattered in a light southwest wind. The beach was yellow, the sand clear of debris. No evidence of the storm remained.

$\mathcal{S}$OMETHING $\mathcal{W}$ICKED $\mathcal{T}$HIS $\mathcal{W}$AY $\mathcal{C}$OMES

Daniel Duane

$\mathcal{U}$nlike any other athlete, a big-wave surfer never knows when, exactly, his marquee game will come. Keeping packed bags by the door and an open plane ticket ready to go, he might wait months—even years—for that once-in-a-lifetime moment. And when it happens, he has to drop everything and move. On a Thursday late last January, Evan Slater, a surfer from Encinitas, California, heard that a howling North Pacific storm had just blown the biggest waves in ages through Hawaii's Waimea Bay and that they were due on the West Coast by morning. More big surf had already hit in the last two weeks than in most years: SurFax, a service that crunches Pacific weather data to provide clients with a daily wave forecast, had recently quipped, "We're reminded of the Simpsons episode, where Homer goes to Hell and he's strapped to a machine that continually force feeds him donuts. He liked it." But this new swell was something else altogether.

Outside Hawaii, only two places in the world reliably turn waves like these into high-quality big surf—"rhino waves," as they're known—and choosing between them requires water knowledge and good judgment. The westerly direction of the swell that Thursday coupled with a sloppy local storm seemed to rule out the first, Maverick's, a deepwater reef near Half Moon Bay in northern California, so the smart money was headed for Killers, at Baja's Todos Santos Island. Some of the best big-wave riders in the world were already waxing boards, canceling appointments, and preparing to travel through the night. Which is the way it goes: These breaks all fire during the winter, are relatively far apart, and don't even perform their normal magic (much less the rare juju on its way that day) more than a few times in a normal year. A committed rush disciple just might have to face the ocean's wildest offerings in less than peak condition: jet-lagged, sleep-deprived, and all-around disoriented.

The tom-toms usually start with someone like San Francisco's Mark Renneker, a 46-year-old big-wave-riding oncologist and surf-meteorology obsessive. Calculating wind speed and direction for the far-off storms that generate waves (the one behind this swell, for example, got started off Japan), and then factoring in wave heights gleaned from ship reports and buoy readings, Renneker might come up with the right numbers on a Friday afternoon and begin working the phones. Maybe let the guys down south know that tomorrow looks like a Maverick's day. Or perhaps, like this time, that Killers was the only sane choice; clear skies likely all day off Ensenada, and the tide dropping just in time for the estimated noon arrival of the 4,000-mile swell.

In surf parlance, the term "big wave" means a wave of at least 20 feet. The word "feet" in this usage, however, bears only a mystical and as yet unveiled relationship to dozens of inches. Developed in Hawaii as a way of sandbagging visiting haoles, this traditional wave-measurement scale rigorously underestimates actual surf dimensions—such that "20-foot" actually means waves with faces of at least 30 feet. The more reliable method simply measures body lengths: knee-high, head-high, double overhead, triple overhead.

But however you look at it, the surf generated by that Thursday's swell was enormous. Even as it began to build, professional surfers were flying to Hawaii for the invitation-only Quiksilver big-wave contest, held at Waimea Bay in memory of Eddie Aikau, a Native Hawaiian surfer who drowned in 1978 while sailing in a storm. The event requires at least 20-foot surf; by Tuesday night, the Hawaii wave buoys had jumped from 11 feet to 23.

By Wednesday morning, 40-foot waves were overwhelming Waimea every ten minutes, prompting comparisons to the legendary swells of surf history—most tellingly, to the Swell of '69. That was the year Greg "da Bull" Noll, a big-wave pioneer, caught what everyone was content to call the largest wave ever ridden, in spite of (or perhaps because of) the lack of photographic evidence.

Regardless, the Swell of '69 was the biggest of the sport's first Golden Age, the moment when surfing's Neil Armstrong planted its first extraterrestrial flag. Big-wave riding has arguably entered a second Golden Age now, with aggressive young talent and new techniques stretching the limits of both wave size and performance—not just surviving monster waves, but riding them in high style. This swell, like that of '69, ranked as the biggest that a new generation had yet seen.

The contest organizers held the surfers at bay all morning, waiting for the waves to get *small* enough for this, the world's premier big-surf event. Aside from the sheer power of the swell, something else may have been weighing on their minds. For years, big-wave surfing had seemed curiously safe; despite its aura of lethality, nobody had died since the 1943 drowning of Dickie Cross right there at Waimea. But then, in December 1994, Mark Foo, the famous Hawaiian big-wave rider, surfed giant waves at Waimea and then caught a red-eye to face the very same swell at Maverick's the next day. Taking off on a big—though not monstrous—wave, Foo lost balance and fell. His body and shattered board were found an hour later, floating south of the break. A year later to the day, a veteran surfer named Donnie Solomon tried to push through a big wave's lip at Waimea only to get pulled back "over the falls" and drown. And finally, just last year, a fit and experienced surfer named Todd Chesser got caught shoreward of a big breaking set on Oahu. Held under repeatedly, he lost consciousness and eventually died.

In the end, the organizers called off the Quiksilver at midday Wednesday. Walls of whitewater were rolling across Hawaiian highways, uprooting palm trees, and blowing furniture into backyards, sending Oahu's Civil Defense to Code Black. Haleiwa Harbor and all North Shore beaches closed. But before the clampdown, a few surfers jumped on jet-skis and headed for distant offshore reefs. One pair, going full speed on their 700cc Wave Runner, got run over and nearly drowned in a 30-foot wall of foam. Another team that included Ken Bradshaw, the foremost big-wave rider of his generation and Foo's companion the day Foo died, made it out to a break called Outside Log Cabins. The size of the swell ruled out traditional paddle-in surfing, but Bradshaw made a kind of history that day by getting towed like a water-skier into a wave he later "conservatively" called 40 feet. By this he probably meant that it had a 70-foot face and a barrel big enough to hold a small savings and loan. The surf-world buzz repeatedly described Bradshaw's wave as "cartoon," even "beyond cartoon," and a growing consensus was calling it the largest wave ever ridden on the North Shore.

Now buoy and ship reports showed that same swell roaring across the Pacific, holding speed and size unusually well and promising what Thursday's SurFax called "a rhino stampede."

At dawn Friday morning, huge waves poured over Ensenada's mile-long harbor jetty. Fisherman—who knew well that rich gringo surfers would need boats—crowded the docks shouting, "Big boat! Big, fast boat! Come with me!"

Crawling out of a white, surfboard-loaded Suburban, we breathed urine, fish, and desert grasses riding the morning breeze. In addition to their almost comical taciturnity, there's a loose humility to young big-wave surfers, their eyes more quietly distant than aggressive. There was big, blond, easygoing Keith Malloy, a 24-year-old professional surfer and friend of the late Todd Chesser; Santa Cruz's Josh Loya, a quiet Maverick's regular who'd caught a late flight into San Diego; and blond Evan Slater himself, who was building a career as an editor at *Surfer* magazine but still chased big waves at every opportunity. Stretching like cats, they pulled muscles into readiness, didn't talk much about the fear they must have been feeling—just a little chatter about how many boards to bring, which wetsuit.

An open fiberglass outboard puttered into the dock, and the nine- to ten-foot boards went in first. Rounding the end of the huge black jetty, the boat began to skip and pound, bouncing off chop and climbing open-ocean ground swells. From the wave peaks, Todos Santos Island appeared hazy on the horizon. Running well outside the island's shoals, we motored into sight of Killers, a submerged reef that breaks giant waves into rideable shapes. There, a blue mountain rolled under several speck-figures lying on long surfboards.

"Hey, that's Taylor," Slater said quietly, referring to Taylor Knox, a successful pro from Carlsbad, California, "and Snips," meaning Mike Parsons, the unofficial mayor of Todos. Mike Stewart, the best bodyboarder in the world, was out there, too.

A good-size wave rolled over the reef then, but never quite broke. "Tide's still kind of fat, huh?" Malloy said.

"Yeah," Loya responded. "Wind's offshore, though."

A jet-ski driver circled, ready to pull guys out if they got in trouble.

"I like seeing him there," Malloy muttered. Foo, Solomon, and Chesser had all died in conditions no more dangerous than those before us.

Slater peeled off his sweatshirt and pants, pulled on his wetsuit. Loya checked the knot on his ankle leash and touched up his wax job, not wanting to risk the slip of a foot.

As they got ready to go, I brought up the K2 Challenge. Late last year, K2, the ski and snowboard manufacturer, offered $50,000 to the surfer who got photographed riding the season's largest wave, wherever that might be. I was wondering where these surfers stood on the matter, how much it motivated them. After all, the Challenge forbade jet-ski tow-ins, and if ever there was a day to paddle into the biggest wave of the season, this was it.

Malloy just dropped his huge spear in the water and jumped after it—no comment. Slater tried to be polite, but was too focused on following Malloy. Only Loya had anything to say. "I'd rather move to Oregon and grow dope for a summer," he offered. "The odds are a lot better."

The topic seemed to make all of them squirm, and as they paddled off, I thought about why. For one thing, the Challenge, due to end March 15, had the potential to lure unqualified surfers out of their depth. But probably more troubling to guys like these was the way it clarified the blurry lines between the purity of the surfer's pursuit and less noble aspirations. In other words, the $50,000 potentially waiting in the trough of every big wave undermined the dearly held belief that real surfers never do it for money.

Soon after Slater, Malloy, and Loya reached the other surfers, the wind at Killers went completely slack, and the surface took on the character of royal-blue oil. Parsons caught a "smallish" 15-foot wave, but mostly the guys just floated in a small pod, waiting. Looking out to sea. Perhaps wondering what was happening at Maverick's, wondering if they'd picked the right spot.

As it turned out, about 20 surfers were paddling in circles at Maverick's at the time, trying not to get killed. Offshore wind usually improves waves, but Maverick's heaves over so brutally that wind coming up the front slows down your entry, stalling you right where you least want to be: in the lip, which can drive you to the rocky bottom 25 feet under. A westerly swell like this one also produces both a current drawing you into the impact zone and waves that, when they catch you there, blast you toward a hideous cluster of rocks. Mark Renneker later reported that either two or three consecutive waves—nobody was quite sure—spun one surfer around like a propeller and denied him air for over half a minute. A Brazilian named Deniks Fischer wiped out so badly he tore every ligament in his knee, burst an eardrum, and was left temporarily numb from the waist down. Screaming for help, he got rescued only by a boat crew throwing him a life preserver.

Conditions at Todos looked much better, though when the tide finally began to drop at noon, I felt a faint onshore breeze. Nothing spoils surf faster. It picked up even more in the next few minutes, and I could feel the tension in the water. If the swell didn't hit sometime soon, and if that wind kept building, this whole mission would end up a colossal waste of time.

Suddenly, Killers turned on. Loya lay on his board and paddled for the horizon as two outsize sine curves bent out of the benthos and bore down on the crowd. The others followed. Malloy wheeled first and caught one, absolutely free-falling for perhaps ten feet, somehow landing on his board. Loya took a high line on the next, cutting fast along the wave's summit ridge. The tide had begun to run out now, and for 30 or 40 minutes waves broke with cannonlike booms. Slater, flying in front of one, seemed a tiny doll skipping before a flash flood. Terrance McNulty, an underground big-wave hero from San Clemente, caught several genuine monsters. Now that the huge stuff had arrived, drowning became a very real possibility; someone—from the boat, we couldn't see who— got blown toward the island by successive rows of foam, then dragged himself back onto his board only to be blown off again. The jet-ski prowled the impact zone for long seconds before it could get to him. But the surfers kept at it, riding 20-foot waves to their dying shoulders and then sprint-paddling back for more. The sun kept shining, the wind held its breath, and one massive blue wall after another drained a foregoing pit and poured forward.

And then the biggest set yet appeared, and something extraordinary happened. Slater turned and paddled with one wave. The bottom kept dropping below him, blackening into a wall of shadows as Slater pulled and pulled, trying to get his board sliding down the thing's face. Just as a thick lip bounced into being, Slater hopped to his feet in one motion. Halfway down, as the floor vanished, his legs straightened and he began to free-fall, down and down as the mouth of the wave spread wide. Then he landed square and his knees compressed. Laying his board over on a rail, Slater carved to the right, sending out a spray of foam as the jaw clamped shut with a shocking detonation. It was the largest wave I'd ever seen surfed.

But the moment soon passed. First, a beast broke far outside the crowd and blew everyone off their boards, putting them through a serious rinse-cycle and dragging them 50 yards deeper into the impact zone. When they'd all clawed back up to daylight, a ripple of fear came off the foam. The wind had kicked up yet another notch, cross-chopping the surface in a way that can buck you off a wave and make paddling to safety impossible. The window of optimal conditions had closed.

That's when a wave of another order of size appeared and did something quite different. Instead of breaking in the usual place and peeling to the right, it broke like an avalanching cornice and rumbled left, which meant that as our boatman yanked frantically at the engine cord, the guys in the water had some serious thinking to do. This kind of reversal—a wave normally a right becoming a left—can be terrifying, upending all the knowledge you've been counting on to keep you safe. You thought you were only flirting in danger's way, and it turns out you're lying on its train tracks.

As that backward mountain of foam rolled toward the already tired men in the water, our boat's engine engaged. We shoved up the face of an incoming berm, down its back, and then over another one. When the waves had passed, the surfers fought their way back to the surface, panting. Lying on their boards, they breathed awhile, shook it off, noticed that the wind had turned on strong again and that whitecaps already flecked the outer waters. Loya appeared beside the boat first, and then Slater and Malloy. They hauled themselves in, dripping, coughing, and flushed with pleasure, and we headed for shore.

In the end, you just have to trust that there's nothing else in the world like pushing your board off the edge of a heaving 30-foot wall of water, harnessing all that titanic impetus, and doing something beautiful and pointless with it. Far from a man-versus-nature showdown, it's an utterly wild kind of play. Timothy Leary once said that in the far future humans would attain a state of purely aesthetic existence; surfers, he felt, had already arrived.

When all their boards were piled in the boat and we had started for home, the guys sat down and actually talked for once. About what? Maybe the fact that they had just done everything Solomon, Foo, and Chesser had died trying to do, and had come away unscathed? To the contrary. In fact, the chief issue was whether they should change back into their clothes now or leave their wetsuits on for the ride back to the harbor.

Wondering if this could really be it—the total occupancy of their minds after several brushes with death—I remembered something a friend once said to me. I'd remarked at the unflappability of a particular big-wave rider on a similar day. With a knowing smirk, my friend had said, "Just ask how he slept last night."

So I did.

Slater smiled his egoless smile. "You want to know the truth?" he asked. "I thought I was driving to my death this morning."

And then he turned to Malloy. "You really leaving your wetsuit on? Won't that be kind of clammy?"

In This Light

Marybeth Holleman

When despair for the world grows in me,
and I awake in the night at the least sound
in fear of what my life and my children's lives may be,
I go and lie down where the wood drake
rests in his beauty on the water, and the great heron feeds.
I come into the peace of wild things
who do not tax their lives with forethought
of grief, I come into the presence of still water.
                                        —Wendell Berry

It is bigger, brighter. Its tail streaks farther across the night sky. When I look at it through binoculars, I have to move them slowly, steadily, panning like a photographer at a race, to see it all, to see the sunburst head and the tail that arches and fans like a single wide brush stroke. This comet seems so different from where I now stand than from my porch at home, but it is the same comet, Hale Bopp, that I have come to expect on a clear night, come to expect as much as I expect to see Orion's Belt and the Big Dipper, even though I know that in a few weeks it will disappear, not to return in my lifetime.

I turn to the west and see the quarter moon, filled out with earthshine and so brilliant that through binoculars I see its craters. Turning to the east, I find Mars, a red beacon in blackness. All this shines above me from the porch of a cabin on Green Island in Prince William Sound, Alaska, in the middle of March. In just one week, in the wake of the spring equinox, this comet will reach its zenith, this celestial gathering will reach its brightest night, and this place will have eight years between it and the Exxon Valdez oil spill that coated the beaches before me and killed throngs of seabirds and sea otters and fish in the waters beyond me.

Green Island. I've never been here before, but I've heard of it. In April 1989, a month after the tanker hit Bligh Reef, birds started arriving by the thousands, some to stay and some just passing through on their spring migrations to northern nesting grounds. People awaited them, firing gunshot into the air to keep the tired birds from landing, for instead of the respite the birds sought they would find only deadly oil.

Now here I stand eight years later, watching a giant comet within a few million miles of Earth, Mars in direct opposition with the sun, and the moon on its way to a near total eclipse. What does this mean, this brilliant celestial event and this dark anniversary converging?

I didn't plan this trip to coincide with these prodigious events, but the oil spill has profoundly affected me, as it has irrevocably harmed the Sound. Memories of those dark years haunt me, as does the knowledge that it is not yet over: oil still lies beneath rocks and animals still suffer. I cannot separate place from event. At times the entanglement of place and event tightens its grip into an obsession that blurs past and present.

Underlying this despair, hard as bedrock, are love and desire. Prince William Sound is more dear to me than anywhere else on earth, and I crave time in it. I have wanted to come to Green Island for years. Though I've spent time in the Sound for over a decade, this is farther out than I have yet been able to travel.

We are staying in a cabin that sits on a bight of land on the western edge of the island, sandwiched between two beaches. The front beach faces Montague Strait, with Naked Island in the distance; the back beach faces a wide quiet finger of water flanked by the main body of the island and a narrow spit. Green Island lacks the towering peaks of Knight and Montague islands to either side of it; instead, true to its name, it remains green year-round with a dense forest of spruce. It is low-lying, marshy, dotted with ponds, perfect for migrating birds. And it is lovely.

The morning after our arrival, the beach facing Montague Strait rumbles with waves thumping against long rows of tangled kelp and sea grass and driftwood washed up in winter's storms. Wind roars through the trees around us. The seas, though, lie low enough for us to venture out in our canoe. We push off into the wind—Rick, my son Jamie, and I—hoping to paddle around the point to see Montague Island. Montague is the largest island in the Sound, and protects the Sound from Gulf of Alaska storms. It and Green and Knight Island to the north caught the vast majority of oil in the arms of their fjords.

I am anxious to lay eyes on Montague, having only seen it from the air. The choppy seas make for slow going, though, and Jamie complains of cold. While March may hold the spring equinox, here it is still winter—snow crusts the shoreline, ice covers fresh water, and the slightest breeze sends a chill. Then my dog Keira, who is following us on shore, disappears into the woods. Things seem more rough than the water's surface.

We are almost to the point, so close I can imagine rounding that steep headland and coming into full view of that magnificent island of snow-capped peaks, forty miles long and wild with brown bears and deer. But Rick worries about Keira—who is notorious for not returning from her wanderings—and Jamie whimpers with cold. We turn our backs to Montague and head to the cabin. After beaching the boat, Rick heads off in search of the dog. Struggling with my disappointment at not making it to the point, I follow Jamie down the beach to the headland nearest the cabin.

It is low tide, and every crevice, every cirque in the rock, holds salt water filled with life. Jamie and I climb from one tidepool to the next, peering into them to discover what lives within. Once our eyes adjust, we can see rockfish, anemones, starfish, sea urchins, barnacles, limpets, and snails among forests of sea lettuce, kelp, and eel grass. We find one long, narrow pool packed with starfish, orange and burgundy and yellow stars among bright green waving eel grass. I use a long yellow float that Jamie found and pry up one starfish, turning it over so that its pale belly shows.

"Watch and it will turn itself back over," I whisper to him. A few pale tentacles wave around, reaching out for a firm footing. Gradually more and more tentacles reach, rippling across the thick arm like swells in the ocean. Almost imperceptibly the legs stretch and turn, and the body of the starfish migrates onto its side.

"C'mon, let's go," says Jamie after a few minutes. "I want to climb up to there." He points to a rock face that leads up to the forest.

"We have to wait. The starfish is vulnerable this way. I don't want anything to happen to it because we turned it over," I tell him.

"What could happen?" he says, interested again.

We continue to stare into the tidepool as the tentacles wave and reach. The change is slow but certain. It is almost, except for two feet, turned over when we start climbing the rock, squeezing itself back in among the other stars.

My hand presses against smooth gray rock. My fingers reach for a small hold where rock juts out, where rain has eroded a dimple, a crack. My eyes focus on patterns of granite inches away.

"Put your foot here, and then put your hand here," my five-year-old son tells me. He leads, watching me closely as I follow him up the boulder. "Go the same way I do," he reminds me.

I do. He finds the best route.

We crouch on top of the boulder, feet on soft moss, shoulders touching, and look out from the headland to the waters of Prince William Sound. The waves of morning lie down to ripples on the surface. The rock we climbed a few minutes before to look into tidepools is slowly surrounded by the incoming tide. I point to it.

"Look," I say, "see how that rock is becoming an island? See how the lay of the land changes every moment?"

We climb down from the boulder, pick our way across the rocks not yet submerged by the tide, and return to the sandy beach. Jamie finds a wave-washed spruce limb and prods the kelp berm at the high-tide line, digging for treasure among the debris of storms. I find a boulder half-submerged in sand, smooth, gently sloping, facing the sun. Leaning against it, I close my eyes and feel the heat rising from black sand and rock. My head and back are cradled in the curve of rock; my feet, free of boots and socks, dig into warm sand. I drift in place.

"Mom, come look at this," Jamie says. I get up too quickly, and see stars, lost for a moment in a universe of my own.

Jamie points to a dead sun star. Its bright orange color is fading, bleaching away, and its skin peels off in strips, eaten by the spring tails and beetles hidden in the kelp berm. We turn it over and see the skeleton beneath, white cartilage radiating out in twelve thin lines, each with matching patterns of thinner strips across, the whole thing like a snowflake magnified. When we check on the sun star the next day, I am surprised at how quickly it has become something new. The skeleton is complete—no skin, no color, no body remain. Just white arms radiating upon black sand, a star skeleton.

Standing up, I see Rick trudging down the beach toward us, head down, without Keira.

"Don't worry," I tell him when I see his face, trying to sound more certain than I am. "It's an island, and we're the only people on it. She'll come back."

Spruce shadows lengthen over the beach, so we walk over to the quiet lagoon on the other side of the cabin. Jamie plays at the water's edge, throwing in rocks and singing. I start to read from a book I'd brought, but the words on the page can't draw me away from this place, so I join Jamie and stand at the water's edge, staring down into it.

Something moves in the clear water, something small and translucent. A feather? An embryonic stage of a marine animal? It wiggles back and forth, propelling itself slowly through still water. Its body is soft and oval-shaped, with flaps on either side and a row of three finlike appendages. It is ethereal. I show it to Rick and Jamie.

"I think it's a nudibranch, a sea slug, called *melibe,*" Rick says.

"I thought about that," I say, "but I've only seen nudibranchs in photographs of tropical waters. I didn't know they lived this far north."

Suddenly I remember seeing something in the water when we were paddling in this lagoon the day before. The image returns as quickly as a flash of light. We were rushing to get back, and I didn't stop to look longer or mention it to anyone.

The water was so clear, I had never seen it so clear, not in all the times I've been in the Sound. I could stare deep into it, as if I were looking through a telescope, no surface movement to distort the image. Long thick strands of green kelp waved up from the bottom, dark green palms rising from burgundy stalks. Attached to and floating among them drifted tiny translucent pink things. My eyes focused on one, and then I saw more than I could count, like underwater flowers blowing in the currents instead of the breeze, blossoms that have blown off their branches to float through the forest of kelp, stars in the water.

By evening, clouds obscure Hale Bopp and Mars and the waxing moon, but as I set our dinner on the table, I look out the window to something I've never before seen: Keira returning on her own. She trots up the path, tongue lolling, ears back, a satisfied grin on her wild husky face.

The next morning, we paddle out from the front beach again, this time heading toward the western point, hoping to paddle around it and to some islets on the other side. Keira is off on another adventure, but we no longer worry for her return.

I dip my oar into flat clear water, looking 50 feet or more into it, once again astounded by clarity. Colors intensify with the sun's rays reaching far into the water. Jamie sits in the middle again, calling out excitedly at every discovery.

"Look, another starfish! A purple one!" he cries. "And there! An orange anemone!"

As we paddle, a pair of magpies, their black feathers shining blue in sunlight, follow us from the shore, hopping from rock to rock, flying a few feet.

"Our escorts," Rick says, and we laugh, delighted.

At the point, we paddle through some sea stacks, coming right up on a couple of sea otters and a raft of seabirds. Among them are cormorants and guillemots, but what are the ducklike birds with the striking markings of silver and white and burgundy? They are harlequin ducks, birds I have never before seen, but have heard about just as I have heard about this island.

Harlequins suffered greatly from the oil spill, and they suffer still. They haven't been able to breed successfully for eight years. I feel that familiar but confusing mixture of sadness and pleasure, sadness over the loss and their continued suffering, pleasure at seeing them here nonetheless, seeing their brilliance like the comet, like the tidepools.

I want to reconcile these feelings, but how? Not by glossing over pain, not by denying joy. How, then? Like oil and water, they don't seem to mix.

At the headland, we pull the canoe up on some boulders covered with pop weed and walk up to the high-tide beach. Strong, thick blades of beach ryegrass are just starting to push new leaves through the layer of snow and last year's grass. I sit in the sun, basking like a seal on a rock, and then open my eyes quickly as I hear a sound at once strange, familiar, and unfortunate.

An outboard engine. A small aluminum skiff carrying three people in bright orange float coats zooms toward us. The person in front holds a clipboard, so I know they are scientists studying these creatures, seeing what happens in the aftermath of an oil spill. Perhaps they are counting the harlequins, or maybe sea otters or scoters.

I do not want them here. They intrude into our solitude. Even more, they intrude into my thoughts, the roar of their engine like the roar of sorrow and frustration and rage over what happened and what continues to happen. It is as if their boat rushing toward me carries all my memories of the spill. Carries, too, my anger that now, because of the oil spill, dozens of humans zip around out here counting and capturing and prodding and poking into the lives of these animals, animals who have already suffered so much.

I watch as they motor through slowly, staying far out from land, watch as the otters dive and seabirds fly at their passage, watch as they pick up speed and disappear in a rush of noise and wake into the horizon.

When their wake dissipates, we climb back in the canoe, paddling in the same direction as their passing. For a while, the possibility that we'll come upon them again looms like a storm cloud before me. Today, though, I am lucky; we do not see them again.

We come into view of the islets, a beautiful maze of cliffs and trees and beaches. We stop and eat lunch on a rocky beach. Harbor seals are all around, eyeing us curiously and playing hide and seek, though they do all the hiding. I begin to wish I could see one of the seals or sea otters under water. It is so clear that, back in the canoe, we can see down to the bottom where they were moments before. How wonderful it would be to see them swim under water, where their rounded bodies, so awkward on land, must slip through water like sunlight slipping through atmosphere. But I don't voice my desire; it seems too much to ask for, a thing only of imagination.

All day long we paddle in the equinox sun, reddening our faces and hands and forearms. All day long we look down into water, out over water, up into sky. Paddling through narrow passageways, we talk quietly, briefly, our voices as relaxed as the water's surface. Puffins ahead of us flap out of the water, then land again behind us, settling on the surface. Every now and then, a salmon leaps through the glassy surface. My senses are filled with the life that vibrates around us.

Late in the day, beyond the islets and the seals, in the middle of the strait, we see a flash of black dorsal fins lit by a low sun. A pod of orca whales, eight or so, arc their way down Montague Strait. Through binoculars I see a large male out front, then a group of females and calves close behind. Their white saddle patches glow pink in the evening sun. We watch as they surface again and again, heading toward the snow-capped Chugach range in the distance.

We round the last headland and come back into view of the quiet lagoon that leads to the cabin. To my left I see another sea otter perched on a rock. He stretches up, looks our way, then slips into the water, leaving a small splash. I consider paddling over quickly in hopes of seeing him under water, but I do not suggest it. This day has already given so much. Sometimes, though, deeply felt desires are heard most clearly. I watch to see where the otter will resurface, hoping at least to see him again.

Look. The sea otter is under the water right beside me. He slides around the front of the canoe, bubbles streaming from his fur and from his nostrils as he streaks through water. Air escapes from fur more dense with fine hairs than any other animal in the world. It pours out of his fur in long waves. He moves beside the canoe like a comet in the night sky. He zigzags back, rolls and stops in mid-roll, curled into a half-moon. Sea otter looks up through the water at me. And I, I am saying, over and over, "Look! Look! Look!" Then he rolls again, shimmers away under the water, and is gone.

The next day, a few hours before the float plane returns to pick us up, we walk on the front beach again. The sun star skeleton is nowhere to be found, washed away in the night's high tide. I imagine its fragile bones scattered along the shore like rays of sunlight.

Past the smooth rock I leaned against, Rick begins turning over rocks, finding what he looks for: oil. He shows me the splatters on boulders that look like asphalt gone awry. He pulls back one big flat rock to find a puddle whose surface rainbows when exposed to light. Eight years later, puddles of oil still slick the beach.

"I've got to bring some of this back," he says. "People all over the U.S. need to see this. They need to see that Exxon's lying about how clean the Sound is."

He collects some in a trash bag, wiping his hands on his coat as he works. These streaks of oil on his coat will be there forever. I know. We both have pants stained with crude oil from eight years ago. I don't want to see oil-stained clothes again. I bring him a towel to use, but it's too late.

The questions I asked our first night here resurface, looking up at me through that pool of oil. What does this mean, all this beauty and horror mixed together?

I pick up an oiled pebble and start to put it in his collection bag, but then I stop. I drop it, straighten up, and look out at the water. All the moments of absolute being—the boulder with Jamie, the blossoms of melibe, the sea otter under water—reverberate through me, mixing with the grief like salt water mixes with fresh water, diluting the pain, drawing it out like the moon to the tide.

For a moment I shed questions. For a moment everything fits and I feel only peace. Look. All this is changing. The comet will be gone in a few weeks, not to return for thousands of years. The Sound was harmed by the oil spill; it continues to suffer and to heal. As do I. As do we all. Look now. All I have is this moment, in this place, at this time. All I know is what I see. Moon, water, comet, trees, starfish, otter, light.

$\mathcal{T}$HE $\mathcal{B}$AY

William W. Warner

$\mathcal{I}$t is so known through the length and breadth of its watershed. The Bay. There is no possible confusion with any other body of water, no need for more precise description. It is, after all, the continent's largest estuary. Its waters are rich, the main supply of oysters, crabs, clams and other seafoods for much of the Atlantic seaboard. Its shorelines cradled our first settlements. It is the Chesapeake.

North to south, from the choppy wavelets of the Susquehanna Flats to the rolling surges of the Virginia capes, the Bay measures almost exactly two hundred miles. Alone among its vital statistics, its breadth is not impressive. The extremes are four miles near Annapolis and about thirty miles near the mouth of the Potomac River. In all else the Bay is champion. Its shoreline is prodigious. Put together the great rivers on its western shore: the York, the James, the Susquehanna and the Potomac. Add the labyrinthine marshlands of the Eastern Shore, always capitalized, since it is a land unto itself. The combined shorelines string out to about 4,000 miles, or more than enough to cross the country at its widest. Some say the figure doubles if all tributaries are followed beyond the reach of the tide. The Bay's entire watershed extends north through Pennsylvania to the Finger Lakes and Mohawk Valley country of New York, by virtue of the Susquehanna, the mother river that created the Bay in Pleistocene time. To the west it traces far back into the furrowed heartland of Appalachia, but one mountain ridge short of the Ohio-Mississippi drainage, by agency of the Potomac. To the east the flatland rivers of the Eastern Shore rise from gum and oak thickets almost within hearing distance of the pounding surf of the Atlantic barrier islands. To the south, Bay waters seep through wooded swamps to the North Carolina sounds, where palmettos, alligators and great stands of bald cypress first appear.

To qualify as an estuary, a body of water must be well enclosed, provide easy entry and exit for open sea water and enjoy a vigorous infusion of fresh water from one or more rivers. These are minimum requirements. The fiords of Norway are estuaries, but they are uniformly rocky, deep and thus biologically impoverished, which is why Norwegian fishermen spend most of their time on offshore banks. A good estuary with high biological productivity requires other things. Shallow water, for one, which the sun can penetrate to nourish both plankton and rooted aquatic plants. Extensive marshland is another. An estuary without it lacks the lace-work of tidal creeks and shallow coves which traps nutrients and protects and feeds the larvae and juveniles of a host of fish and invertebrates.

Also, to be summa cum laude in estuarine productivity, there must be circulation. A good mix, one is tempted to say, is almost everything. Not just in one direction. There should be two-layered or horizontal circulation in which heavier salt water from the ocean slides under the lighter and fresher surface water from rivers. Inexorably, that is, with a net flow upstream on the bottom and downstream on the top which surmounts the temporary effects of wind and tide. Ideally, there should also be some vertical mixing, which is not found in every estuary, since it requires significant contrasts in depths and water temperatures.

By all tests the Chesapeake does well. Its very configuration, its long north-south axis, encourages and concentrates horizontal or two-layered circulation. The result is a splendid salinity gradation or, to be more exact, twenty-five parts salt per thousand of water down near the Virginia capes, which is almost ocean, to zero or fresh water at the northern or upper end of the Bay. Fresh water infusion is constant and indeed vigorous. Often, in fact, it is too much of a good thing, as when the rivers of the western shore rise in spring floods. Mightiest of these is the Susquehanna, the longest river of the eastern seaboard. Next in order along the Bay's western shore come the Potomac, James, Rappahannock, York and Patuxent. We must note these next-in-rank carefully, because each is a considerable estuary in its own right which replicates the salinity gradients of the main Bay. The York, although at the smaller end of the scale, is a good example. Water lapping the beaches below Yorktown's historic heights is unmistakably salt, or seventeen to twenty parts per thousand. Only thirty miles upstream it is completely fresh.

Vertical mixture takes place thanks mainly to a deep channel running almost the total length of the Bay. Geomorphologically speaking, it is the fossilized bed of the ancient Susquehanna. It lies at the bottom of the Bay at depths of eighty to one hundred and twenty feet, still well defined after 15,000 years of silting and sedimentation. In its first life it was the course of an upstart river searching and scouring its way to the sea, nourished by Pleistocene glaciers not far to the north. As glaciers melted in the post-Pleistocene, rising ocean waters drowned the river valley to create the Bay much as we know it now. Today ship captains running to Baltimore know the old river well; it is the route of seagoing commerce. Trouble is in store for those who don't or who ignore the pilot's warnings. Its shoulders are sharp, and sure stranding attends any deviation from course.

To the Bay's host of marine organisms the fossil river is equally important. In late summer and early fall fresh seawater—fresh in the sense of oxygen content—creeps in along its bottom and branches up the tributaries with unusual strength, since rivers are low and their obstructing flow weak. Above it lies tired or biologically exhausted water. All summer long the surface waters have supported immense communities of plankton, not to mention sometimes harmful algae, greedily consuming oxygen. Now these waters are oxygen-starved. But it is autumn and they are cooling more rapidly than the deep water below. Being heavier, they sink. Conversely, the intruding seawater below carrying fresh oxygen slowly begins to rise. The mix is thus two-way. In the process the microscopic plant and animal plankton, heavily concentrated near the surface in summer, are swirled up and down and thus distributed more uniformly. Some of the Bay's most prominent year-round residents—the blue crab, the striped bass, the white perch—take their cue and make rapidly for the deeps. There they can feed amid the deeper groves of plankton and enjoy warmer water as autumn slowly turns to winter. (Theoretically, oysters and clams would do well to follow suit, but locomotion, alas, is not within their powers.) Crabs especially appreciate the deep water in autumn, since it prolongs the time left to them before cold water will force virtual hibernation in the post-Pleistocene ooze. The great channel is therefore a winter haven, a place for rest and limited feeding free of the temperature extremes of surface waters.

In spring vertical mixing again takes place through reversal of the autumn factors. Reoxygenation starts at the surface. In response the fish ascend and the crabs start a slow and measured crawl up out of the channel. The crabs' eventual goal is the shoal areas where eelgrass abounds and where the new spring water courses over the shallows with every tide. They go there to hide and to feed and to feel the rays of the warming sun. And think about other things associated with spring.

"Feller hasn't run ashore, he don't much know this Bay," a waterman once said to me after he pulled my ketch off a tenacious sandbar. It was the nicest thing anyone could possibly say under such embarrassing circumstances and it made me feel much better. What he meant, of course, is that the Chesapeake does not lack for the shallow water that is another prime estuarine requirement. The average depth of the Chesapeake, mother river and tributary channels included, is twenty-one feet. For most of the Bay, fifteen feet or less would be a better figure.

Shallower still are vast areas along the Eastern Shore, the waters surrounding the great marsh islands of Tangier Sound, for example, which Captain John Smith called the Isles of Limbo, where vigorous sounding will fail to uncover anything deeper than five feet. Captain Smith was glad when he left, and today's less venturesome sailors shun the marshy islands like the plague. Yet these very shoal waters have their place, if not for yachtsmen. They provide an optimum habitat for such rooted aquatic plants as wild celery and widgeongrass, the choice of waterfowl, or eelgrass and sea lettuce, which although acceptable to ducks and geese, are only preferred by small fish, crabs and young seed oysters. Almost invariably the shoals supporting these water plants are bordered by marsh. The marshlands in turn support a much greater growth of plants, plants which want to have their roots covered by water some of the time, but cannot tolerate it all of the time. Dominating these, heavily outweighing all other species in sheer tonnage and outdistancing them in distribution, are the spiky *Spartinas* or cordgrasses. *Spartina patens,* that is, which ripples in windrows or lies in natural cowlicks on the firmer ground, and *Spartina alterniflora,* taller and denser, which grows on the quaking mudbanks and along creek borders first invaded by tidewater.

The interaction between the two plant communities, one just below the water and the other barely above, is admirable. The marsh grasses are the storehouse or granary. The agents that mill them and their associated plant and animal life, principally algae and insects, are death and decay. We cannot readily see the crop so produced, since it ultimately takes the form of pinhead particles of detritus and bacteria-manufactured nutrients dissolved in the water, but it beggars anything that happens on dry land. Most of the Chesapeake's marshlands produce an annual average yield of five tons of vegetation per acre. Those in the southern reaches, along the lower Eastern Shore, go as high as ten. Down every tidal gut and through every big "thorofare" and little "swash" or "drain," as the breaks in the marsh islands are called, there comes an enormous and nourishing flow of silage made from this decomposing *Spartina* crop. Waiting to receive the flow, well protected by wavy forests of eelgrass, are many forms of life. First recipients are plankton and the larvae and young of larger forms, who need it most. In the latter category are enormous infant populations of fish, clams, oysters, jellyfish and worms. Predominant among adult forms are the blue crabs, who have a fine time of it preying on the small fry, including, sometimes, some of their own.

The animals of the aquatic plant communities give something back to the marsh in return, although not as much as they receive. Since they consume great quantities of marsh-produced nutrients, they also therefore release considerable amounts of nitrogen and phosphorous after their rapid browse-feeding and digestion. The waters so fertilized return to the marshes twice every twenty-four hours, as sure as the moon and sun make tides. The same waters, of course, also bring salt, which is what permits the cordgrasses to reign as uncontested monarchs of the marshland. Alone in the plant kingdom, the *Spartinas* thrive on it. Or, more accurately, despite it. Thus interaction.

Most of the Chesapeake's *Spartina* marsh is concentrated on the lower Eastern Shore in a broad belt extending south from Maryland's Little Choptank River. "South of the Little Choptank," the watermen tell you, "the fast land disappears." It is their way of saying that only isolated islands or small clumps of firm ground dot the vast marsh landscape of these parts. The larger islands are called hammocks; often they support whole fishing villages or a considerable growth of pine and hardwoods. The smaller ones, with barely enough soil to nourish a single bush or tree, are dismissed as "tumps." Seen from the air, the region appears very much like an Everglades of the north. It is the largest undisturbed marshland in the mid-Atlantic states, undisturbed because it is far from ocean beaches and thus largely overlooked by developers. May it remain so.

Such are the Bay's estuarine assets. Each makes its contribution and together they combine to produce marketable marine resources of incredible volume. The Maryland portion of the Bay alone produces more oysters than any other state in the union, with an annual harvest of approximately three million bushels. (Jurisdiction of the Chesapeake is divided; Virginia controls 985 square miles of Bay waters and Maryland 703.) Together the two Bay states supply one-quarter of the United States' oyster catch, worth about $22,000,000 dockside. Since its inception in the 1950s, the Bay's soft or "steamer" clam industry has provided over half the national catch of this species, moving all of New England to second rank.

But it is in the stocks of the familiar Atlantic blue crab that the Bay's bounty stretches belief. No body of water in the world has been more intensively fished for crabs than the Chesapeake, nor for a longer period, with such successful result. Since its beginning in the mid-nineteenth century, the Bay's blue crab fishery has made the United States the leading crab-consuming nation of the world, followed closely by Japan only in recent years. The national catch of all species annually averages anywhere from 250 to 350 million round weight or "whole crab" pounds, worth approximately $80,000,000. Crabs are thus our fourth most valuable fishery, exceeded only by shrimp, salmon and tuna. The blue crab regularly provides fifty percent of this national crab catch. Second in domestic rankings is the Alaska king crab, which has come rapidly into vogue since World War II. Other popular market species include the famed Dungeness crab of the Pacific Coast and the Alaskan tanner or "snow crab." Perhaps almost as tasty as these, although taken in much lesser numbers, are the Florida stone crab and the rock and Jonah crabs of Maine.

Blue crabs are now fished commercially from Delaware Bay down the Atlantic seaboard to Florida and around into the Gulf Coast as far as Louisiana and Texas. The biggest catch by far comes from the Chesapeake Bay. The Bay annually offers up anywhere from fifty to eighty million pounds in poor years and good years respectively, or approximately half the total catch of the species. This means that anywhere from 150 to 240 million individual blue crabs are removed from the Bay waters each year, since the average market specimen weighs one-third of a pound. Not only that, our dependence on the Chesapeake for the succulent soft crab is almost total or ninety-five percent of the national catch in this form. This is not a matter of biology or habitat, but human industry. Skill, hard work and infinite patience are required to hold crabs in "floats" or pens until they moult and successfully bring them live to market. People in other places don't want to do it. Only the Core Sound area of North Carolina, where early season softs are a short-term specialty prior to the opening of the shrimp season, and certain localities in Florida and the Gulf states, where there is a local restaurant trade, are exceptions. Practically speaking, therefore, but for the strong work ethic of Chesapeake watermen this most delectable form of crab would never come to market.

As might be expected, the Chesapeake's grand mixtures of fresh and salt water are also ideal for anadromous fishes, or those that spend part of their life in the sea and part far up estuaries for spawning and early growth. Most prized by both sport and commercial fishermen is the striped bass, always called rockfish in the Bay country. Here again honors go to Maryland. Its fresher half of the Bay regularly leads all other states with an annual catch of four to five million pounds.

There is yet another record of sorts among the anadromous fishes that is often forgotten, since the catch has dwindled to relative insignificance. Searching here and there in the fresh-fish shops of tidewater Virginia, one occasionally finds giant slabs of glistening meat lightly marbled with yellow fat. It is not swordfish, as size might first suggest, but sturgeon. The annual catch is around 17,000 pounds. Dockside value seldom exceeds $3,000, or barely enough to rate mention in the Department of Commerce's logorrhea of fishery reports. Before the turn of the century catches of over a million pounds, from which one hundred thousand pounds of caviar might be extracted, were not uncommon. There is a message here.

The Bay has other treasures, not all at the head of lists. Enormous herring runs, sufficient to support a sizable canning industry and provide the herring roe Virginians like to eat for breakfast with scrambled eggs. Mink, muskrat, nutria and otter, sad to include, trapped in the lovely marshes of Maryland's Dorchester County, in numbers second only to Louisiana. Sky-darkening flocks of migrating and wintering waterfowl, in the thickest concentrations of the Atlantic flyway.

Enough superlatives. They mislead. The Chesapeake does not impress those who know it best as the grandest or most of anything. For all its size and gross statistics, it is an intimate place where land and water intertwine in infinite varieties of mood and pattern. None has captured the essential Bay better than its principal discoverer, Captain John Smith. After rounding the sand dunes of Capes Charles and Henry, he wrote:

> . . . a faire Bay compassed but for the mouth with fruitful and delightsome land. Within is a country that may have the prerogative over the most pleasant places of Europe, Asia, Africa or America, for large and pleasant navigable rivers. Heaven and earth never agreed better to frame a place for man's habitation.

Although more than one historian has called the doughty explorer America's first press agent, none has seriously suggested that he was far off the mark in his description of the Chesapeake. It is true, of course, that ice occasionally grips the Bay, and winter storms are not unknown. The summer thunder squalls (and sometimes waterspouts) are notorious. A prominent yachtsman who has sailed the world oceans once told me he had never been so taken by surprise, dragged anchor farther, or felt more helpless than when hit by a fast-moving thunderstorm off Oxford, Maryland, in the month of July. But for most of the time the mood of the Bay is gentle and charitable. There are no rocks to claw or rend ship bottoms. Tidal range is slight and currents, when found, are more a refreshing diversion than an obstacle. Fog is rare. Caught in an autumn gale, the prudent skipper knows that he need only run a short distance before the storm to find a wide choice of snug, completely enclosed anchorages, where gallery forests of pine and oak come down to the water's edge and where geese and wild swan still fly over at masthead height with every dawn.

Delightsome, fruitful, pleasant. So it is, most would say, to this day.

$\mathcal{T}$HE $\mathcal{M}$ARVEL OF A $\mathcal{T}$IDE

Gilbert Klingel

$\mathcal{A}$LL living, when looked upon in a large sense, is a tide. Ebb and flow is one of the inevitable characteristics of existence. The growths of nations and their declines, the boiling sweep of conquests and their recessions, the rise and fall of cultures are manifestations of the turn of tides in the affairs of men. The Dark Ages and the Renaissance that followed were opposite halves of a single flow of energy just as the devastation of the hordes commanded by Chepe Noyon had its counterpart in the brilliance of the court of Kublai Khan. Only time pours ceaselessly in one direction; but even the march of the hours leaves behind a trail of risings and fallings, of comings and goings. The geologic eras bear bountiful evidence of the fluctuations of existence. Great waves of life washed up on the shores of eternity and fell back again; the extinct dinosaurs and amphibians, the fossils of armored fish and the billions of long buried trilobites are proof of this. Even individual lives are only tides in miniature; birth, growth and swelling maturity, decline and dissolution are separate phases in this phenomenon.

I have often wondered if the ancient and very primitive religions which recognized the existence of Selene, the goddess of the moon, did not have as their origin an instinctive recognition of the immense power of that satellite over the ceaseless pulsing of the tide-controlled sea. The phases of the moon and the correlation of the creeping of the waters into bays and lagoons could hardly have escaped the attention of early man, who was highly conscious of natural phenomena and who was just becoming aware of a sense

113

of power and articulation. The moon worships date far into the recesses of unrecorded history. Many of the primitive peoples of today to whom the printed page is an inexplicable mystery have a keen appreciation of the relationship of the tide to that orb and regulate their activity accordingly.

The flowing of a tide to anyone familiar with the sea, and with the least grain of perception, is an impelling and inspiring event. The tides of time are discernible only from a distance, but the surging and falling of a sea tide is a potent and tangible happening. Perhaps the inexorable character of a tide is its impressive quality, but I think the emotional response to the occurrence goes deeper than that. The newly formed embryo of a human being bearing its telltale marks of ancient gill clefts harks back to the time when our ancestors, no matter how far removed, strove and battled fin and tail with the tide. If you have never leaned over a ship's rail and watched the soft swirl and eddy of the tide-urged water flowing past a rudder you cannot fully appreciate what I mean. If you have, and were at all aware, you will know that the sight of a moving tide is a stimulating experience.

Here at my typewriter, far from the flow of moving water, the feel of a tide is a difficult emotion to catch and imprison on a sheet of paper. If a tide boomed and crashed like the surf it would not be so hard. But a tide is *silent;* it cannot be heard except faintly when interrupted by a rudder or a ship's bow; it cannot be smelled nor touched. A tide is best seen though it is more readily *sensed* than visualized. Its very vastness makes it difficult to grasp. In my mind's eye I see barren sand bars lying idle in the sun with fiddler crabs moving about, or boats lying on their bellies in the sand; I picture seaweeds trailing toward the mouth of a river or whirlpools eddying about a buoy and I say "this is a tide." But it is not. These are only small manifestations of a tide. A complete tide is a stupendous awakening, a gargantuan breathing of the whole ocean, or a monstrous wave running the circuit of the earth extending from pole to pole. It is a swelling giant that sends millions of creeping fingers into the hollows of the land, bringing life to those hollows and as regularly withdrawing it again. A tide is the pulsing bosom of our planet. The Norsemen grasped the idea better than we when they believed it to be the breathing of the earth-serpent, Iörmungander, a monster so enormous that it encircled the globe and held its tail in its mouth to make room for that appendage.

"Beneath the lashings of his tail
Seas, mountain high, swelled on the land."

It was a tide that wrecked me on Inagua when I thought all danger from the ocean was past, and it was to the tide that I turned for one of the most entertaining days I spent on that island. Near Mathewtown, toward the south and in the direction of the opening of the Windward Passage, the coast of Inagua makes a last turn before sweeping away in a long spit toward the desolate frozen sand dunes of the weather side of the island. At the last point of the turn the rock cliffs by the settlement crumble away, and a little beyond, the interminable arcs of the barrier reef take up their existence and fling away toward the infinite horizon. Here the full force of the tide, sweeping in twice a day from the wastes of the Atlantic Ocean and from the turbulent deeps of the blue Caribbean, meets in a boiling mass of currents and counter-currents. When all the remainder of the coast was calm and smooth this point was flecked with foam and with the peculiar lapping waves of tide-tips. This was the final meeting place of east and west where the debris and flotsam of two oceans mingled before being swept into the blue depths or piled on the high white beach which was already littered with the fragments of a hundred thousand sea tragedies.

The diving at this rendezvous of the seas promised to be good, so I lugged the heavy helmet with its hose and line down to a little shelf on the very edge of the breakers. Instead of diving from a boat I decided to crawl from dry land to the depths on foot, so that I might experience the full sensation of the transition from dry to wet and examine the structure of the cliff wall and its life on the way. A small oblique opening in the sloping rock made an easy entering wedge without making it necessary to battle the full force of the surf. In addition, the opening was well padded with algae on its upper slopes and was reasonably free of the ubiquitous spiny sea urchins.

With a tremendous heave I hoisted the eighty-pound helmet on my head and settled it on my shoulders. It was so top-heavy that I staggered and nearly fell. The native boy that I hired for the task, started the pump, and, like a drunken man, I felt my way across the padded algae and stepped into the first gradient of the slope. The foam whirled slightly about my knees and then about my hips. In a second I had advanced to my shoulders and the intolerable weight was suddenly lifted. Once more I assumed control of my feet. I paused a moment at eye height gazing at the strange sight of a world divided in half and enjoying the unusual perspective of being exactly at the level of the water. Most impressive was the definiteness of the division; above was dry air and sunshine, all the familiar sights flowers and white clouds; below was a strange blue cosmos of tumbled rocks, vague shadows and dancing bubbles. The surface was as rigid a barrier for most life as if it had been made of hard metal instead of the light-transmitting, yet opaque film that it appeared from beneath.

The amount of life that clung to the film itself was surprising. On the upper side it was dusted with yellow grains of pollen drifted from the bushes on shore, and with down and winged seeds that had floated too far on the trades. There were also a few dead bugs, the frayed and broken wings of a butterfly, and some beetle elytra, little else. For the land creatures the top of the sea was death and failure. But a mere fraction of an inch beneath, the reverse was true; the under film was a marine maternity ward. For clinging to the burnished ceiling was a host of just-created things: baby fishes scarcely a quarter of an inch in length, transparent as glass and as helpless as the current-swirled plankton; microscopic lacy crustaceans aglow with jets of iridescent color; round globular pelagic eggs with long filaments and dark specks of nuclei; small blobs of pulsating jellies just released from their rock-dwelling, hydroidlike, animal-flower parents; and other myriads too small to be identifiable to the naked eye but made apparent by the rays of sunlight they caught and refracted. This final yard of open sea before the beginning of dry land was a veritable hatchery of sea-life.

Swiftly I dropped into the wedge and entered the frothing line of bubbles. These hurled about in all directions and I had to seize a rock to keep from being smashed against the sheer wall. The waves retreated and came plunging in again forcing me to cling tightly, digging in toes and fingers like one of the Grapsus crabs against the swirling retreat. Six times I crouched against the onslaughts before there came a lull and I was able to step lightly into space and float downwards to a ledge eight or nine feet below. I had hardly landed when the seventh wave came in and I had to fall on my knees to keep a firm hold. Once more there came a period of quiet and again I jumped, pausing momentarily on a round mound of meandrina before I gave a final seven-league step and landed thirty feet below the surface on the level white sand at the base of the cliff that was the foundation of Inagua.

Catching my balance and my breath I looked about. Seaward a smooth plain of dazzling white sand leveled off into a blue immensity, dipping slightly at the point where it went out of vision. To the right the southwesternmost crags of the island lay piled in gigantic fashion, torn loose in great blocks by some heavy force. On the left a similar but smaller bluff jutted out into the azure world. Like the first it was scarred and pitted, festooned with a tremendous mass of living objects. Long fronds of exceedingly lacy algae alternately drooped listlessly, then flung skyward as the advancing pulse of a wave hit and rushed upward, deflected by the stone. Looking at the combers from below I was interested to observe that it was the wave form that moved, not the water itself; the great bulk of blue liquid seemed to throb forward slightly but always came back to its original station. I ascertained this by watching some floating bumpers that hung close to the watery ceiling. Only in the last few yards did the inverted wave-mounds fling themselves in their entirety at the cliff. In the open the wave shapes advanced ceaselessly; their power seemed to be transmitted from particle to particle, but the particles remained in their relative positions. Were this not so the destruction that would be wreaked on the land would be so tremendous that the islands and the continents would be quickly eaten away.

In order to take in the entire vista of the base of an island resting on its bed of sand I moved forward towards the open plain and stepped from the shelter of the twin bluffs. Instantly, and unexpectedly, I was met by a blast of water that threw me off my feet, rolling and twisting on my side over the smooth sand bottom. My helmet filled with bitter salt water. I gasped for breath and fought to stand erect. With a jerk I came to the end of the light rope that I was trailing between my fingers, then was startled to find myself yanked off my feet, and streamed out on the end of the line like a rag in the breeze. Fortunately my flight into open water brought me erect again and with a final splash the liquid subsided in the helmet so that I was able to catch my breath once more. The savage current caught my lightly balanced body, swooped it in a great arc nearly to the surface, swirled me towards the shore where it slackened and let me drop again on the sand.

Then I became aware that beyond the shelter of the crags a great assortment of objects was floating by at a dizzy rate. I had noticed them before but they had made no impression. Between the cliffs the current was barely perceptible except as a cool back eddy from the main stream. Once more I tried to breast the flow but was thrust back as if by a heavy hand. There was a solidity to the pressure that was unequaled by any other flow of energy with which I have had experience. Wind in a violent storm pushes and buffets one about, but water moving at one-twentieth the speed of a gale of wind would level everything in its path and tear up the ground besides.

The sand out in the swath of the tide was moving too. Close to the bottom the grains were rolling and bumping, creating small dust storms—a strange phenomenon under water—and long curving ridges and valleys a foot or more in depth which formed in endless parallel arcs at right angles to the course of the water. On a larger scale they were precisely like the smaller ripples seen on the mud bars when the tide is out. The whole ocean bottom seemed on the move, as though it were alive and were creeping towards an unknown destination.

Crouching in the shelter of the outermost boulder, I made myself comfortable and sat down to contemplate this stupendous event. For it was exactly that. All along the hundreds of miles of coast all over the world this same action was taking place. Great rivers of liquid were surging past thousands of headlands into bays, creeks, rivers, and lagoons, over shallow bars and in the hollows of deep channels, rolling countless sand grains and bringing oxygen, food, life and death to millions of swarming creatures. I remembered another tide I had watched in the murky green waters of the Chesapeake Bay in Maryland. In comparison to this Inaguan tide, it was a dull slow affair, but before I was through witnessing it from the windows of a steel cylinder hung from a barge anchored in the mouth of the Patuxent River near Solomons Island, I was completely overwhelmed at the mass of life it had brought past my small sphere of vision. The Chesapeake at that time was full of ctenophores, wraith-like comb-jellies belonging to the genus *Mnemiopsis*. The range of vision from the window of the cylinder was limited because of the haze to about six square feet. With a companion I began counting these organisms as they swirled helplessly by on the rising current. For six long hours we tabulated ctenophores and found that an average of 48 went by every minute or over 23,000 for the entire period. Then by computing the width of the river and the square surface of the tidal flow in a line across the river at its narrowest point, we reached the almost astronomical figure of 1,218,816,000 ctenophores! This did not consider any of the other forms of life which abounded in the water. This was only one small river, so unimportant that it does not even appear on a map of the Eastern United States. When we realize that every inch of this tide-impelled water all over the oceans from the poles to the equator is swarming with similar billions of living things we can only be silent with awe.

The Chesapeake tide, however, had none of the gigantic sweep and force of this Inaguan occurrence. It was a small scale flow, performed in a landlocked bay. This, of Inagua, was a full-fledged deep sea current with the pressure of two immense oceans forcing it on. While I watched, it increased in intensity until even the backwaters of my quiet eddy began to circle and tug at my bare flesh. The algae on the outer rocks were all streamed in one direction, straining at their fastenings as though they would momentarily tear loose. There was none of the gentle swaying and graceful undulations of the sea fans that I had seen on the reef. The actions of the marine plants and organisms gave the impression that a vast underwater hurricane was brewing and that they would all be shorn away into the blue abyss beyond. Some had been pulled from their anchorages, for large heads of orange-colored algae went swirling past and were lost in the haze. Clinging to one of them was the curved, ringed torso of a spotted seahorse and the saffron colored carapace of a small crab. They were battling bravely to maintain their positions on the rotating fronds, but they were probably going to a certain death. Sooner or later the buoyant tissues would lose their freshness, become limp and watersoaked, the particles of enclosed gas would escape and the seahorse and crab would coast with the plant to the deep sea bottom far off shore away from their accustomed habitat. Somewhere down in the blackness they would be snatched up by a hungry deep sea creature or would slowly deliquesce amid the abyssal ooze and slime.

While the tide was disaster for the tiny cosmos of the orange algae-head, it was the high road for the larger more vigorous fishes which took full advantage of the current to carry them on errands best known to themselves. A few fish attempted to breast the tide but large numbers permitted themselves to be carried on its strenuous course. How like people they were, taking the path of least resistance, going full speed towards an intangible goal, to be returned again when the tide changed. In just this way human action follows the main stream of thought, climbing on the fashionable bandwagons of a particular movement. Large numbers of big hogfish, gaudy fellows splattered with reds and deep oranges went by in a steady stream. Several times vast schools of blue-striped grunts, gleaming with brilliant iridescence, obscured the sand, so closely packed and so numerous were they. These were followed by a scattering of immense amberjacks which may have accounted for the excessive hurry the grunts were in. Some very stout-hearted fishes were breasting the current, but they were not making a very good job of it. Most numerous of this rugged group were the common and vividly colored spot snappers. They moved along in a narrow file, or in congregations of thirty or forty, close to the bottom, taking advantage of every depression or place where the rush of water was moderated even slightly. Their fins vibrated at high speed as they crept along, gaining a few feet, holding their own for a space, then inching forward again. What could have been so important to cause all this expenditure of energy I could not guess, though I rather suspect that the fishes themselves did not know. In many respects they are like sheep and blindly follow the leader. It is even questionable if the leader is fully conscious of its activities, for if by some alarm or other interruption the direction of a schooling mass is changed, the leader relinquishes its place and becomes the led, imitating the motions of the nearest member of the school. There is much that is not understood about the phenomenon of schooling in fish; it has been suggested that the occurrence is a form of natural communism organized by a scheming nature as a means of protection. It is a simple task for a marauder to follow and seize a lone individual, but much more difficult to grasp that same individual when it is one of a great mass of darting, scurrying forms. Numbers mean confusion to the enemy, a sort of primitive and defensive "united we stand, divided we fall." It is a curious fact, however, that very few of the big carnivores resort to gregarious living; the greater number of fishes of this type are the preyed upon. However, like all communisms, the individual is sacrificed for the purposes of the mob, and we have the spectacle of spot-snappers following their leader in a useless and energy-spending task.

Not all of the upstream creatures, however, were as foolish as the snappers. Some of these wiser ones were exceedingly cunning in their method of attaining their end. These were mostly small fishes, like the red, dark-eyed squirrel fish, and the silvery burnished moonfish and lookdowns. They went well out of their paths to avoid the current, circling in the lee of rocks, catching the back eddies, pushing through narrow holes and crevices, pausing frequently to catch their breaths, as it were. Of all these the lookdowns were the most amazing. They were characterized by the constancy of their numbers. Whereas the other fishes came singly, in vast schools or in isolated groups of six or seven, the lookdowns always appeared in twos. There is magic in numbers. Seven is a favorite numeral in certain folklore, thirteen forebodes evil, and all good things are supposed to come in threes. The number two will always bring to mind the silvery bodies of these fish. When I first saw these peculiar creatures during some diving in Florida, they were swimming in pairs and I have seldom observed them otherwise. Always two by two, side by side, moving as one individual, they are an underwater Damon and Pythias. Their duality is complete. If one dipped downwards, its companion did likewise; when they turned they turned together; moving or quiescent, what one did so did the other. I can think of no logical explanation for this piscine twinning, for these fishes are not known to pair off and build nests in the manner of some fish.

Even in appearance the pairs were identical. They seemed to have a sad expression, and their name was in keeping with their faces. The forehead sloped steeply downwards and they looked as though they were continually searching for some treasure lost on the bottom. From the tips of their backs long lacy filaments went trailing off in graceful arcs. Not the least remarkable characteristic of these fishes was their thinness. When swimming directly toward or away from one, all that was visible was a narrow line extending in a vertical direction. It was fascinating to watch the thin line suddenly form into a broad oval and then as quickly fade as the fishes wheeled and turned. A sort of now-you-see-me and now-you-don't.

Although the tide was whirling a vast horde of larvae fish and transparent spawn towards the outer wastes of the open ocean, it was also bringing a bounty to the many fishermen crouched on the rocks. Not human fishermen these, but an array of fantastic creatures of considerable variety. They were armed with an astonishing assortment of hooks, entangling snares, poisoned arrows and cleverly designed nets. Among the netmen were those most enchanting, highly successful and amazing creatures, the barnacles. Superficially, nothing is more stupid than a barnacle. Yet these doughty animals are clever enough to maintain themselves all over the world, from the frigid Arctic to the equally frozen Antarctic. There is almost no place in the sea where one cannot expect to find them at their interminable net casting. They think nothing of taking a world voyage on the bottom of some dirty tramp, or to go frolicking off on the hide of a whale. Certain species of whale barnacles are so fastidious that they will most often reside on the whale's lips and the front edge of its flippers, while others are said to prefer the throat and belly to the exclusion of the rest of the animal. Still other species are known to take to the air on the persons of flying fish, and not the least unusual are certain forms that attach themselves to the umbrellas of large dead jellyfish.

As seen from underwater barnacles are creations of considerable beauty, not from their color, for they are always drab, but from the exceedingly graceful and lacy form of their fishnets. These nets, which are really legs which have been transformed by the mechanics of need into living seines, must be seen to be appreciated. A barnacle's legs—even though these appendages resemble feathers more than they do legs—are as important to a barnacle as hands to a person, fins to a fish, or wings to a bird. Although walking is unthought of, their entire existence is dependent on their limbs; their breathing is possible because these organs circulate the water necessary for the separation of oxygen; and the status of the barnacle's stomach is directly in ratio to the functioning of the legs. A barnacle lives because it kicks.

Contrary to popular belief, a barnacle is not a shell fish, although it spends almost its entire life period tightly encased in a shell. Instead it owes allegiance to the great Class *Crustacea* and in its family tree are the lobsters, the shrimps, and our other friend of the epicures, the edible crab. The name of its subclass is the Cirripedia, which means, literally, the "feathery-footed."

Biologists, not being above error, for a long time considered the barnacles as aberrant relatives of the mollusks, and it was not until some thoughtful soul undertook to study the early stages of this creature that the truth became apparent. It was discovered that, after hatching, the young barnacle was so unlike the adult that it seemed impossible that the two could be parent and progeny. The infant had no shell at all; it swam and it looked like nothing on earth quite so much as an outlandish mosquito. It was studded with hairs and bristles, with spikes and long trailing appendages. But it obviously was a crustacean, for it was segmented and resembled the young of certain other crustaceans. In time the microscopic monstrosity molted, then again and again, altering its shape until oddly enough it grew a small shell on each side of its changed anatomy. At this period of its development it wandered about seeking a place to settle down to begin housekeeping as a full-fledged, calcium-enclosed barnacle. When, by instinct or simple chance, it discovered a proper locality it turned on its back, firmly cemented itself in place, surrounded itself with a house and began kicking—an activity that it continued to the final chapter. And its legs—which in any other crustacean would have become claws, paddles for swimming, or hooks for grasping—spread out, fringe apart and wound up looking like so many feathers.

I worked my way out to the boulder where there was a considerable colony of barnacles and watched them snaring the manna brought on the tide. They looked like so many active volcanoes, with puffs of light brown smoke beginning to issue from the tips of the cones only to be suddenly snatched in again, as though the eruption had gone inexplicably in reverse. Peering closer I could see that the momentary puffs of smoke were really the interlacings of the feet which were extruded and then quickly withdrawn fully expanded and curved inward to prevent the escape of any life that they had snared. The excess water escaped between the interstices of the fibers.

With my fingers I touched one of the delicate cirri, as the feathers are properly termed. With a snap it was retracted and the entrance barred with two plates of solid ivory. These plates fit so closely that they are airtight and watertight, sealing the barnacle in its shell until it once again desires to open. Thus barnacles can survive low tides when then are helplessly removed from their native element. Crashing surf, preying enemies are all the same to the barnacle. I have often thought that barnacles have their advantages. How nice it would be if we could escape undesirable situations, tax collectors and such, by merely closing our doors and going to sleep!

By this time the chill of moving water began to penetrate every fiber of my being. Some of the current seemed to be welling up from the depths for it carried bands of warm and cold. As the tide increased the cold became more pronounced until I was shivering. So I called a recess for a half hour.

When I again dropped below a great change had taken place. The current had become so violent that I had difficulty in keeping my position, even in the shelter of the boulders. Practically all the fish had disappeared. Those that were still about were swimming close to the rocks or were snuggled down in depressions where they were slowly undulating their tails. Great numbers had retreated into crevices and fissures in the cliff where they hung motionless. No big fish were in sight, except a half dozen large blue parrotfish that were bunched together in the shadow of a crag. The water had become a veritable avalanche and its speed was so great that even the fish did not consider it prudent to fight against it but took refuge in a philosophical retreat.

I did not descend again until just a few minutes before the tide began to change. The water which had flowed so swiftly before was barely moving. It was nearing the full flood. The aqueous dust storms had all subsided and the limit of visibility had extended thirty feet or more. Only the long curving rows of sand ripples remained to remind one of the deluge. I could stand without danger of being swept away.

In ten minutes all motion ceased and a perfect calm settled over everything, except at the surface where the waves still rolled over the rocks. The greatest change, however, was in the fishes. They no longer hung hidden in deep holes or lay quiescent in hollows on the bottom. The grunts were back again from their indefinite errands, though the amberjacks that pursued them did not return. Most of the fish were busily feeding. A number of brilliant triggerfish had mysteriously appeared from nowhere and were gliding from place to place munching on small tidbits which they scraped from the algae-adorned rocks. Their strange dorsal spines, I noted, were folded well out of the way, and were raised only occasionally. These spines, which comprise the first dorsal fin, are constructed in a most ingenious manner. At their bases is a complicated locking device, so cleverly arranged that when the first spine is erected it cannot be lowered from without until the third is depressed. When this is done the entire fin automatically folds down with it. I watched them carefully for a long time hoping to catch some hint of the reason for this strange contrivance. It is considered as a protection against enemies, though this theory does not account for the unlocking action of the third spine. Unless this is first lowered, however, when pressure is applied the other spines will usually break before they give.

Between the triggerfish were swarming large numbers of porkfish, handsome striped creatures, gleaming with iridescent color. Like the triggers they were feeding off the algae, but their method and food was quite different. The triggerfish were scraping low lying mosses; the porkfish confined their activities to the larger, more rounded heads of vegetation where they seemed to search carefully, probing between the fronds, snatching up the small crustaceans, worms and other invertebrates that made the algae their homes.

With a five-pointed spear that I took down with me I tried to add one of these porkfish to my collection. I missed it completely but on a second try snared one through the top of the back. Before I could grasp it to place it in the mesh bag I carried tucked in my belt for the purpose it had twisted loose, and squirming in pain it floated lopsidedly past the cliff wall. Before it had drifted very far there was a rush of fins and it was seized by a rock hind, a large mottled fish covered with reddish spots which, unnoticed by me, had been lurking in a wide crevice. The hind returned to its shelter carrying its victim with it and I went to try for another porkfish. To my surprise they would not permit me to approach. Previously they had swum freely about my legs, but now they kept their distance. Before I had been considered some strange new kind of fish; I was now regarded as a potential enemy. I have observed similar behavior among the snappers.

Most fish, however, are quite unconcerned about the death of their neighbors. Tragedy may strike within a few inches and they will continue feeding or idling or whatever their activity might be, as though nothing had happened. The next fish that I tried to spear exhibited a most surprising reaction. The barbed point scraped along its side, removed several scales and retained a small speck of flesh on the point. The victim, which was a yellow grunt with a flaming scarlet mouth, darted away, then turned, snatched up the floating scales and bit at the flesh on the point of the spear. Even when I jabbed at it again it did not flee but glided to one side and nosed the blades which had become buried in the sand! I marveled at the contrast between the two species; one perfectly sure of itself and the other timid and untrusting once danger had been proved.

Spearing fish is not as easy as it might seem. Although most fishes appear utterly relaxed, they are ever on the alert for anything that moves with directness. I have jabbed a spear into a school of fish, so densely packed that to miss seemed impossible, only to find that my barbs did not touch a scale. Yet the school, itself, moved scarcely at all. Usually there is a localized flurry which lasts for a brief moment and subsides.

After my failure at snaring the grunt my attention was attracted to a pair of small dull-colored fish which were cavorting between two sponge covered masses of dead coral. They were blennies of the same type that I had found at Lantern Head. They were the most unfish-like creatures I have ever seen. They skittered about the rocks assuming the most unusual attitudes. Heads up, then down, vertically or horizontally, they slithered in and out between the algae like restless insects. In a moment they gave a most remarkable performance. They had climbed down—they seemed to walk rather than swim, so closely did they stick to the moss—to the sand at the base of a boulder. Here they faced each other with only an inch or two of space between. For a second they remained motionless, then began a strange little hopping dance, using their pectorals as stilts. Round and round they went in a circle with their mouths as the axis. Occasionally they halted as though attempting to stare each other down.

Their mouths, which up to this point had been tightly closed began chattering as if in conversation. Once again the hopping and skipping began and continued for some time. When they again stopped, instead of chattering, they protruded their mouths until they touched. It was a perfect kiss! No such amatory caress was intended, however, for, shortly after, the blennies touched lips once more, established a firm contact and began shoving. The kiss was really a trial of strength, and apparently was their method of establishing ownership over a certain territory, for after quite a bit of pushing one of the blennies suddenly turned and fled, leaving the victor triumphantly poised over its tiny kingdom of a square yard of sand and an equal amount of coral encrusted rock. This seemed a very safe and sane way of settling the question of ownership without resort to bloodshed.

The instinct of curiosity, I am certain, is very highly developed in certain fishes. Sharks possess it in a great degree and so do the gurnards and sea-robins. This victorious blennie was the most inquisitive fish I have ever encountered. When I sat down in the sand close to its domain it came over and very carefully inspected each of my fingers outspread in the loose soil, tiptoeing delicately from one finger nail to the other. It nudged each very gently and then proceeded to crawl over my foot where it examined minutely an old scar inflicted by the sharp edge of an oyster shell years before.

Life in this tide-swept land clung almost exclusively to the rocks. The outer sand with its curving ridges was too completely unstable to house any permanent organisms. It was a watery no-man's land, a barren sheet of white against a background of blue. However, in the temporary quiet of the full flood, a number of fishes were deserting the rocks and making short excursions into the open. With the exception of the larger and more able types, few strayed any great distance. The sergeant-majors, blueheads, and the demoiselles were restricted to within eight or ten feet. Within this range they seemed very confident, frequently passing within easy reach of much larger forms. They knew that with a twist of a fin they could dart into the safety of a crevice. The only small forms that strayed with impunity into the open sand were the trunkfish, which no doubt felt secure behind their solid casings of jointed armor, and the porcupine fish, which are the nearest things to a living pincushion except the sedentary sea urchins. These were utterly without fear, and little wonder, for even to touch one would be to invite a painful puncture.

The open water was also inhabited by a small group of swell-fishes, drab prickly fellows with gullets capable of tremendous extension when they are alarmed. These fish are supposed to be very stupid, yet in the Chesapeake Bay I have observed close relatives of the West Indian forms attacking large blue crabs in mass and biting with their sharp teeth through the crabs' hard shells, a task that would be exceedingly dangerous if attempted singly. No creature that is capable of such organized action can be considered stupid.

Most of the fish that patrolled the outer waters were large carnivores that swept ceaselessly back and forth waiting for some rock-dweller to venture too far. They were not very numerous, but most were capable of great speed. Among this group were a cornet-fish about three feet long, not including the long filament attached to the end of its tail, an equally long trumpet fish which chased a tiny butterfly fish into the shelter of a crag, and the long slim torso of a barracuda.

For a half hour the water at the base of the submarine cliff remained quiet and motionless. The fishes glided about, moving and turning in an easy effortless way. Then faintly, imperceptibly, the tide began to swing. At first I did not notice it, so gently did it start. But soon I became aware that the algae no longer drooped listlessly. They began to point their delicate fronds in the direction of the distant and invisible island of Mariguana. I noticed that the sea fans on the rocks were bending too, and that, unlike the sea fans on the great reef, they were all aligned at right angles to the shore instead of parallel to it. Here the tide, not the surf, was the dominating force. Out on the sand the long ripples began to reform, reversing the position of their slopes, gradual on the upstream side, steep on the lee. The parrots, demoiselles, and other rock feeding species began to drift over to the sheltered side of the boulders where they temporarily resumed their interrupted feeding. The easy relaxation of the past half hour began to disappear. The underwater gale was approaching, and in preparation the fishes and even some of the invertebrates, including a half dozen wandering hermit crabs, began to vanish into little holes or fissures where they drifted into that wide-awake yet apparently restful sleep of the creatures without eyelids. The trunkfish and swellfish came out of the sand to settle down on a smooth spot where the swellfish buried themselves until little more than their eyes were showing. I could not help but wonder what sort of perilous life the creatures of this outermost point must lead, forever hedged in by marauding, patrolling enemies, limited above by the boiling surf, and twice daily forced to battle, or sustain, an almost irresistible deluge of flooding water. I was reminded of the people of Flanders, or of Alsace, who are periodically overwhelmed by floods of conquest or counter conquest, who bravely or hopefully continue living there, building new homes to replace those destroyed by shells or gutted by flames, and who after a time see them destroyed once more and are faced with the necessity of doing it all over again. Yet the comparison is not a completely true one, for a sea-tide is a river of life, not of death, a manifestation of nature which is a normal state of affairs for millions of creatures all over the world.

It was fitting that, as I returned to the dry earth again to avoid the rush of water rapidly welling to its climax, the last creatures I saw before my helmet broke the surface were the *Aurelias,* the moon-jellies. They were the first and only moon-jellies that I saw near Inagua. Their appearance at this opportune moment was significant. More than any other living creatures could have done, they expressed in their filmy iridescent tissues the symbolism of a flowing tide. There were six of them slowly drifting with slight pulsations of their hemispherical umbrellas on the bosom of the current towards the open sea. Pale and glowing they resembled the moon after which they are named; in a translucent shining galaxy they floated aimlessly off into watery space. Like the currents of the ocean they were giving themselves completely and passively to the pull of the invisible moon; the responsive tide was their life, their complete world and their means of conveyance.

$\mathcal{A}$ $\mathcal{D}$AY IN THE $\mathcal{L}$IFE

Nancy Lord

$\mathcal{I}$ wake before the alarm, as I always do on fishing mornings. Nights before fishing, I'm never really asleep but only waiting, monitoring the wind and water. For hours already, I've listened to the creek trickle and the songbirds warble. Now I sit up and look outside. The skiff—which I always check first—is still on the mooring, slack on its line and milk-cow tame. In the northeast sky, behind layers of low clouds, the sun glows with an oyster-shell light. The water lies as flat and dull as a pewter plate, its edge solid against the shore. It's my kind of fishing day. It might also be a very good one. We're in the third week of July, and the sockeye run should be close to its peak.

Ken stirs. "Wicked surf," he teases. He knows I've worried all night that the weather might change. He's never in his life worried about something he couldn't affect, and he prides himself on his ability to fall asleep the second he puts his head down and to sleep through the ragingest storm.

I get up and dress, then make myself a bowl of instant oatmeal. I learned a long time ago that if I didn't eat before going out to fish, something would happen that would keep me from eating until way past the point of low-blood-sugar grouchiness. It's one of the laws of fishing, like another I generally obey: take raingear or it'll be sure to rain. Ken, however, doesn't need to eat. He waits until the last minute to get out of bed and throw his clothes on.

Chestwaders, flotation vest, raingear, hat, glasses, gloves, lunch box. I run down my mental checklist. Make sure Ken has his knife. We go out the door.

The tide is still coming in—an easy tide to set on. It's a good day of tides, all in all—large enough to move fish but not so large that the water will suck out as we watch or leave our low-water sets in rock piles. We carry our nets to the water's edge; then we carry the rowboat down, and Ken rows for the skiff.

Ken motors in and we load the nets. He does leads and I do corks, piling them into the center and port bins so they'll set out neatly over the stern, in order. We work quickly and silently, except when I ask "This one?" before grabbing a new end and Ken grunts in response. Most inlet setnetters divide their allowed gear into three thirty-five-fathom nets—indeed, that's the rule for most areas—but we fish more nets of shorter lengths, as short as ten fathoms. Throughout the day we move, switch, replace, and tie these together, depending on location, stage of tide, height of tide, wind, waves, current, time in the season, and how things are going. Ken's the master at devising these fishing plans, and I'm the crew that follows directions and just sometimes suggests we move a net sooner or let one soak a little longer.

No fishing day is the same as any other, and we always think we can be a little smarter about how we fish, work harder, and catch more salmon.

Ken ties one end of the corkline to the setline at the high-tide mark and climbs back into the boat; I pull us out along the setline; Ken lowers and starts the motor; and at exactly 7:00 A.M. we set our first net. Leads and corks tumble out over the stern as I watch for snarls, and then, when we reach the end of the net, I wrap a bite around the setline and tie the net off.

We both turn expectantly to see what's happening behind us—whether fish are hitting the net, whether this will be a fishy day. I continue to watch behind us for splashes as we speed to the next set, but the corkline lies in a perfect gentle crescent against the current.

Our first sets go like clockwork, right down the beach. I love fishing when it's like this—the smooth, voiceless teamwork, the echoing clank of orderly corks over the stern, the practiced feel in my hands. I don't think so much as I *am*. The body knows; the memory is in my fingers, my shoulders, the knees that brace me. My physical self knows the grip of line, the quick tightening, the double hitch pulled over itself. If I stopped to think about what I do, I would surely fumble.

The nets are out, and I stoop to scrape seaweed and sand from the bare boat bottom. I'm sweating inside neoprene; the sun, breaking through the clouds, has lit the fireweed and monkey flowers on the hillside into a blaze. *The red salmon come when the fireweed blooms.* So they say; so the old-timers said about the sockeyes, the money fish. We are ever hopeful.

To a fisherman, every fishing day is like Christmas, every net like presents to be opened. We never know what surprises we might find, only that there'll be something there and that it just might be, this time, the stuff of our dreams. That's why we fish on days when we catch just ten fish, and in storms, and on those days when nothing seems to go right—because the only thing predictable about fishing is that we won't catch anything if we don't have web in the water.

This morning our nets are not, however, loading up with fish. Ken blames the weather. It's too good; we need a storm to move fish up the inlet and in against our shore.

We start back through the nets, pulling leads and corks between us across the boat. Ken snaps loose a silver, worth just half a sockeye. The next fish is a silver, too. I slip a finger under one gill to peel away web and then shake the other side free. Every fish is its own puzzle to pull through, spin out of a twist, unbag, ungill, shake off. After years of practice the hands know, but my brain still clicks through its calculations, seeing the patterns.

Ken looks glum, but at least we've got fish in the boat. This is another maxim among fishermen: we have to have one fish before we can have ten, and we have to have ten before we can have one hundred. We pull more net and Ken grabs for our first sockeye. "Now *that's* a beauty," he says.

The fish, still fighting fresh, leaps around the center bin as though it would throw itself from the boat. It smacks against the aluminum, splashes water, dances on its tail, and comes to rest against one of the still-twitching silvers. It is, in fact, a very good looking fish, with a rounded body and a dainty-featured face, marred only by the gillnet's score across its head. It's the color of distant water, a soft gray-blue that deepens over its back into a metallic, nearly cobalt shine. Mirrory scales divide into contour lines like shifting plates of antique, tarnished mail.

The fish flops again, spattering blood that's hemorrhaging in thick, tomato-bright clots from its gills.

Wherever this ocean fish was headed, it was a long way from beginning its transformation to spawner. In another week or so we'll begin to catch an occasional wasted-looking sockeye, as flat as if it had been driven over by a truck and rose-colored, with a monstrous green head and hooked snout, all the better to scare its competitors once it reaches its spawning grounds. One will spill eggs like jewels into the boat, and we'll wonder if it lost its way home.

The fish makes a last flop and then lies quietly, its mouth working open and shut as though it's gasping for breath.

I'm well aware that some people think this cruel—killing fish like this, killing anything. They forget—or they never understood—that killing is part of how we live, the fish as well as the fisherman, the fish eater as well as the most committed vegan. Something dies that another may live. To me, the morality lies somewhere else—in what happens after the killing. When salmon are caught as "by catch" in other fisheries and discarded overboard, or when someone takes a fish but leaves it on the bank or in his freezer to get freezer burned, that's when behavior must be faulted.

These days, I frequently find myself examining that most basic of Dena'ina beliefs—that all things have wills and give or withhold themselves by choice, depending on whether a person shows respect or is insulting and wasteful. Among Peter Kalifornsky's Dena'ina belief stories is one about a young man who didn't listen to his elders about the proper treatment of animals. He left bones lying all around, and he killed mice cruelly and threw their bodies away. Other mice spoiled his meat, chewed up what was in his traps, and scampered over him in his sleep. At last he dreamed of going to the place where the animals wait to be reborn, and there he saw the ones whose bones had been walked over. They were horribly disfigured by his mistreatment and unable to return to human space.

Such lesson stories clearly helped enforce what the Dena'ina considered proper behavior and served the culture well in the long run. Would that our own laws and practices worked so well to feed people within a conservation framework.

What's a better end for a salmon—being chewed on by a seal, rotting to a slow death after spawning, or flopping into a fishing boat? From a salmon's point of view, the question has no meaning. The salmon's brain can't consider the options. The salmon doesn't think; it reacts. Nor does it feel pain as we know pain, not with its simple nervous system. The sockeye in the boat isn't gasping. It only looks that way to people, who know what it feels like to *them* to struggle for breath.

In the belief that a quick death is a humane one, sport fishermen often club their catch on the head. We knock only the lively kings with the back of the gaff, to keep them from bruising themselves—or us—as they thrash. The smaller fish are difficult to club without damaging their flesh, and they fade away quickly as it is. In any case, most fish we bring into the boat are already dead; once they're in the net, the web caught in their gills prevents them from working water through properly to extract oxygen. In fishermen's language, the fish "drown."

The best way to handle a fish—to be quick and to ensure good quality for whoever's going to eat it—is immediately to slit it gill to gill and drain out the blood and then place it on ice. Some commercial fisheries have moved in this direction, and the better care brings a higher price. Change is slow, though, in those fisheries that have traditionally dealt more in volume than in quality. Our processors still want salmon untouched by a knife, and they won't bring us ice.

We do the best we can. We don't step on our fish. We don't let them go dry on the beach or get beaten into noodles in the surf. We keep them out of the sun.

Our count now is up to eight—four sockeyes, four silvers. There's the sockeye with the metallic shine and another that's smaller and greener, the silver with a thick tail and two lankier ones that look like twins. These are the fish in a "mixed-stock fishery," where salmon headed for a variety of large and small, glacial and clear, fast and slow-running rivers and lake systems mingle before turning right or left and separating out. Bluebacks belong to one river, bullet shapes to another. That's the beauty and the essential genius of salmon: the custom design that matches each separate stock to color and stream flow, the natural conditions in their different home waters. As the big kings evolved to dig spawning beds below the scoured depths of powerful rivers, the sleekest sockeyes perfected their ability to move through shallows; the strongest, to throw themselves up falls; and the greenest, to blend into mossy depths.

I soak a piece of burlap over the side and cover the fish, a little brown mound in the center of the boat. Across the inlet, the sky is streaked with rain. The time is 7:40.

"How many?" Ken shouts as he cuts the motor. This is one of our games—to guess the number of fish in a net. Ken has not only much better eyesight than I do but also an uncanny ability to predict what lies under the surface of the thick, flour-roux water.

I always make a conservative guess. That way, when there are more, I feel lucky to have them. "Three," I say, leaning from the bow to grab the corkline. I already see two heads.

Ken guesses six.

There's a silver along the leadline right away, and then the next pull of net brings in a big, headless sockeye, all gnashed red meat and dripping eggs. Ken curses and we both look around.

The seal's right there, just fifty feet off the outside buoy, bobbing up to get a better look at us. The way it stretches from the water makes it look as though it's standing on something solid, on tiptoe. Ken and I both yell, and I grab an aluminum post and bang it three times against the boat. I always think this should sound to a seal like gunfire, but it never seems to have much effect. This seal—a harbor seal, the most plentiful of Alaska's seals—merely ducks under and reappears seconds later a little farther downstream. "Go away," I yell as I might at a dog loitering around a picnic table.

The seal lowers itself to whisker level and stays where it is, watching us. It has a bowling-ball head, dark and shiny, and saucer eyes. Most people think seals are cute; they would have a completely different opinion if seals had hard, little eyes and ferocious fangs—if a seal looked, for example, anything like a bat. Seals, in our modern classification system, are closely related to Bambi, and everybody loves Bambi. As a culture we Americans have Bambified ourselves away from any real understanding of individual species and their importance in the ecological picture.

Sometimes, grudgingly, I, too, will admit to being taken with fawns, bunnies, puppies, the baby seal that once swam to our boat wailing and still wearing its umbilicus—all soft and cuddly animals, cartoon creatures with fluttering eyelashes. *Bambi* was the very first movie I was taken to as a child, and I was struck to the soul with empathy. It was many years before I came to understand that there could be cultural systems—even within my own country—with beliefs different from and as strong as any I grew up with. This understanding came to me with pinprick clarity the day a Native woman told me about the time *Bambi* played in her village: when Bambi and Bambi's mother came on the screen, all the boys in the audience raised their arms as if to shoot.

At least cartoons were recognized as cartoons then. A more recent movie, about a seal named Andre, stars as Andre not a seal at all but a young sea lion. Every few years we spot a sea lion in the inlet, and even from a distance—with most of the animal underwater—it's easy enough to distinguish it from a seal. Much larger, more brown than gray, a sea lion swims and rolls along the surface, tossing its flippers. It has a pointed, doglike face and visible ears. Out of the water, it has longer limbs and an altogether different, more upright shape. Perhaps it was the sea lion's superior posture that attracted Hollywood, or perhaps they're easier than seals to train or have some other cinematic advantage; I don't know. Hollywood didn't care about correctly depicting a marine mammal, and most viewers, more familiar with E. T. and the Little Mermaid than with either seals or sea lions, didn't have a clue.

Ken keeps an eye on the seal as he works to free the mangled fish. With the head gone, there's no good way to grip it, and the web is tight in the flesh and tangled with bones.

It's not that we begrudge the seals having a meal; it's just that we think they ought to get it on their own. We can only guess how many gilled fish they steal from us. Often there's little evidence— just an empty or near-empty net. Their usual technique is to grab fish by the heads and pull them cleanly through, though sometimes they tear the heads off salmon that are too fat to slide through the web, and rarely, like vandals or epicurean wastrels, they swim along a net and bite out just the sweet bellies.

Ken finally frees the fish and it drops into the boat with a lifeless thud, like a sack of wet sugar. Since we can't sell it, we'll take it home for ourselves. The seal has ducked out of sight—on its way, we imagine, to our next net. We rush to beat it there, though we know our slapping around in a tin boat is no competition to a creature born to the water and shaped like a torpedo. At most, we can try to keep our nets picked clean, to avoid leaving fish dangling like so many buffet items.

Seals—though in recent years they've grown both more numerous and bolder along our beach—have, of course, been a part of the life here for as long as anyone knows. The traditional Dena'ina relied on them for their skins, meat, oil, bladder—all their various parts, down to their whiskers. It took twenty seals to make one large skin boat.

After Americans brought the canned salmon industry to Alaska, seals—despised for eating fish that could otherwise be caught by fishermen—were systematically slaughtered. For most of the past hundred years the government paid a bounty on their noses and even, for a time in the 1950s, dynamited seals at the mouths of salmon rivers. At the peak of bounty hunting in the 1960s, 70,000 seals were taken in a single year. Not until 1972 were seals protected; the federal Marine Mammal Protection Act prohibits the hunting of seals and other marine mammals except by Natives for subsistence purposes.

Today, although seals are notoriously hard to count, biologists estimate there are about 250,000 harbor seals statewide, a population considered healthy. Alarm has arisen only recently over apparent sharp declines in the Gulf of Alaska and the Bering Sea. Those two areas are—perhaps not coincidentally—the locations of aggressive harvesting of bottomfish by factory trawlers.

When we began fishing, we rarely had problems with seals raiding our nets. Most seals in the area kept to the south of us, to the clearer water of the river sloughs and the easy hauling out along the bars. Whether population growth has pushed them north or they've simply learned how to find an easy meal, I don't know. I imagine the sound of our outboard calls seals to our nets in the same way the grind of an electric can opener calls a hungry dog to a kitchen.

Not too many years ago, Alfred and Ann Topkok, Natives originally from the coast near Nome, fished a few miles north of us. We sometimes saw Alfred boat past our camp as he went to hunt seals, and when we visited them at their camp Ann showed us baby booties she sewed from the spotted silver pup skins.

Alfred and Ann are gone now, and the local seals are probably less hunted today than since before the Dena'ina first arrived on these beaches. Perhaps they are also as fearless as any seals, ever.

When the tide's high, it's time to move nets.

We tear over the flat water at full throttle, the shore alongside us a narrow band, the water everywhere high and capacious, swirling in muddy boils. Darkening clouds make a patchwork of the wide sky. I lift my chin and breathe deeply of the rushing air, lick my lips clean of salt and splashed gurry. We pass under a low-flying flock of gulls, and for a time we neither gain nor lose on them but keep their exact pace, floating with them in the same ethereal dimension. We stare at each other, the birds and I. Their wings sweep up and down. I could be a feather, a barb of a feather, one of the one million fluted and hooked barbules of a single feather. I could be the floating lightness of down.

This, too, is a part of fishing.

We take a break and go ashore, clipping our bowline to a net. The sun has broken through and beams down warm on the sand, rumpled with old bear prints above the tide line. I shed my gloves and vest, peel neoprene to the waist, open the lunch box, and take a long drink of water. I make myself comfortable against a rock and unwrap a Fluffernutter sandwich, an obscenely high-fat, high-sugar, sticky concoction of peanut butter and marshmallow cream. Ken and I both ate these as children and somehow came back to them for fishing food, though even the thought of eating one in any other circumstance makes me gag.

I've taken just two bites before Ken spots a seal at one of our nets and we rush back out.

We pick fish, and then we sit on one net and then another, waiting for more fish, watching for seals. The water's so still we can both see and hear salmon moving past—jumpers behind us, a finner leaving a ripple, small fish squirting through our nets. The jumpers leap elegantly into the light; like dancers or basketball players, they defy gravity to hang in the air, stop-time. We watch one launch itself several times, closer, closer, closer to a net, and then we don't see it again. Another, instead of slipping back tail first or landing on its side, traces a high arc, like a diver springing from a board to make a clean, headfirst entry into a pool.

Why fish jump is one of those questions that may forever entertain us with possible answers. Surely one good reason is to escape predators—in this case, the seals that continue to pop up around us. Some biologists, noting more comely females than hump-backed males among pink salmon jumpers, believe that at least some jumping has to do with females trying to loosen their eggs. I think it's entirely possible that fish may appreciate, on some level, the sensation of leaving the water, of feeling air ruffling through their gills and the blast of all that white light on their eyeballs.

Off to the south, a skiff at Kustatan glides out toward the rising bar.

As we pick one fish, two more hit the net, kicking up splashes of water. Ken shouts, "They're really poppin' now." This is what our former neighbor Lou used to say before he quit fishing and we bought his sites, and it's become part of both our lexicon and our folklore, our ritualistic good-luck chant.

The tide goes out. We pull nets from the beach and reset them between offshore anchors. When we return to pick the first of them, I've only just lifted the corkline and begun to gather web when a huge, purple face floats up out of the murk.

"King!" The word squeaks through my teeth. We rarely see king salmon after the beginning of July. Ken squeezes into the bow, and I let my side of the net go as he studies the way the fish lies against the net and begins to bunch web around it. Kings are too large to gill, and when they don't simply bounce off a net they often only rest up against it or are snagged by a single tooth. They can be gone in a flash.

Ken loves nothing in fishing more than catching king salmon, and he is at his most intense at this moment. This is his art. He works quickly, delicately, wrapping web around the passive fish and then grabbing for the bundle.

The fish comes alive. It thrashes with violent, tortuous twists of its body, spraying water ten feet high, which falls on us in sheets. But Ken has hoisted it over the side, and it dumps into the boat to finish beating itself out among the little fish. It's not as large as its shapely head made it out to be—perhaps thirty-five pounds—but it's a fresh ocean fish, still gleaming, its spotted tail unfrayed.

It's rounded like an old-fashioned pickle barrel. Near its tail, a couple of scaleless circles the size of nickels mark where lamprey eels caught a ride through a far sea.

On average, our kings are smaller than this, but they can reach Bunyanesque proportions. Earlier this summer, a sport fisherman across the inlet caught an eighty-nine-pounder. A catch like that on rod and reel must surely be a thrill, but the burgeoning sport fishery that's developed around kings threatens those who fish commercially. Across the inlet more than here, commercial seasons have been shortened—targeted to sockeyes and timed to avoid the early- and late-running kings. In addition, fishermen there have begun their own campaign of releasing live kings from their nets; they hope this altruism will keep them from losing more fishing time. I try not to be overly pessimistic, but if history is any indicator, the battle over fish won't be won by the commercial side. There are many more of them than there are of us. Already the "sports" get the main allocation of silvers as well as the kings, and now they're casting into the political system for more sockeyes, our money fish.

We head for the scow to make a delivery and lighten the boat. As we motor past George and his crew, bent over a net, I slip my hands into our king's gills and hoist it high for them to admire— and envy. George pushes the air with his hands and yells across the water, "Throw it back! Throw it back!"

After we've tied up alongside the scow, Ken and I pitch our salmon. We grip them by their heads, tossing sockeyes into one tote, silvers into another. We keep our own silent counts. The fish drip slime; stiff and discolored now, they handle like sticks of firewood. Ken lifts the king last, steps up onto the scow, and drops it in on top of the sockeyes.

To our north, Mount Spurr towers whitely over the land. A volcano as raw as the beginning of time, Spurr belched ash and steam and nearly brought down a passenger jet just a couple of years back. Its Dena'ina name, which translates to One That Is Burning Inside, attests to its eruptive fame; of the four volcanoes in the region that have been active in my time, it's the only one whose traditional name refers specifically to its status as a volcano.

Today, as we chase fish in its shadow, scientists are poised on Spurr's rim with a NASA robot—the world's most sophisticated, designed for exploring Mars. The spiderlike machine, named *Dante II,* will descend into the crater on its computer-programmed legs and then beam up video and geochemical data to a satellite. I take a minute to marvel at the juxtaposition—fishermen on water as perilous as it's ever been, engaged in the same basic hunt for food that people have pursued since day one, and space technology on the mountain, as state of the art as it gets. What a world we live in, that can accommodate both in the same here and now.

The reason we chose setnetting over other fisheries in the beginning was largely for its simplicity: its basic, low-tech nature. All we really needed was a skiff, a net, and a couple of pairs of hands. When the world's oil was drained, we told ourselves, we would row our boat with oars; we would work with the tides. And yet, I'm surely no Luddite. I follow the space program with a keen interest in all its inventions and discoveries. I want to know about the farthest stars just as I want to know about the bottom of the ocean and the inside of a salmon's brain. If the "crater critter" designed for Mars can also totter down into an active volcano and add to our collective understanding about rocks and gases, that's gravy.

Rachel Carson wrote that the picture of the sea that existed at mid-century was "like a huge canvas on which the artist has indicated the general scheme of his grand design but on which large blank areas await the clarifying touch of his brush." That picture, surely, still has plenty of blank space. Why do fish jump? Where do the belugas go when they leave the inlet? What's the reason for the sudden sharp decline in the numbers of seals and sea lions in the Gulf of Alaska? Only recently have marine biologists discovered that the deep ocean floor, long thought to be a biological desert, is in fact home to a diversity of species rivaling those thought to exist on the planet's land surface—somewhere between ten and one hundred million different species. Imagine the possibilities for undersea discoveries in light of the fact that an entire species of large terrestrial mammal—the goatlike *sao la* of Vietnam—escaped scientific notice until 1992.

Although I don't doubt that someday humans and their machines will reside away from the earth's surface, I also believe with absolute certainty that no artificial creation or substitute world will ever be as infinitely interesting and lovely—not to mention munificent—as this one and only earth.

We motor past George again, and this time *he* holds up a fish. It's a pink salmon, we can tell even at a distance—skinny as a knife blade, weighing less than two pounds. If we were closer I'd hear George saying, "I caught one of them spotted-tail fishes, too."

At low water we move nets again, back around the point. These offshore sets we make with regular anchors, whose buoys have popped to the surface now that the tide's out and the current has eased. It takes my whole body to lift each anchor while Ken motors into the current; from the soles of my feet to my aching shoulders, every muscle pulls. For each set, I hook the anchor on the gunnel and tie off the outside end of the net to its buoy. We motor to shore; I hop out and fetch the onshore buoy and tie the inside end of the net to it. Then we motor out again, spilling net behind us. When the net is straight and tight, I drop the anchor over.

This time, though, we screw up. One of the nets catches on itself, and a lump of corks and web flies out of the boat all at once. Ken slows and tugs on it, but it doesn't come free, and then the current swings us into rocks, where we bang the prop. We pull back on the net to try again, but as we back up with the motor in gear the net flags, and suddenly there's that abrupt clothy sound that's always like a kick to my gut. The prop has caught web and ground to a stop. Ken swears and slams his hand against the boat, then climbs onto the seat and balances over the transom to begin twisting and untwisting and peeling the tightly wound web from the prop. I'm grateful for the calm weather—that we're not caught in surf and having to hack away with a knife while the boat pitches.

All afternoon, seals continue to plague us. We pick nets and find only viscera or telltale catches in the web, and one very large new seal-shaped hole. We break sticks, throw back flounders, and shake out the aptly named jellyfish that roll in the net and fall to pieces like Jell-O taken too soon from a mold. We pause to eat again from our lunch box. I peel an orange with hands that smell as foul as the insides of my leaky rubber gloves. A seal surfaces well outside the net with a flopping fish in its mouth. It bobs high and looks as though it's juggling the fish as part of a circus act, though it must only be trying for a better grip. We continue to pick fish—one by one by one. We're catching more sockeyes than silvers and are glad of that.

Ken chants, "One fish, two fish, red fish, blue fish." I try to remember the words to a Russian peasant rhyme that counts dresses and sacks of flour and magpies. Gulls squabble over something in the rocks and are silenced when an eagle lands in their midst. Eagles are, above all, scavengers, which is one reason Ben Franklin didn't think they were particularly suited to represent our country. "He is a bird of bad moral character," Franklin wrote of the eagle after it was selected as our national symbol over his own favorite, the turkey. "Like those among men who live by sharping and robbing, he is generally poor, and often very lousy." In places with clearer water, eagles are known to dive for fish, but here they rarely even circle the water when salmon are finning or jumping. We've never seen one catch its own fish, though we did once see one carry off a wiggling one.

When the tide comes in, we move our nets back up the beach.

At 6:30 we begin to pick up nets, and at 7:00 P.M. on the dot we pull the last piece of web from the water and head in to dump the whole pile on the beach. We deliver again to the scow, tossing our afternoon fish into our totes while George and his crew do the same into theirs. The tender will be by later, sometime during the night; we have only to leave our permit card and some outgoing mail in the "mailbox" tacked to one end of the scow.

While Ken fills our gas tanks from a barrel we keep on the scow, I pour water over the fish and fit the covers back on the totes. I summon a last spurt of energy to wash down the boat, coil lines, rinse the burlap and stretch it to dry. My legs are bruised and my shoulder creaks. The muscles in my hands are tight, and my little finger got squashed between an anchor and the skiff's rail. My chest aches from being pressed into the bow every time I lifted a corkline. I hurt with the hurt of a full day's work, hard work done well.

Before we leave the scow, I take a look into George's totes.

We highboated him again, just barely. We have two hundred sixty-two fish for the day.

Back at the cabin, I strip off my fishing clothes and wash my face and arms. I scrub aluminum stain from my forearms until they're pink, and then I pick off fish scales with a fingernail. Each scale pops off like a brittle flake, leaving a circle on my skin like a slightly gathered pockmark. There's something satisfying in this picking of scales, even in finding a last, crisp scale days later on the back of my arm. Better than gold stars, they're the medals that remind us how we live with fish.

"We work hard for our fish," I say to Ken. "We work harder for two hundred than we do for a thousand." It's been a long time since we caught anything near a thousand fish in one day, but it's true that when there are more fish to pick, we pick more and work our gear less. It's trying to maximize possibility that's so hard.

Ken yanks off his hip boots and drops them with heavy clunks in the center of the floor. He has mud on his cheeks and fish slime glistening in his beard, and his hair is so matted his scalp shows through. The back of his neck has darkened one more shade. He smiles a tired smile and says, "You can expect to find a little extra in your paycheck this week."

The leftover pizza warming in the oven has begun to fill the cabin with its burnt-cheese and tomato smell. Ken asks, "How many sets do you think we made?"

The individual pieces of the day are becoming a blur to me, but I know Ken recalls every set, every circumstance of every set, every pick of every set. He has a memory that can recall the play of a bridge hand six months earlier, and he carries a map in his head for every city he's ever visited and every road he's driven, just as he knows every contour of our beach and its every rock.

"How many?"

Ken lists our sets in order, holding up a finger for each. "Cove, Point, Emmet's, South Point, Eddyset with a short net, Eddyset with a full net, 12K, short net at Point, Eddyset deep, Lou's, Emmet's deep, Point deep, short net at Slide, full net at Slide, Rock, Campset, Emmet's, Cove."

Eighteen. The recitation is like poetry to me, but it's poetry I want only to wash over me at the bottom of deepest, absolutely motionless sleep. Eat, then sleep. The next fishing day is four days away.

FROM *Striper*

John Cole

$\mathcal{A}$ breeze from the northwest feathers my cheeks as I walk from the Model A to Ted's back door. He is up. I can tell because the bare-bulb light over the door shines blindingly in the predawn darkness, casts long shadows over the dooryard where Ted's big silver truck is parked, complete with a seine-heavy dory on the attached trailer.

I wait there in the light, at the bottom of the cement steps with their steel-pipe railing. No one has told me, but I would bet that Ted built the forms, poured the cement and made the railing—probably traded a fish or two for the pipe. I wait for Jim to clamber out of the "A." He takes his own sweet time, checking to make certain he has his gloves, his oil coat, his wool-knit pullover cap, and his brown banana for breakfast.

He walks out of the dark in his waders, a black shape waddling into the circle of light, moving quietly across the decades of crushed clam and scallop shells that make a parking lot of Ted's front yard. He stops and looks at the stars, hard and bright in the cloudless sky. He points up at them. "Nice morning, Cap. They don't come better in October."

As far as I'm concerned, they don't come any better any time of the year. It is all I can do to sleep through the short nights that we have left when we leave Ted's at six or seven in the evening. We have to be back at four every morning, and sometimes, when we get fish on the "sunset" haul of the day before, we don't get home until nine or ten. Five hours sleep seems to be enough for me; it has been ever since we joined Ted's crew.

We saw him and Ding and Smiley and the rest of the spring crew quite often after that morning he pulled me from under the *Peril.* The summer came and Jim and Peter and I quit seining. Peter and I spent the summer digging clams, and in the early fall we went scalloping, waiting for the bass to begin their migration. Jim was still on his summer job as a mate on one of the charter boats at the Montauk Yacht Club. Between us, we'd agreed to begin bassing about the first of October.

But before that, we got a phone call from Ted.

"Want to give the bass a try?" That was the first thing he said. I wasn't sure I understood.

"Well I'll tell you, Johnny, Ding and Lindy got their own rig this season. They're leaving me with Smiley, that's all. I thought you and Jim and Peter could come with me. Bring that Model A, we'll get a winch with a Briggs and Stratton for her. She'll do OK if she don't have to pull a dory. You'll get a quarter-share for the car, plus a share for each of you. I always treat my crews fair. You ask anybody about that."

It wouldn't have made any difference to me if I'd been told I wouldn't get any sort of a share. The idea of fishing with Ted, one of the best of the Poseys—who were the best of the fishermen—was enough to set me to yelping with glee. That huge truck, that long seine, those powerful winches, the equipment and skills that had been acquired over four generations of fishermen—I was going to get in on all this after just a year on the East End. I could hardly believe my luck.

Like me, Peter was all smiles. He was most of the time anyway, but the notion of fishing with Ted gave him a prospect he rolled over in his fancies during the entire last week we were clamming. He'd stand there in the bow of the *Emma,* yanking at the handle of his bull rake, grunting with each pull, fashioning a running monologue on the days we were soon to see.

"Jawn, when we get started with—grunt—Ted, we're just as likely to get—grunt—a hundred-box haul as we are to get ten—grunt. Good Gawd, Johnny, what are we going to do—grunt—with all that money?

"I'll tell you, John, what I'm going to do. I'm going to—grunt—get me a set of waders that don't leak, and—grunt—I'm going to throw this bull rake so far out in the bay no one will ever be able to find it. Not even me—grunt—if I'm ever stupid enough to think I want to go clamming again."

But Jim wasn't so sure joining up with Ted would be a good thing. "Why do you think he called us, John? Did you ever puzzle over that? Here we are, three guys who've only been on the beach for one season. We might as well be men off the street as far as our experience is concerned. But Ted calls us.

"Well, he does know us, knows who we are. Maybe he thinks you're rich, Johnny, coming from that big house on the dunes. Maybe he wants you to finance a new rig. Ha, wouldn't that be a laugh!"

Jim grabbed me by the arm. "That's what did it, Cap. Not your money, your muscles." He squeezed my biceps—a meager lump at best. "Wiry, that's what you are, Cap," he laughed. "Like a steel cable, them arms are." He broke up at his joke.

"No, Ted needs us, that's why he called. He needs the Model A. He needs some young studs who are crazy enough about fishing to get up at three or four every morning, work in the cold and wet all day, row that great ark of a dory of his against the chop, get covered with sand and fish gunk, not eat any lunch, and haul seine all day, some days for nothing more than a couple of sand dabs and sea robins. Probably average out we'll make something like fifty cents an hour for working twelve-hour days, seven days a week. Now what do we get out of that, Cap? What do we get out of that?"

I'd been thinking a good deal about what I was getting out of fishing, but my thoughts would not have given Jim the answer he was looking for. He was half joking; he wanted some reply like, "A busted back and a flat billfold," but I had been thinking about what I had learned, about the people I had met, about how good I felt when I got a word of praise from Jim on my rowing, or when I looked at three full bushels of clams after a day's digging and realized that I had done that work quite on my own, out on a bay one hundred miles from New York City—a bay that tens of thousands of people looked at every month without ever seeing more than the reflection of the sky on its surface, if they even saw that. I knew what I was getting out of fishing, even though I didn't understand some of the reasons for my total involvement with an occupation that had been alien to me for all but one year of my life.

I was getting a kind of companionship, a fellowship, a friendship I had never known before except with my two brothers. I was getting outdoor physical activity that was putting muscles on my thin frame, in spite of Jim's joshing. I was working long hours, but they were hours totally free, free of the hierarchical, rank-happy system I had found in the Army Air Force, and free of the subservience that had been an inevitable part of the public relations job in the city. And most of all I was getting a rush of enthusiasm such as I had never known, or even visualized. Nothing in my total experience had prepared me for the excitement I found in fishing day after day with no letup in my thumping adrenaline level, no matter how much one day was like another, how small the catch, or how seemingly pointless the hours of waiting on the beach for a school of striped bass to show on the surface.

That's what I was getting out of it, but I said to Jim, "I don't know, Cap. I guess we'll get a busted back and a flat billfold. But we'll do the same on our own, so why not try it with Ted? At least he's got winches. We won't lose any more hauls because we can't hold the net when a set is running."

"OK Cap," Jim said, "I'll give it a try, for this one season." I was surprised at this limitation, but I knew Jim meant what he said. I began to understand just how much he wanted to become his own fisherman, to become better than the Poseys. For him, fishing had no mysteries. As Jim saw it, if he worked hard enough, long enough and smart enough, he could decipher the sea.

As we stand under the light, waiting for Ted to come to the door, Jim looks at his brown banana. "Finest kind," he says, "finest kind."

When we're inside, Ted pours us each a cup of instant coffee, tosses a piece of toast to each place at the oilcloth-covered kitchen table. We're free to spread the toast with peanut butter from the jar in the table's center. This is Ted's home kitchen, and he has given us breakfast each morning for the week we have been fishing with him. It's the same breakfast every time, and it's nothing special; but there aren't many other skippers who would do as much.

Ted looks at me as I munch my toast. "You have beefsteak last night for supper, did you Johnny? I can tell you did. The blood is in your cheeks. Nothing like beefsteak to make you horny, is there? Come on now, Johnny, tell me. Did you have some?"

Now there is blood in my cheeks. "Yes Ted, I did. But I don't believe it makes me look any different."

"Course it does. Course it does." He looks at the door. "There's Peter, coming now. I wonder what happened to that damn Smiley. Good weather like this, we want to be out early. Get that first set in before sunup, before those bass even know we're on the beach."

Peter comes through the door, large and loud. "We're going to get them today. Oh yes, we are. I can feel it, Cap. I just know it. Aren't I right, Ted?"

"They can be there any day. They are there, every day. We just have to find them, is all. Can get a hundred boxes just as easy as one, As long as we set that twine around fish, we can catch five tons . . . or ten tons, if we want." Ted gets up from his chair, pulling up the suspenders on his waders. "But we can't catch bass here in the kitchen. That twine's got to be in the water. Now if Smiley was here, we could leave. Isn't it something. He lives closest, but you fellows are all here before him."

We move outdoors, in single file through the door—four bulky, black figures in our chest-high, big-footed waders—and walk over to the narrow tar road that runs through Poseyville. It's called Poseyville because, on this stretch of cross highway about two city blocks long, the entire Posey clan has its homes, its fishing shacks, its boats, its gear, its families, its vegetable gardens and the leavings of a century of fishing the waters of the East End.

Set between East Hampton and Amagansett, two of the Island's wealthiest villages, Poseyville looks like a landscape that drifted in from the sea, or was left in the wake of a tidal wave that washed over the land. It looks as if it should have been cleaned up after the storm, but somehow the apparent mess has stayed, has escaped every civic broom. There are homes worth literally a million dollars less than half a mile from here, belonging to the heirs to some of the nation's largest fortunes. There have been repeated efforts over the years by some of the homeowners to "do something" about Poseyville: to zone it out of existence, or buy it out— but the Poseys have maintained a state of such continued and puzzled refusal to every offer, that even the most persistent reformer has given up.

"What would a fellow want an old place like this for? . . . Where would we go? . . . It would be too much trouble to move that old boat. I don't know if she could take it without parting her seams. . . . I got this place all paid for. Why get into debt for a new place I might not like? . . . Been working years on that strawberry patch. Ain't going to leave it now. . . . My brother Bill lives right across the road, and Frank right behind him. If we moved, they might not be as close. . . ."

So Poseyville persists—a collection of small houses, some of them unpainted, scattered over the fifteen or twenty acres as if they'd tumbled from a tipped bushel basket. For every home there is an outbuilding cluster: one for nets, one for baiting codfish trawls, one for tools, one for general "stuff" collected off the beach, after line storms, or from the town dumps. And every yard is cleared of grass. The bare earth, often dusted with beach sand, makes it easier to repair nets; twigs and stalks of grass do not get tangled in the twine. In every yard sits a collection of trucks, cars, nets, scallop dredges, dories, power boats, skiffs, clam rakes, harpoons, lobster traps, pumps, trap stakes, fish boxes, bushel baskets, kids' tricycles, dog houses, anchors, flag buoys, oars, eel pots, buckets, rope, and the remains of the sea: flattened horseshoe crabs, clam, oyster and scallop shells, jawbones of sharks, marlin and swordfish bills, crab claws, squashed sea robins and blowfish, giant tuna tails, and a sheen of fish scales everywhere, lending their pearly luster to a landscape that looks as if it had been raised from the ocean bottom just days before to dry out in the sun.

Poseyville persists. It does so without defiance, without debate, with scarcely an acknowledgment from those who live there that their place is a kind of innocent aberration, a square of reality surrounded by the well-tended make-believe circles of the super-rich. If the Poseys are conscious of their well-heeled neighbors—and they must be—they never let on. Instead, they go about their fishing as they always have. They never talk about the architectural palaces that rise from the dunes, except as ranges which help them mark the best fishing places. "Just to the east of the windmill on the Ford place, there's a good set when the wind's easterly. . . . Watch out when you're setting in front of the Simon place. Get too close to that big window and you're likely to get hung up on the wreckage of that coal schooner."

Nonplussed by being so unnoticed, would-be reformers realized they didn't have a chance. And now that the Poseys are totally surrounded, the high rollers and big timers take a certain pride and reassurance from the settlement in their midst. There may be Rembrandts on East Hampton walls and Meissen porcelain on Amagansett dinner tables, but the Poseys, launching their dories in the sea, driving by with a truckful of fish, walking past Main Street boutiques in their oilskins and waders, now that's real. "I tell you, Henry, it's great to see them doing things the old way, isn't it. Reminds you of what it took to get this country started."

Ever since I have joined Ted's crew, I have been treated with the same detachment. I get kidded, but it is meaningless joshing, as repetitive as the lines about beefsteak putting color in my cheeks. "Why are you fishing, Johnny, a millionaire like you?" "Aw, he's just down here for a hobby, ain't you, Jawn. If he wanted, he could buy your rig, Ted, couldn't you Johnny. You must have a bundle put away somewhere. . . ." Lines like that, every day, one after the other, automatic, without intent or envy—meaningless, innocent, an acknowledgment of the difference of my background, nothing more. It is a statement from the Poseys that they know about the gray house on the dunes, the white chimneys and the rest. They know, but they don't care; they really don't. They watch me row, watch me pull on the oars, haul seine, tie knots, mend nets, wash fish, shovel ice, lift boxes—that's what they watch, that's what they care about—and it is all they care about. They are purely fishermen.

After fifty years of late October mornings like this, Ted is still impatient, champing, fuming about Smiley. We stand in the road, looking west to the small house where he lives alone. We can see a light in the window; then it goes out. Ted snorts.

"About time he left. He'll be promenading in here soon, looking for some breakfast. Well, he ain't going to get any. I'm going to warm up the big truck, get started. Johnny, you and Jim take Smiley with you when he gets here. He can squeeze in. I'll take the rig to Hither Hills. The boats did good at the Point yesterday. Maybe those bass have worked around. You know how to get there, don't you, Johnny?"

"Yep. Go ahead, Cap. We'll wait for Smiley."

Sitting with Jim in the "A," close and quiet there in the dark after Ted's truck has left the yard, charging off in its own envelope of ear-shattering sound, I can see the darker shape of Smiley moving toward us along the road. With his long, black overcoat over his waders, he walks slowly, taking short steps; he looks like a dark column, teetering, but angled our way, so every teeter edges him a bit closer. There is something about Smiley I have never understood. He lives alone, unmarried, unlike any of his Posey kin. He talks about drinking as if he does it all the time, but I have learned he doesn't put away half as much as he claims. I think Ted keeps Smiley on the crew partly out of family pride; Ted must assume that if Smiley had to shift entirely for himself, he couldn't get a job.

I don't know about that. I think Smiley likes crewing for Ted. Because he is the skipper's brother, Smiley gets away with a good deal of loafing, yet he gets his full share when the checks arrive from Fulton Market. So Smiley overdoes his own incompetence, babbling more than he has to, voicing more inexplicable sentences than he otherwise might. It's a game with him—a promotion of his own weaknesses, exaggerated for effect. Smiley knows Jim and I have him figured; the recognition is there in Smiley's twinkling eyes whenever he's playacting with us. He is well named; every time I see him in that getup, I can't help smiling. He must be the only fisherman on the entire East Coast who wears a long, black chesterfield coat to work every day. This morning, I laugh aloud as he approaches the car, his cursing and rumbling as staccato as the roll of a snare drum.

"Jesus Christ, that goddammed Ted. You'd think, by Jesus, he'd learn something, wouldn't you, after forty christly years in this business. What's he in such a hurry for, tear-assing out of the yard an hour before sunup, leaving me standing there in the middle of the road. Think he's going to catch every fish in the ocean, don't he. Well, he ain't. Now I suppose I got to go haul seine without so much as a cup of coffee for my belly. Ain't that a kick in the head."

Jim picks up a thermos. "You can have some of this on the way down, Smiley. Come on, squeeze in here with me and John."

"Yes, yes. I'm riding in style this morning. We'll get there, we'll get there. Don't hurry none. We got another half-hour before we can haul, another half-hour easy, ain't that right, Johnny?" Smiley gets in, sitting there, stiffly upright between me and Jim. It's a change for him; he usually rides in the back of Ted's truck where he often stands, just behind the cab, like the leader of the expedition surveying the route ahead. I don't know how old the man is, but looking at his face as we drive along under the street lights on the Montauk Highway I can see that he is older than I had thought. The lines are deep; the multiple folds of his eyelids blink over blue eyes bleached and battered by the years. He is an old man who has risen early on a cold, autumn morning. He is a plucky old man, denied the respect his age entitles him to, and riding along with a couple of young men who have been fishing one year to his sixty. But he doesn't complain about us, or the car, not for a moment. I ask him if he thinks we'll get any fish so far to the east.

"Can't tell, Johnny, can't never tell. Them bass don't tell us where they're going. They could be anywhere, sliding over the rocks down at the Point, easing around along the beach. Ted always likes to fish to the east in October. Fish gather up at the Point, don't you know. Ted wants to be first when they come around. Ted always wants to be first."

Smiley is right. Ted is waiting for us when we pull onto the beach at Hither Hills, just to the east of the state park's public campgrounds. The silver truck is backed down; the hulking dory is poised at the sea's edge, bow pointed toward the horizon where there is just the faintest shard of light showing in the southeast. Smiley nudges me.

"Told you didn't I? Didn't I? Still too dark to set, and there's that Ted, backed right down. Jesus, that man never knows when to rest."

"Johnny, you get along over here," Ted calls. "Let's get the dory off the trailer. It's slick calm here, no sea at all. We won't need much light to set."

We get the dory off, and Peter and I stand there, ready to row, waiting for Ted to give the word. I can see the morning star shining when Ted says, "Get in, John." We make the set and are ashore before the dawn grows bright enough to hide the star. There is maybe a box of fish in the bunt.

Smiley is still talking as we reload the seine into the trailered dory. He's coiling the cork line, I load the leads as Ted eases the truck along the beach where the seine is being hanked and cleared of crabs and seaweed by Jim and Peter.

"See, Johnny, I told you there wasn't no call for that christly rush. Shit, there ain't enough fish there to pay for gas. Been anybody else but Ted, I could have had my breakfast, ain't that right Johnny? Ain't that right?"

I tell him he's right, and Smiley keeps on talking. "Now we're done here, he's going to get out of the truck and say, 'Where do we go next, boys?' cause we are as far east now as we can get. You wait, that's what he's going to say."

When the net is loaded and Jim has pulled the "A" up behind the truck, Ted climbs out of the cab.

"Well boys," he says, taking off his long-billed cap and scratching his silver hair, "where do you want to try next?" I look at Smiley, and he's got that big grin going, the one that's full of broken and missing teeth, and he's rolling his eyes so the whites show. He is funny; that's all there is to it.

"Let's go anywhere, Cap, as long as the fish are there," Peter answers, laughing. "Let's go east."

"No sets left to the east, too many rocks," Ted says.

I had thought Smiley was just talking. I can't believe there are those miles of shoreline and no place to make one set. "You mean there is all this beach and not a single place where we can haul?"

Ted points toward the cliffs of Montauk. "Even if there was a spot, we couldn't get to it. Can't get a rig down those banks. There's just one beach. That's at Ditch Plain. There's rocks there, but sometimes they get sanded under. I have hauled Ditch Plain and had no trouble. Go back the next day, you get hung up."

The sun is up now; the breeze from the nor'west is picking up. The excitement of autumn is in the air. I look at the flat ocean and feel my heart pound at the prospect of fishing in a place untouched by any other crews. "Ted, come on, let's give it a try."

Ted is surprised at the urgency in my voice. "I don't know, Johnny. The charter boats fish off Ditch Plain, and them surfcasters are always on the beach. They don't like to see us haul seiners down there. Gives them fits if we catch fish and they don't."

"Let's try it, Ted. Just once." It is a mark of my total involvement with fishing that I am trying to persuade a man who has fished most of his life to try a haul in a place I have never seen. Peter and Jim are watching the exchange with big eyes. They are wondering how Ted is going to take the pressure from a green hand on his crew.

"OK. Let's go, then," says Ted. "Let's go find out if Johnny can smell them fish."

Smiley is restored to his spot in the big silver truck, and he waves to me and Jim as we follow behind in the "A," on our way east. As I sit there, warming in the climbing sun that is now shining full through the windshield, I decide Ted is playing a hunch as much as anything. Like all fishermen, he has superstitions, believes in omens. He is trying me on this one to see if I'm lucky.

When we pull onto the beach at Ditch Plain, I can see why few haul seiners would want to set here. The place is unlike what I know as "beach." This is no long, straight stretch of sand running as far as I can see, like the beach in front of the house with the white chimneys. This is a small crescent of sand, bracketed at both ends by rocky points. Offshore of the points, boulders rise like the backs of whales, appearing and reappearing as the swells glide past. In front of us, the beach does not drop off steeply as it does to the west; here the ground is shoal far offshore. If seas of more than three feet were running, they would break a half mile out. This morning, there are scarcely any seas. The water is clear, and I can see shadows of seaweed and rocks: dark, wavering shapes that threaten us with their mystery.

Ted is looking steadily out to sea, checking the wave patterns, trying to see through the clear water to learn if the rocks are sanded or not. We wait for his decision.

"What the hell. Let's give it a try. No weather here today. Even if we do get hung up, it'll be easy enough to pick her up and ease her over the rocks."

Two surfcasters, holding their long, whippy rods like two soldiers with spears, stand on the rocks to the east and watch us as we make the set. The arc of the seine takes in the entire stretch of sand; we leave just inside the western rocks and land next to the bouldered point to the east. Ted guides us every stroke of the way. We row ashore fast when the jack goes over. Peter jumps out, grabbing the gunwale of the dory, pulling her up on the beach with exaggerated vigor. Like me, he is brimming over with the day's energy.

As I walk to the west to begin my hauling with Jim and Smiley, I marvel at the water's clarity. The gentle, small waves are translucent, catching the sun as they rise on the horizon. I look through them, into the sea's liquid green center. A bit of silver lashes in the curve of a breaking swell, then another. I wonder if I am dazzled by the refracted sun, or if it is life I see. There, there is another, then another. This last is not merely a bit of silver; it is a striped bass. I can see the white belly, the golden shoulders, even the stripes along the bronze sides—the sun is so bright, the water so clear.

I have never seen fish in a net like this before. I begin to understand that the fish rocketing along the walls of the waves are dashing from one seine wing to the other, looking for an escape. If there are so many fish in the net that they have begun to feel crowded before we start hauling, then there must be more fish here than I have ever thought possible.

"Hey! Hey! Hey! Jim. . . . We got fish in here." The yelling bursts from me, like shots from a cannon. For a moment, the tumult in me is uncontrollable. I turn back to yell toward Ted and Peter. I turn to the sea, transfixed again as yet another bass cruises high in the curve of a wave. This one lunges to the very top of the crest; its tail breaks the surface, leaving a gout of white water.

"There. There. Look, did you see that!" I run toward Jim and Smiley. Jim, standing in front of the "A," is handling the rope off the winch, beginning to pull steadily on it, hauling the first of the net from the waves, watching Ted's end so both wings will come ashore evenly. Jim has his lips set in the particular way he holds them when he tries not to smile—a set I see often. He nods his head toward the jack, just now pulling through the waves, vibrant with the tension the winches have begun to exert on the seine. There, in the first two feet of the net, a bass is gilled.

"You better get down there, Cap, and give Smiley a hand," Jim says quietly. "We may have a few fish here."

I hear Peter yell from the other end. A whoop, a trumpeting. I look and see him jump, like a huge dancer in waders. He is pointing to a bass gilled, like ours, just beyond the east-end jack.

Oh Christ, I say to myself. This could be it. Don't let the net get hung. Don't let anything go wrong. I stand there, useless for minutes, rooted to the beach as I immerse myself in the moment's frantic beauty. The bass have communicated their general panic. There are no longer mere flashes of silver, watery hints of fish. Now there are constant surgings as the bass search for escape in the white water of the wash.

A wave breaks, shapes glide through its arc. The wash rolls and tumbles to the beach, and from its white, foaming canopy rise the sleek shoulders of stripers. Dorsals cut the foam like knives, spilling a wake that rises inches over the surface and sustains a vertical fragility that catches the sun, so there are bright lines of light, darting here, there, and there. Each one, I know, is a fish, each one a creature of infinite vitality. I am overwhelmed at the glory of the drama. I cannot move, but merely stand and watch, afraid that the thumping of my heart will force me to my knees.

"Hey, Cap. Let's go." There is an edge to Jim's voice. I run toward Smiley, who has not yet tied the next winching knot around the seine. He is, instead, trying to tug one of several gilled bass from the meshes.

"Got a bunch. We got a bunch, Johnny. Must be mostly small fish. Wouldn't have so many gilled, otherwise. Small fish get us the best price, ain't that right, Johnny?"

I don't know what to say to Smiley. He is working as he always does, with no special effort. Is it possible that he can remain apart from this realization, this actualization of an event so many fishermen talk of, but so few ever witness? Or has this happened for Smiley so often that he is unmoved? I look through the waves once again. Those shapes in their curvings draw me like a magnet. I could look at swimming fish forever. But now the clarity is gone. The arc of the net is inscribed there in the sea's transparent aqua-marine—a dingy half-circle, slurred and soiled, muddied. I do not understand.

"What the hell? Are we mudded? Is the net hung up?" I yell at Smiley, even though I stand next to him.

"Sand rile. That's a sand rile. Must be some fish in there to make a rile like that." Smiley pulls yet another gilled bass from the twine.

A sand rile—I don't know the term, but I understand it. Incredible. The fins, the tails, the turnings, the twistings, the massed surgings of thousands of striped bass have set the very sea bottom in motion. As they do in the tumult of a violent storm, the sea sand and the water mix, kept in murky suspension by the constant, gathered force of the creatures imprisoned in the shrinking curtain of twine, pulled, inch by inch as the winches turn, toward the water-less beach.

Peter whoops again, louder now because, as the net arc tightens, the two wings come closer together.

"By hand, by hand," he yells. "Ted says by hand!"

I can't believe the instruction. "Jesus, Smiley, haul by hand? We can't move all those fish."

"Ted doesn't want to lose the set. Them damn winches. Get a bunch of fish like this, get hung up before you know it. Them winches pull the twine right apart." Smiley begins tugging on the cork line. "Come on, Johnny, we can do it. Never used to do it any other way. We ain't always had them winches, you know. Sit down there on that beach and pull on that lead line.

"Oh, feel them fish, boy. Feel them fish."

I sit on the hard, damp sand, my feet toward the sea, my shoulders bent forward over my knees and my gloved hands clasped around the lead line. I pull, my back is in it. The line strums, vibrates like a steel rail a mile away from a thundering locomotive. The compressed fish are trembling against the twine; the message of their growing terror is here, strumming the line in my hands.

"Keep it down, Cap, keep it down." Jim is behind me, helping. Peter is on the other lead line, across from us, grunting, whooping, heaving, roaring. The fish are everywhere in the wash now. It is impossible to tell sea from creature. The two are blended in the turbulence of breaking waves and running bass. The frothing is endless, perpetual. The wash hisses like water boiling on a stove. Spray flies as if the wind were blowing a gale.

Ted's cry rasps dry over the wet sounds. "Pull, boys, pull. We got a bunch here, we got a bunch. Don't let's lose them now."

He is holding the cork line higher and higher on his side, moving further and further out into the waves, trying to keep the bass from weighing down the twine, spilling over the top like living grain from the side of a sack.

"Get down there, Smiley," Ted yells. "Get down like me. God dammit, Smiley, they're going to go over your corks. Get over there, Jim, give him a hand.

"Jesus Christ, there they go." Ted is screaming now. He is up to his chest in the waves, fish all around him. He is trying to keep the corks up, by himself, deep in the surf, almost lost in the confusion of the thumping fish, the surging swells and the now tortured twine, stretched beyond its limits by the sheer numbers of the stripers.

The bunt rolls in the wash, swelled grossly by tons of twitching bass. It is full. There is no place for the fish in the quarters to go. Ted sounds to me as if he is crying.

"They're getting out. Shit, they're going over the corks. Come on Jim, for Christ's sake, keep the corks up, keep the corks up." Ted's voice is now a hoarse scream, shrill, strange, desperate, almost unintelligible. His face is crimson under the long-billed cap. He is at the brink of dementia, so far out in the surf that the waves wet his shoulders as they rise, rippling the sodden, bulging bunt.

Smiley shakes his head, in a kind of regret as he watches his brother. Peter whoops and pulls. I keep my hands locked tight on the lead line, strumming still. Jim is in the ocean with Ted, trying to hold up the corks. The net will not move.

We can do nothing. We are at a stalemate with the fish and the sea. Small rivulets of bass escape here and there, over the corks, under the leads. Ted weeps and screams. I fear he'll have a stroke, but we are all paralyzed with the functions of our duties. None of us can let go of what he holds, otherwise all may be lost.

We hold what we have, there in the high sun of the bright October forenoon. The sea swells and surges, hisses and swirls. The bass in the quarters struggle and run; they leave, like dew from the morning grass. Now it is there, then it is gone, with no moment of departure.

As we scream, yell, whoop and curse on the Ditch Plain beach, we realize, after a while, that the bass are gone from the quarters. We have the bunt to contend with now. It is, at last, a dimension we can comprehend.

Ted comes out of the sea. He is soaked. To me it appears that he is in pain. He walks to the silver truck, starts it, turns its front end to face the sea, and, roaring in low gear, edges the front bumper directly toward the bunt.

Jim and Peter unwrap the heavy line around the truck's bumper, make it fast to the net as close as they can to the swollen bag. Ted puts the truck in reverse, the monster machine roars, jerks, bounces, and edges back slowly, slowly. The bunt, packed too tightly for the fish to wriggle or twitch, eases from the wash, moving inch by inch to harder, drier sand. Ted hauls it about twelve feet this way, then the truck begins to dig its own stopping place as the huge tires spin. Ted shuts down the engine, gets out of the cab. He does not let go of the truck, though. He hangs to the door opening on the driver's side, exhausted. I trot to him.

"Johnny, tell Jim to take the 'A' back home. See if Ding is off the beach. If he is, tell him to bring his truck and crew here to help us. We'll never get these fish off before dark by ourselves."

"All right, Ted. Are you OK?"

"It's one of my spells. It will go away, or kill me. One or t'other."

I go to tell Jim. "OK," he says, "but you better watch Ted. My father died of a heart attack one hot day, conducting on the train. Fine one minute. Boom, gone the next."

The notion that Ted has been weakened, could be hurt, is a jolt to me. I am worried as I watch Jim pull off the beach to go get Ding's crew. I tell Ted to stay in the truck while Peter and Smiley and I open the cod end and start carrying the bass, one by one, to higher ground.

There seem to be hundreds, thousands, of fish. We keep carrying them, tossing them into a growing pile in the back of Ted's truck, but the bunt seems to get no smaller. Peter sings, yells, talks to the fish as he trots back and forth in his waders, sweat running down his tanned neck. A knot of surfcasters has gathered at the point. They watch, not moving, for a spell, then two of them walk to the bunt's open end while Peter and I are at the truck. As Smiley stands there, unbelieving, the casters reach in and each takes a fish. Ted waves his hand.

"Hey," he calls. "Hey, those fish are worth something, you know." If the casters can hear, they act as if they don't. They keep walking. "What the hell, Johnny, I'm too pooped to chase them. Ain't it something what some people will do." He slumps back, leaning against the cab.

We have the truck loaded by the time Ding arrives. The bass, stiff now, dry and sand covered, are piled like stovewood. There is no more space, and Ding looks at the mound in the truck and at the bunt, still impressively full, on the beach.

"Jesus, I guess you did get a bunch. Whoever had the notion to set Ditch Plain, anyway? What are you doing this far east, Ted?"

Ted waves his hand toward me. "Johnny was the one. He wouldn't rest till we come down here."

Ding looks at me and laughs. "Shit, we'll never hear the end of that, now will we."

It is three o'clock before we get off the Ditch Plain beach. We have been up, working, for almost twelve hours with no food, and we still have the fish to wash, weigh, box and tag. We have fish in the dory along with the net and Ding's trucks are full. Ted gives us half an hour for food, and Jim and I stop at a restaurant for cheeseburgers and milk.

At 10:30, we are done. The floor of Ted's fish house is an inch deep in sand and scales. In the cool room, where shaved ice is piled in drifts on the floor, there are ninety-two boxes of striped bass, tagged for shipment to brokers at Fulton Fish Market. That's more than nine thousand pounds, almost five tons of fish. They are money fish: five- to ten-pounders that bring the highest market price. We have handled more than a thousand fish, three and four times over. I figure twice that many escaped the twine. We must have had the net around more than three thousand fish—close to fifteen tons. We never could have handled them, even if we had landed them all. At thirty-five cents a pound for what we did catch, I figure each share could be as high as $500.

Five hundred dollars for one day. I cannot believe it, but, borne on some manic frenzy for more, I wonder as I leave if I'll be able to stir at four the next morning. I ask Ted what time he wants us.

He is sitting on the concrete steps, under the light, his gray head down on his arms. When he looks up at me, I can see the same sort of oldness in his eyes that I had seen in Smiley's.

"I, I may not be going, boys," he says to me and Jim and Peter. "I don't want another of them spells. One more, and I might have to stay off the beach for too long.

"If it's weather, you can take the rig. Jim can drive the truck. Take Smiley. The four of you can handle it. You ain't going to get another bunch like today. Ain't likely.

"Supposed to breeze up tomorrow, anyway. You might get one set in the morning. If you want, take the rig. You won't have to go far. Right down here to the radio towers will be as good as any. You'll never get Ditch Plain. Ding has already got his crew down there. He didn't get nothing to the west today. They'll spend the night on the beach to keep that Ditch Plain set."

"OK, Cap," says Jim. "We'll be by. We'll see what the weather is like."

I can see no stars the next morning; the breeze is not from the northwest, it is from the east, bringing with it the wetness and sounds of the sea. Ted's light is not on. Peter arrives as Jim and I sit there in the "A," then Smiley shows up. I marvel to myself at the way this man in his seventies can endure. Jim climbs into the big silver truck, starts it, and I follow in the "A."

The southeast chop has not had time to build, we discover when we reach the beach at Napeague, opposite the radio towers. Working on an ocean flattened by days of wind off the land, the stiffening breeze generates short seas that topple almost as soon as they are formed. In the gloomy dawn, the ocean is dotted with gobs of white, but there are no swells rolling ashore. It will be hard rowing, but we can set with no trouble.

None of us wants to. I have that feeling standing by the dory with Peter, waiting for Jim to leave the truck. We are exhausted from the day before, numb. But none of us will admit it; each of us dreads learning from the other crews that we missed a good fishing morning by not making a set. Besides, if the wind stays in the east, there's a chance there won't be fishing weather for several days. That's when we will get our rest; at least that's what we say to ourselves, there by the ocean on this lowering morning.

Jim and Smiley come down to the boat.

"Smiley can make the set," Jim says.

I am surprised. "Why not you, Cap?"

"Smiley doesn't know how to drive. We need someone in the truck."

"Don't worry, Johnny, don't worry. I know what I'm doing. I know. You think I been on this beach as long as I have and I can't set a net." Smiley hunches up his coat and gets ready to clamber over the gunwales as Peter and I get in and Jim pushes off. It's lucky no seas are running. We bend the oars trying to pull against the chop; the dory founders as if she has a sea anchor dragging. Peter grunts, strains, but finds enough cheer somewhere in him to yell, "It looks fishy to me, Cap, it looks fishy to me. We'll get around another ninety boxes."

Smiley is slow setting. He takes small handfuls of the lead line; doesn't, or can't, throw them far enough. Peter and I are rowing the net overboard—pulling hard enough so the forward motion of the dory pulls the net into the water. With the net still wet and sandy from the day before, the rowing is slow, hard, labored. I can feel myself tiring fast, and I wish, more than anything, for the set to end.

We reach the bunt. We are halfway there. Peter and I stop rowing, leaning on our oars, waiting for Smiley to heave the bag and the buoy. It is his only function, really. Neither Peter nor I is fully certain of the way the bunt and the buoy must be arranged to fish properly.

Neither, it turns out, is Smiley. We are losing ground on the set as the onshore wind pushes at the dory and the chop slaps on her beam, jostling her back toward the beach. The seine arc is flattening.

164

"Smiley, come on," says Peter, leaning toward the stern from his oars amidships, but not wanting to stand in the boat that is pitching and rolling now that we have no headway.

Smiley stands there, studying the twine, his gloved fingers fluttering over the bunt as if he could read a braille code there that would instruct him. He picks up the buoy, starts to flip the rope one way, then another. I know now that he has forgotten, or never knew, the proper way.

He cannot fool himself or us any longer.

He picks up the bunt. The heavy twine drapes down the front of his black overcoat. He grunts with effort.

"Shit. I'll throw the goddamn thing. It's gotta be OK. Ain't that right, Johnny?"

Smiley swings his armful of twine back, then heaves the heavy netting toward the horizon. As he does, the dory pitches, wallows, then rolls.

Smiley and the bunt go over the gunwale together. For a second or so, the air under his overcoat keeps him up. I am looking into his pale face, white there in the dark sea. His thin hair is spread in the water, the way it was the first day I saw him in the back of Ted's truck.

He doesn't cry out. There is no time. The bunt, with its extra lead weights and rings in the cod end, sinks fast. Smiley goes under with it. Nothing marks his going. The chop beats at the side of the boat as Peter and I sit there, paralyzed with our comprehension of what is happening.

Peter moves first. He stands, lunges for the net, starts hauling the bunt back in the dory. He heaps it, dripping, in the bottom, hauls further back, first to the quarters, then to the wing. Smiley does not surface with the netting. The dory is sloppy now with the sea water the net has shed. We roll in the chop. I can see Jim standing, still, on the beach.

"Should we go over?" I ask Peter. "I can strip and swim."

"No, too deep here. Besides. the net is down there. You can get tangled in that."

"Peter, Peter, what can we do?" I am trembling, shaking, shivering. I want to vomit.

We sit there, stupidly, in the rolling dory. It's as if we are waiting for the miracle, for Smiley to surface, shed of his coat and waders, to swim toward us like a summer swimmer, and clamber over the side of the boat, the way I used to climb over the sides of the *Emma*, playing with my brother Chick.

The gray sea hisses in the wind.

"We can't do a thing," Peter says, thumping down in his seat. "We can't haul the net back. We'll sink the dory. We've got to go ahead, finish the set, get this twine out of the boat. How else are we going to get ashore? We may not make it now, with the wind breezing up all the time.

"Come on, John. We better row."

We bend to the oars. The seine slides over the gunwale, cork by cork, lead by lead. When we turn the corner and the wind is on our stern, Peter stands and heaves great handfuls of lead line overboard. With the chop pushing the boat toward shore, I can row alone now.

We don't stop when we approach the beach. I row, Peter hangs on to the line and we surf ashore sloppily on the shoulders of one of the small seas. Jim is there waiting. He grabs the dory bow, runs a line through the bow ring. He runs to the truck, backs it, and jerks the dory to high ground. He has said nothing since we came ashore.

Peter walks with me to the far wing. We are helped by the southeast wind and, somehow, we get the seine ashore; Jim works his end single-handed, running from the winch to tie on his own hauling line. There are maybe three boxes of bass in the bunt. Smiley did have it set up right.

We haul the bunt up on the beach and stand around it, looking at the fish. Jim breaks his silence. He looks at me and Peter with his hard, blue eyes and asks, "Who will tell Ted?"

What the hell happened to yesterday? That's what I want to know as I look up and down the long, empty, windy beach. What the hell happened to the excitement, the good times? How did it get like this—the three of us, here with this wet, sand-heavy seine to pick up, with this lumbering dory to load, alone here on this raw morning without any sun? How could we have worked so hard, come all this way to be in the boat when Smiley goes overboard, when Ted's brother drowns, with us in the boat? What in the christly hell are we doing here? We don't belong here. And Smiley is gone—the old guy that I liked so, the fool who was never a fool. And now we have to decide who will tell Ted. God.

The wind picks up as we load the net. There will be no fishing this afternoon, nor tomorrow. That thought eases our depression a bit as we finish our work on the beach and begin the mournful procession back to Ted's—Jim driving the truck with Peter beside him; me alone in the "A," still seeing Smiley's presence in the empty seat next to me, still in a kind of shock as the realization of the loss works deeper into me.

Ted is sitting on the steps, waiting as we roll into the yard, the clamshells and scallop shells crunching under the tires. He walks over and peers into the back of the truck when Jim stops and shuts off the roaring engine. Ted glances at the sand-covered pile of bass, makes his eyeball appraisal.

"About three boxes. Well, could have been worse. Breeze up too much for another set, did it?"

Jim is the one who answers. He waits a long moment before he does. "Yes, Cap. Blowing hard now, from the southeast. That's the end of fishing today, tomorrow too, the way it looks.

"But we would have come back anyway, Ted." Jim walks closer; his face is inches from Ted's. "We had an accident, Ted. Smiley, well, Smiley went overboard, trying to heave the bunt. He stumbled. A sea hit the boat. He just went, Ted. We couldn't do a thing."

Ted stands there, nodding. "It happens, boys. It happens. My nephew, Arthur, drowned last spring putting in trap stakes. Fell from his sharpie. Drowned in a few feet of water. Couldn't swim a stroke. Neither could Smiley, neither can I."

He turns to walk to the house, then stops, turns back. "You didn't find him, did you?"

Jim shakes his head.

Ted climbs the steps, turns back to us again. "Wash and pack them fish. I got to call my brothers. We'll have to have a service of some sort." He steps inside, shuts the door, leaving us standing there in the yard, listening as the southeast wind rumbles with the sound of the surf, breaking harder now against the beach a mile from where we are. In the sound, I see Smiley going over the gunwale. He's out there now, somewhere, I tell myself as we walk toward the fish house to finish the day's work.

There is no fishing the next day, or the next. The wind backs into the northeast and stays there—mean, cold, and wet—too rough even for the scallopers.

Because of the weather, nearly every Posey in town is at Smiley's service. They crowd in the pews at the church, dressed mostly in dark suits that I have never seen before, and wearing heavy, black shoes. The ruddy faces look even ruddier indoors, and the hands holding the prayer books seem huge, swollen so by the sea that the stiff, broad fingers have a difficult time turning the thin pages. The service is short, somber. The men file out, not talking. Ted comes over to me.

"I'll call you when it's weather," he says. That's all.

It is November before we can fish again. The northeast wind held for two more days after Smiley's service, then blew southeast for a day before finally turning northwest once again, bringing back clear skies and knocking down the heavy surf that had built steadily during the storm.

It takes a while after a blow for the ocean to settle down. The four of us—me, Jim, Peter and Ted—can set on the first afternoon of the first clear day, but the seas are still significant, coming in hard, sharp and murky. When we haul the net, it comes ashore dirty. Bits of debris are caught in almost every foot of twine; it takes us an extra hour to pick the meshes clean. If I were the skipper, I wouldn't bother setting so soon after a storm, but the Poseys don't make choices about when to fish and when not to. They go whenever they can launch their dories through the surf; sometimes they try even when they should not. There are many stories about dories being flipped and pitchpoled in the surf—just as many tales of disaster as there are about success at unlikely times, such as this breezy afternoon in early November with the sea the color of coffee.

But we score no success. Our two sets are dry hauls; there is nothing in the bunt. It comes ashore like a long, empty sleeve, and I am glad when the sun sets and we head off the beach. The western sky is tinged with green at dusk—a signal that Jim and I both recognize from our previous winter of wood cutting. Riding home in the "A" I remind him.

"See that, Cap? See that green sky? We'd better wear our longjohns tomorrow, or we'll freeze our ass for sure."

"Yes, yes," says Jim, but he goes no further with the banter. There hasn't been much talk since Smiley's drowning. We are a working crew now, not a laughing crew, not a crew of friends. We are merely four fishermen, going through the motions, waiting together for the memories to ease.

The first revival of Jim's spirit, and Peter's for that matter, comes the next morning after Ted backs down and we drop the dory off the trailer at the edge of the ocean, ready for the dawn set. Jim leans over the gunwale, picks up the bailer and starts cracking the ice in the boat's bilges. He nudges Peter.

"Look at that, Cap. You want to watch that ice. When Ted tells you. 'Get in, Peter,' you're liable to go flying." He thumps the bailer down again, grunting. "Must have been some cold to freeze that salt water. Well, maybe it's cold enough to move a pod of them bass along this way. We could use a haul one of these days. December will be here before we know it."

"Don't talk about it, Jim, don't talk about it," Peter says. "I don't want to even think about December yet. All I want to think about is fish."

We make the set on a cold, calm sea that reminds me of the first days Jim and I fished together, with Swede, in his dory at the Main Beach. It was still and cold on those mornings.

I can see every cork on the seine as I walk west to help Jim. My imagination is working: I persuade myself that there are at least fifteen boxes of bass inside the half-circle. But I don't say anything to Jim. There is no sign that we have fish. No stripers are gilled, there are no swirlings in the surf, no breaks flashing on the flat sea. But my anticipation persists. I am glad, in a way, to feel my heart thumping again.

By the time the extra corks on the bunt buoy are just in back of the surf and the quarters are coming through the wash, I know that my hope is wishful thinking. There just is not enough activity in the water to indicate that we have any fish, much less fifteen boxes.

But as the winching stops and we go to hand-haul the bunt ashore, I feel a kind of weight on the line. Perhaps we haven't made a dry haul after all. Then I see a shadow in the surf, a darkness in the net's cod end. I yell.

"There's one. We got something."

The next sea breaks, moves the bunt further ashore, then recedes, leaving the bag almost dry—dry enough for me to see what we have caught. I recognize Smiley's long, black overcoat, there in our net. I want to be someplace else, anyplace.

We keep hauling. There is nothing else we can do. After six days, the sea has given us back Smiley. I don't want to look. I want to run. I want to stop trembling, I want Ted and Peter and Jim to disappear. I want the sea to take back what it has brought us. I want this entire, wretched, sickening time to be wiped from memory, from my mind, from my life.

"Jesus, oh Jesus." Ted says it softly, on his sighing breath. I hear it, and then I hear the rumble of trucks. Ding and his crew are coming from the east, toward us. I am relieved by that. Ding will know what to do.

Ted calls, "Johnny. Come on, Johnny. Help me carry him to the truck. Come on. Help me."

Ted opens the cod end, loosens the rope that runs through the rings. He and I hold the feet of Smiley's waders while Peter and Jim pull the bunt away from him. Jim comes down and takes one rubber-covered ankle, I take the other. Ted goes to the other end, wraps his arms around the black overcoat just below the armpits and lifts. I keep my eyes on the black rubber foot in my hands as we walk to the big silver truck and slide Smiley in the back. I am surprised at how heavy he is. I would have thought not much would be left after six days in the water.

Ding's truck pulls up alongside and Ding looks down from the cab into Ted's truck, but he says nothing. Ted climbs into the silver truck, starts the engine and lumbers off the beach. Ding turns his truck off and climbs down. He yells back at his crewman Lindy. "Come on, let's give these fellows a hand loading."

We get the dory on the trailer, and all of us pull the net toward it, ready for loading. Ding and I are across from each other, he pulling on the cork line, me on the leads. The sun is high now, bright, spilling some warmth onto the beach. I don't know what to say. I don't want to talk about Smiley, about anything to do with this day.

"Ding," I say, "tell me, what did you get that morning after you waited all night to make that Ditch Plain set?"

Ding stopped pulling, surprised. "You never heard about that? We didn't set. Couldn't. The surfcasters were there, shoulder to shoulder, lined up from one end of that beach to the other. Somebody sure gave them the word. I wasn't going to take a chance in that place with those bastards on the beach. No telling what they would have done.

"We left. Went west and made the Gurney's set. Got about eight boxes, is all."

$\mathscr{H}$ AWAII

Rick Bass

$\mathscr{I}$ had expected fully to hate Hawaii. I had expected that I would be homesick for Montana and the good crisp weather of mid-December the whole time. I imagined it as a place seething with traffic, sun and glimmer. I imagined it as America's ultimate hype: not only a rip-off, but one for which you had to travel interminably in order to be ripped off. I imagined a sort of pig pen, where nothing was sincere, everything a parody of itself, and everything for sale.

I was also afraid that the islands would be overrun with game-show winners, and the terrible vacuous smiles of newlyweds. But I thought if I headed into Hawaii's high mountains (some of the peaks almost fourteen thousand feet tall), and into the upland rain forests and out across the tortured, barren lava fields, then maybe I could stay out of sight of the lemming hordes of beach tourists. And with the exception of the megafleet of turbo-helicopters that followed me everywhere, my theory was correct, and I found solace and rest, and had a lovely time.

Look out! Here comes the geologist! Run!

The Hawaiian Islands consist of seven separate islands. The islands were formed one at a time, assembly-line fashion, as the Earth's tectonic plate slid slowly over an undersea rift, a "hot spot" in the Earth's crust. The lava, the energy of the earth, blasts up through the tectonic plate, mounding up millions of square acres as the cone of the underwater lava mountain grows, reaching for the shining lights above.

The lava reaches the ocean's surface then (after a mile or more of mountain-building), but still it keeps welling up, spreading, until it is a giant cone-shaped mountain. (As in the case of the youngest and easternmost island, the Big Island of Hawaii, such a mountain can be 14,000 feet above the sea.)

The Hawaiian Islands' hot spot tends to give birth to slow-building, cone-shaped volcanoes—"gentle" volcanoes. Other hot spots around the world are more sporadic in their mountain-building. They don't have the regular pressure-release flows and rifts that the Hawaiian Islands have, and instead build up terrible pressures beneath their caps until finally, one day, the whole top of the mountain blows. (Krakatoa.)

So the tectonic plate drifts—is pushed—westward, at the rate of about four inches a year. The first island to be formed in the chain of Hawaii was, of course, the westernmost, about 1500 miles west of the hot spot (which now lies beneath the newest island, the Big Island). At four inches a year, this makes the westernmost and oldest island 70 million years old.

Seventy million years may sound old, but even that is young—*infantile*—compared to the rest of the world. Most geologists believe that the "mainland" of the seven continents—which were once one huge continent called Pangea—is about four-and-a-half billion years old.

The Big Island is only 500,000 years old. Someday it will drift west, too—it's drifting west even now, at that four inches a year—and some day there will be an eighth island. (Perhaps just as the westernmost island disintegrates and disappears . . . The chain of islands, the skyline, moving up and down in this fashion like the pistons of the earth, the pistons of life . . .)

Look out! Here comes the geologist!

Although this story is about my visit to the uplands of the two youngest islands, I think it's important for the reader to understand what lies ahead for each island—the process of its death wedded immutably to the process of its birth. There is no word for it other than fate.

Each island that rises from the sea will heat up each day in the near-equatorial sun. Each mountain will also block the cooler trade winds, which blow from east to west. This creates thunderstorms on the windward (east) side of the mountain, which creates life— lush rain forests (there are places in the Hawaiian mountains that get an estimated 600 inches of rain per year)—but these rains, in addition to producing a quick explosion of varied life forms, also guarantee quick death. The island literally washes away to the sea, cut and carved by the rains. Nutrients are also swept out to sea.

Coral reefs form around the island, nourished by the high-nutrient runoff. These reefs make a protective ring around the island, slowing the island's destruction by the surf, while the island's forests blossom.

But in the meantime, the rain is cutting the mountain down— the rain that the mountain itself creates—until it crumbles to nothing, and becomes like the hole in a donut, with the circular coral reef—the atoll—the only evidence that all that glorious life ever blossomed. There are atolls like this all over the Pacific—ancient ghosts of what were once islands.

I came into this story determined not to view Hawaii as "paradise," to never, ever use that word, for it is a stereotype, and when a writer resorts to stereotypes, he or she—and the story—are sunk, like one of those old, westernmost islands.

And for a while I saw the islands as a terrible, beautiful, floating prison—each island destined for an extremely short life, drifting to oblivion—but then immediately after that I saw, while indeed that was true, there was also no other word—it *was* a paradise. A short one, like the one day of life given to the mayfly in midsummer, but paradise, nonetheless.

You go to Hawaii, and if your eyes are open, you come away marveling not so much at how tropical and lovely Hawaii is (though you do that, too), but more amazed, really, at how special and lucky your own life is, back on the mainland. Deadlines and the distractions of your doomed municipal financial inconveniences may be forming lava mounds in your brain, but you look at the long odds the islands have of ever making it, and the larger odds of any life forms arising from or on those islands—they're 2000 miles from any mainland—and you suddenly realize how peachy we've got it, to be upright and walking around on two legs, on firm ground, and *in the world*.

You don't think of magma (it's only called lava when it escapes to the Earth's surface)—of the molten rock at the center of the Earth—as being the source of life. But the way it rises and blocks those trade winds and secures water and creates life (carbon and hydrogen), you realize that it *is* the source. You realize that the earth *desires* life—that rocks desire life—that it is all a partnership, and that it starts with the fury and passion of magma.

I went to the Big Island first—the youngest one, the only one that still has active lava flows. (The next-youngest island, Maui, which lies just west of the Big Island, had its last eruption in the 1700s; it's since drifted far enough west to no longer be affected by the hot spot that gave it its birth.)

I don't know if I can describe how glorious, how *serene* it felt, to be standing in the high rain forest on that incredibly young, incredibly healthy, raw, hopeful mountain, in the village of Volcano, just outside Volcanoes National Park. I'm used to walking around in mountains that are almost a billion years old. But to be on a mountain that is only 300,000 years old—and to be standing on hardened lava, basalt, that is only ten or twelve years old? You must believe me when I say that I could feel the difference, and that it was immense.

The village of Volcano is green, with every leaf shape so new and different that the effect is like going back in time to childhood, when the woods were new and unnamed then, too.

Elizabeth, my wife, passed up coming with me on the trip I had to make to northern Wisconsin earlier in the month, but has decided to join me on this one. We've got our nine-month-old daughter, Mary Katherine, with us, and she heightens the sense of newness. Things will be as new to me as they are to her.

While traveling through two immense national parks—Volcanoes National Park, on the Big Island, and the even larger Haleakala National Park, on the island of Maui—I would realize how much we rely, for better or worse, on our memories, rather than a willingness to look at a thing—anything—anew. At times I would catch a glimpse of landscape—a certain tree, or a meadow, or even an angle of light—and find in my notes my disturbing, confusing, almost nonsensical attempts to make order—that is, to make comparison—of what I was seeing, and what it was like.

Texas. Arizona. Vermont. Montana. California. Costa Rica. Arkansas. No, Mississippi. No . . .

Elizabeth and Mary Katherine stayed at the lodge the first evening, while I went up into the park and walked around in the dusk. Steam rose from the trees—little rifts in the earth that had worked up to the surface—and it was windy and cold. Water dripped from the green bushes along the hiking trails. It's all or nothing at Volcanoes: beautiful, twisted, folded sheets of hardened lava spread for great distances, as if on the moon, or—if you're in a place spared by the lava flows—then it's lush, dripping with greenery and bird song.

The name for such jungle islands around which the lava flowed and then hardened is *kipakus,* and they are of tremendous ecological significance. Life—and the rapid evolution characteristic of Hawaii, or of any new landform—proceeds at a startlingly brisk, sometimes explosive pace. I really want to leap ahead in the story and begin talking about the bugs, the birds, the seething *life,* but know I can't match the island's accelerated pace. Scientists chasing flora and fauna on the island can't keep up with the furious changes their quarry is making, either—mutations and adaptations—and the last thing one wants to do in Hawaii is get in a hurry anyway.

You just want to rest, and watch. You just want to look. Ninety-five percent of the species in the Hawaiian Islands are endemic—found nowhere else in the world. For them, Hawaii is their sacred home.

Every time I blink, 95 percent of what comes into my field of vision is new. Of course I must go slow, and must stick with the story of the rocks: I must learn that, first.

I head up toward the great Southwest Rift, a beautiful prairie of twisted, rough *aá* (pronounced ah-ah) lava. Bubbles of gas in the cooling lava have given it a vesicular structure, almost like coral: a boulder the size of an ice chest might weigh only a few pounds. (All through Hawaii there are gorgeous stone walls built from lava rock, iridescent black and iron-blood-red, rock fences being swarmed under with greenery, and I'm jealous, wishing to have such rocks available for my stone wall in Montana, which suddenly seems as ponderous and sledge-footed—as *freighted*—as a dinosaur.) After a while, metaphor can become reality, and everywhere I look I see the lightness of the things, the easiness of existence: the youth of the island. It is like looking at a scrapbook of one's parents when they were children. You think, *So this is what it was like.*

The jungle—the *kipakus* and other jungles—are impenetrable in most places, and because the rough lava fields are so treacherous, the national parks in Hawaii have a wonderful system of hiking trails. Back on the mainland, and especially in the West, I abhor trails, which are often just a conduit for passing horse turds up and down the mountain, and ultimately lead to violent erosion. But in this unfamiliar place, they're welcome, and because most everyone else is down on the beaches, here at about 9000 feet, I have them to myself. The crunch of the crushed volcanic rock underfoot reminds me of the cinder running tracks in high school, and I realize that's exactly what it is: ground-up cinders. There's no soil for me to disturb or erode on these trails; it hasn't even formed yet.

I walk out across the Southwest Rift, into the most unusual, coppery sunset I've ever seen—it's 6:00 P.M., almost right on the equator—and then I head back to the park entrance, to the Volcano Bar; to watch a bit of *Monday Night Football.* My beloved Houston Oilers and the aging, heroic Warren Moon are playing. The game is already over back in Houston, but it's on a time delay here; it hasn't even started.

I'm the only customer in the bar or restaurant. This is the only public television in the village of Volcano. A few tourists in shorts walk around in the parking lot, hunch-shouldered against the chill winds, plotting no doubt to amend their itinerary and head back to the beaches a few days early.

A full moon rises beyond the scenic windows of the restaurant, casting an eerie silver-blue glow on the guts of Kilauea crater, which only years ago was a pool of roiling lava; it erupts every seven or eight years. It could happen again at any time—is due, in fact, at any time. A hundred years ago, Mark Twain came here to live for a while and to watch Kilauea erupt, the boiling pit sending plumes of lava 2000 feet into the air. The magma beneath Kilauea is only two miles below, boiling, searching for a rift or fissure—

straining to make one, to launch still more lava into the air, to bring more life into the world.

Two miles down is not very far, for such a force of the world. Any day now.

That night, lying in bed a short distance from the park, I remember reading how the last eruption gave hikers out on the trails only about a three-hour warning.

It could go off while I sleep! It could explode, flow down the road, turn left at the Kilauea Lodge, and turn cottage number six into a *kipaku*. Or worse!

Volcanoes, earthquakes, and other forces of nature—it's delicious, in this unthinking age of arrogance, to rediscover humility. It's silly, but I get up out of bed and look out at the night garden—at all the night-blooming flowers—and I gaze upon their beauty as if it could be my last night on earth. Silly, but delicious. *We are not in control.* Delicious.

The next day, we walk. There are a few other tourists about, but mostly they seem to be restricting their walking to the Visitors' Center parking lot. We walk the Bird Park Trail through a beautiful, dense forest, a *kipaku,* that was surrounded by a lava flow. We move through that strange forest, listening to the chirps of honeycreepers. It's a lovely walk for about half an hour—Mary Katherine looking at the canopy above in wonder, with stripes of green light camouflaging us—but then when we hear the helicopter, something in the woods changes. Certainly it's not as peaceful, and it no longer seems so new or special. It's like being in church and having a crop duster soar past, flying level with the stained-glass windows. I would have to say, in the language of the government officials who try to decide what's right and what's wrong (not understanding that their hearts can tell them this better than any visitor questionnaire), that yes, the helicopter overflights did indeed "significantly reduce the quality of our experience," the experience for which we traveled so far and so long.

But I can say it in fewer words. It's sick. It sucks.

We strike out on another walk, this time across the Kilauea Rim, all lava wasteland and all glorious, both, when you think of it for what it is—hundreds of square miles of just-cooled lava—and for what it will soon become—a seedbed for Hawaii's diversity, Hawaii's writhing, lovely forests.

We say the words out loud—*pahoehoe* (pronounced pa-hoyee-hoyee), lava that is smooth, ropy, almost intestinal, and *aā*, the chunky, savage, bomblike pieces. We look for the wispy strands known as Pele's hair (Pele, the fire goddess, the power and meaning beneath the Pacific Plate) and for Pele's tears, the drop-shaped pieces formed when lava is sprayed a long way from a volcano, flying through the air and cooling into teardrop shapes that harden even before they land.

Most dramatic to me are the incredible, ghostly lava trees, where the lava crept up on a standing tree and covered it, but then drained away, rejoining the rest of the lava flow. The retreating lava leaves only a hardened crust around the now-dead tree, with the tree's branches still intact (but cloaked in that crusty lava), the branches still lifted to the sky.

What happens when the lava flows up and over a tree, but does *not* recede, is just as startling. Called a tree mold, the lava engulfs the tree, but the sap and moisture inside the tree keep the tree from burning up completely. The lava eventually hardens, and the fried tree trunk left standing in the middle of that lava field smolders, dries, rots, and disappears, leaving a perfect hole in the lava—looking for all the world as if someone has drilled wells out in the lava field. Big and little holes, all perfectly round, are the only clue that there was once a green forest.

To look at the lava we're walking across, and to look back into the mysterious recent past, and to understand—to see the clues, the story—is not unlike following the tracks of animals in the snow back in Montana.

The smooth *pahoehoe* lava is hotter and glows brighter than does the rough *aā*, because rather than bubbling its gas out like the *aā* (which is what makes the *aā* so broken, vesicular, and rough), the *pahoehoe* instead retains its gas, which keeps the lava hotter, producing the smoother, more liquid flow.

I tell you, I love this stuff.

We're having a great time—just walking, carrying the baby, loving the feel of good, hard, *new* rock under our feet, walking across the wasteland, reveling in how new it is. The first humans to live on the Hawaiian Islands arrived here only 1500 years ago; the previous 298,350 years (give or take) belonged to lonely Pele, and to the flowers, and the forests. The first non-Hawaiian did not look upon a Kilauea eruption until 1823.

Where I live, I'm used to finding 10,000-year-old relics, such as spear points and arrowheads, left by Paleolithic settlers. I knew that the world—even "our" world, the human world—was old, but I had no idea that it was also so young.

Walking across the crunchy, twisted lava, around the edge of the napping Kilauea, I'm incredibly refreshed, and incredibly humbled. We could do it again if we had to, I think—survive, I mean. Mile-wide meteorites ripping past the Earth every few years, sometimes hitting it, other times missing it by a few thousand miles . . . A dropped gene here or there . . . I know that the odds are long against our survival, that we're the product of either divine luck or divine grace—that we're damn lucky to be here at all. But walking across the lava fields, I find myself exuberant, thinking *yes, we could do it again.*

Looking out at a new world of nothing but rock, with nothing but sunlight above and empty sky (though already, lichens are beginning to form on some of the older lava, and photosynthesis is releasing oxygen into the air, an atom at a time)—looking out at the rubble of lava, at nothing but lava—is like gazing at the pattern, the blueprint, for the possibility of life, for the possibility of everything.

It's a lovely, spiritual moment, or at least it is until the helicopter comes bopping up over the rim of the crater, defiling the sound of the wind and the sight of that open sky.

The helicopter hovers, banks, casts a commercial eye down into the crater, then whirls away, departs like a motorized pterodactyl, and somehow, where before I felt awe, I now feel only slightly foolish, and it is not a good trade, that of awe for foolishness.

Not yet knowing the myths—no, the *truths*—of the island, what Hawaiians refer to as the *kapu* of their island—the do's and don'ts—I pick up a rugged, fist-size piece of *aá* to take home to a friend's son, noting that the rock is the same age as the boy. It is only by chance, however, later in the day, that I hear one of the park rangers telling another visitor about the file the Park Service keeps on people who take lava back to the mainland. It's a drawer full of letters from people who've had bad luck descend suddenly upon them, bad luck in spades, after taking Hawaiian rocks back to the mainland. Broken legs, back injuries, financial catastrophes, car wrecks—all manner of heavy-handed stuff from the goddess Pele, says the ranger; she's rarely subtle. And it's not a psychosomatic manifestation of guilt—the accidents befall the rock-snatchers whether they're aware of the curse or not. It's real; no placebo.

I'm just overhearing this conversation, mind you. No one's got me made. The rock's still in the back of the car, hidden, just riding around with me. I haven't tried to take it away from its home—yet. I'll just think on it a bit, and try to rationalize. Madame Pele, it's for a little *boy,* etc.

The thought stays in my mind, however—the overheard warning—and puts its roots into my brain and slowly strengthens its hold there, expanding ever so slightly all the while, like water freezing in a wedge between two rocks.

And it acts like a filter, changing still further the way I look at the island.

There are stories for everything on Hawaii. I've lost the statistics, but I remember reading that Hawaii's native culture has more stories, more oral mythologies, than any other culture in the world—not just one or two extra tales, but *three times* the "usual" number. And that makes sense, for if you've got such an extraordinary diversity of life, and if everyone gets a story, from turtles to crickets, then of course there'll be more stories. It is a way of honoring life, of honoring the force and power of things.

If it sounds like I am edging toward a defense of native myths, well, maybe I am. I am fully aware of the cynical eye Western culture places on most myths and miracles (save a select few). I'm aware, too, that our earnest desire to explain away the mystery is sometimes as bad as our cynicism—to find, in our oh-so-clever way, scientific reasons for the various myths and miracles.

Our native, myth-based cultures are always right, it seems. I am learning to respect that more and more. Sometimes the myths and miracles are metaphors that have been so carefully crafted (which is what a story does) to match a reality that not even scientists can separate (not even with their electron-splitting microscopes) the metaphor—the myth—from the reality.

And other times, when scientists *can* split the story and explain away the mystery, the two halves of the whole that they hand back to us are so identical, so parallel, that one wonders why there was ever any bother.

And still other times, the myth is more than truth: sometimes, certainly, it is fact as well as truth, and the scientist's microscopes melt, and the ends of their fingers get burned, as they look too closely at a thing that lies behind science.

But it's just one rock—and such a small one!

In Martha Beckwith's massive oral-history collection, *Hawaiian Mythology,* she alludes to the at-times rather insignificant distinctions between fact and fiction, as long as the metaphor is true:

> Hawaiians use the term *kaao* for a fictional story or one in which fancy plays an important part, [and] *moolelo* for a narrative about a historical figure, one which is supposed to follow historical events . . . Nor can the distinction between *kaao* . . . and *moolelo* . . . be pressed too closely. It is rather in the intention than in the fact. Many a so-called *moolelo* which a foreigner would reject as fantastic nevertheless corresponds with the Hawaiian view of the relation between nature and man.

The Pele myth encompasses geological reality—and who knows?— perhaps once (whether 1500 years ago or 10,000) a young woman from a large family (seven brothers and five other sisters) did set out to sea in a canoe, and did settle on the islands, in the manner of drifting plant seeds' and insects' colonization.

Beckwith reports that "Pele is very beautiful with a back straight as a cliff and breasts rounded like the moon. She longs to travel and, tucking her little sister, born in the shape of an egg, under her armpit, hence called Hi'iaka-i-ka-poli-o-Pele (in the armpit of Pele), she seeks her brother Ka-moho-ali'i," who gives her his canoe with the forces of his brothers Whirlwind, Tide, and Current for paddlers.

I said I wasn't going to do that meaningless scientist's stuff, but I'm a white man, European stock, and I can't resist it any more than an otter can resist biting into a fish head.

Consider Pele's sister's strange (metaphorical or factual) characteristic—"born in the shape of an egg." This is, of course, how scientists believe the islands were colonized by almost all the various life forms—the arrival of a pregnant female, or, to use their language (admittedly less lyrical than "in the armpit of Pele"), long-distance colonizers arriving with oceanic and atmospheric transmissions via *whirlwinds, tides,* and *currents.*

The Pele myth is long and involved—she goes here and there, does this and that, finds a love interest (the sensuality of Hawaii is so specific as to be a certain kind of thickness in the air, a green, growing, lushy kind of emotion; everywhere there is the spirit and feeling of "breasts rounded like the moon" and other things)—and Pele ultimately drifts southeasterly, having had an affair (in spirit form) with a handsome young chief. Jealousy's involved, and some forms of the myth say that her little sister chases Pele to the southeast. It's a complex, beautiful story, and finally Pele settles on the most southeasterly island, the Big Island of Hawaii, where "she attempts to dig a home in which she can receive her lover . . . and there is successful in digging deep without striking water, and in an element inimical to her fiery nature."

The question for me isn't Was there really such a woman? but rather Is or was there such a spirit, such a force, in the world? And the answer to that, as any geologist can tell you is, well, sure, hell yes. The Pacific Plate slides northwesterly; the youngest, hottest, most active island is therefore the most southeasterly island, the Big Island. The nest, the force of that hot spot, is real. Spirit, by any definition, must be a kind of force. Do things that exhibit force have a tangible presence in the world—a tide, a current, a wind, a beautiful young woman? Of course they do. So perhaps if spirit exists, then surely we can say that some reality exists even if we can't see it.

Look out! Here comes the constipated theologian! Run! Hide! Let's get on with the fun places to eat, the good things to see and do. But if you come to Hawaii, you need to understand at least a little of the story of Pele, and have a certain respect for it, and for the place—that is to say, the nature and the spirit of it—a place still very early in the stages of its creation, and where anything can happen.

Late that afternoon, Elizabeth and Mary Katherine and I drive down to the sea, roughly 6000 miles from our home in what's labeled the Pacific Northwest. It's the same ocean, but it feels like a different planet. There aren't any calderas brimming with open pools of lava, such as when Kilauea blows, but there is a nice creeping *aá* flow on the east end of the park, running from a rift in the highlands across the down-faulted flats next to the ocean. It is here that lava is running out into the ocean.

And that's where the tourists are—a couple hundred of them driving the twenty-plus miles down to the beautiful shining sea and the black lava sand beach, to hike a mile across a still-smoldering crust of new lava and stand beachside, fumaroles all around, and watch from a cordoned-off distance as this *aā* flow makes its way to the sea.

Even from a distance, we can see a column of steam stretching across the ocean, winding its way to the horizon and beyond, steam from where the 2000-degree lava is entering the eighty-degree water.

Like pilgrims, old and young, the well and the infirm alike, we make our way through the brush down an ancient trail (there used to be a village here, at about the time Columbus was striking west toward the big forests of North America). We pass a still-standing rock wall. A couple of tour bus battalions, all elderly retirees, push on gamely down the trail: *See the lava before you die. See the force that seethes beneath us, which has always seethed beneath us.* There is a wild grimness in their eyes, and a quickness to their steps.

Elizabeth and Mary Katherine and I approach from the upwind side. The steam's all blowing out to sea, but we protect ourselves against a wind change nonetheless. The sulfur in the lava mixes with water when it hits the ocean and forms dense clouds of sulfuric acid, which in great enough concentrations can irritate your eyes and lungs. That same morbid fellow, the park ranger who was so gleefully detailing the various revenges of Madame Pele upon rock-snatchers, has also been telling a tale *(not* a myth) about a recent group of tourists who went past the roped-off viewing area, desiring to get right up to the lava flow. The wind suddenly shifted, surrounding them completely with a great mass of sulfur fog, so that even if their eyes hadn't been burning, they wouldn't have been able to see their hands in front of their faces.

They had to fall to the ground like supplicants, and huddled there for more than eight hours until rescuers went in and found them. It was a good thing they didn't try and outrun the fog, too, said the ranger, because all around them was an oh-so-thin crust, which if they had punched through would have dumped them ankle- or waist- or even neck-deep into gleaming red lava.

So I'm nervous, even behind the single strand of yellow nylon "safety rope." The crusty, hardened lava on which we're standing is still streaked and swirled with iridescent orange hues, and little pockets of rainwater are trapped in its folds and depressions. The rainwater is still steaming and sometimes bubbling.

We can't really see the lava flow, about seventy yards down the coast, but we can hear the steady, crashing hiss as it continues to pour into the ocean—a sound not unlike sticking a hot skillet under cold running water; only magnified a million times; a sound that has no cessation, no cooling relief.

At any given time there are only a dozen or so pilgrims standing on the beach, peering north, craning their heads in a futile effort to see the lure of what lies around the bend: the lava flow. The rest of the hundred or so visitors are straggled out all through the brush, some still coming, and some leaving, perhaps disappointed. Occasionally a great backlash of cool, red *aá* will explode into the sky, rising up and out of the steam for us to see. A collective gasp will go up, as if our hearts have been torn out, or as if we have *touched* the lava—and then that brief sight will vanish back into the steam.

It's the worst thing we do in nature, perhaps—well, one of the worst—preferring the immense and the immediate to the subtle. Perhaps it is some gene that is in us; perhaps predators *need* to think big, to have an eye for the spectacle of boom-and-bust. Or perhaps it's simply further ruination of our lives by the satanic qualities of television. Nonetheless, I'm disappointed at not having seen the Time-Life or National Geographic version of the process, and I suddenly remember, with pride, that my parents were told they were the only visitors in the history of Yellowstone National Park who booed Old Faithful.

We head back, walking south along the black sand beach. It's dusk. Once again there's the feeling that this is the only world there is, the new world, and that we are its settlers: the colonists.

All that is needed is here: water, shelter, food. Myths. The blue waters of the Pacific. Normally I get a bit queasy when I think about eating fish, understanding that all the world's various heavy metals can accumulate in their tissues as if the fish were nothing more than sponges. All I like to eat now is wild game—deer that live their lives high in the mountains, far out of that kind of harm's way.

But these blue waters—they make me desire fish. That seafood phobia, that *repression,* is lifted, so that I find myself wanting to run crazily into the ocean and capture a luscious fish with my hands, if need be, and feast on the sweet, clean flesh right then and there.

It is the cleanest, bluest water I have ever seen. It seems to be speaking to me in a language and on a level that I am not familiar with, a kind of communication from childhood, or the womb, or even before, perhaps: *Eat me; come eat my fish.*

We walk down the glistening black beach in silence, save for the crashing of the surf: a family, our first December. The sand gives way to a new lava that has not yet been broken up into beautiful black sand (Hawaii's white beaches are from washed-ashore coral fragments). In some of these rough passages across the new lava, dramatic stone arches stand right at the water's edge—sea caves and blowholes where the ocean rushes up under the land, racing through an underground tunnel, the ocean spout then emerging square in the middle of the lava flat, farther inland. It's like a journey through the imagination—a child's imagination.

These tunnels—called lava tubes—are formed during a certain kind of lava flow in which the surface of the lava cools as it creeps across the land. This cooling, hardened exterior of the creeping flow (like the scuzz on top of cream left out too long, is how I think of it) insulates the fluid lava beneath it, allowing that lava to stay molten longer (rather than cooling and hardening it). The lava beneath this cooling outer skin continues to flow until it has all gone on its way, leaving behind only the empty, hardened outer shell, that crusty exterior skin, which becomes roof, the ceiling, of the tunnel below. Like veins and arteries, these hollow lava tubes wander all over the island, and sometimes out to sea.

Does anyone besides geologists give a damn about all this? Myself, I find it difficult to understand how such a diverse and different place can exist in the world. There is the old Pangea—all of the seven continents before they split off from one another—like Pele's seven brothers, perhaps—and then there are the Hawaiian Islands, which seem immune to the homogeneity, the at-times barely discernible but always present air of malaise that exists on the continents, sometimes hovering just in the tops of the trees, but almost always somewhere nearby.

But this place—these islands—like only the wildest mountain-tops, or the most sere deserts, has a kind of a grace, a wild grace so tangible that it startles me.

We drive up out of the lava flats, up from the down-faulted block of the island that's not so much a thousand-foot fault as a slump from where the island grew too fast. We drive through lush forests and through wasteland, back up to the Southwest Rift, and around the edge of Kilauea, whose steam clouds glow green in the odd wet light of the setting sun.

The giant moon rises behind us, heightening the feeling that we are on another planet. Never have I seen such lushness, and never have I seen such splendid desolation, and never have I seen anything like this, the two of them side by side, in harmony.

At the Visitors' Center on the way out, while buying a few postcards, I overhear a middle-aged woman from Chicago buying some kind of island amulet—a string of shells, a tinkling necklace.

"Maybe this will make my daughter fertile," the woman tells her companion, and I have the sudden and certain feeling, I don't know where from, that indeed that woman's daughter *is* going to finally conceive, and it seems as natural and uncomplicated a thought as looking at a purple sky to the north and thinking that yes, rain is coming.

As the place where lushness and devastation collide and then prosper, science and religion also have their harmony up here. The Thomas A. Jagger Museum, right at the edge of Kilauea, has been devoting itself to research on and study of volcanoes for years now. (They're *not* the silly-assed people who sent that poor robot over a volcano's rim and down into the magma, a $2-million-dollar boondoggle, cold-hearted premeditated robocide—that was NASA, in Antarctica.)

The Jagger Museum employs real people, dressed in huge silver asbestos suits, looking like knights of old, to take measurements from the volcanoes, and they use lasers, too, to try and measure the infinitesimal swellings and stretchings of the Earth's surface (so goes the theory, anyway) that occur just hours before an explosion.

This is good. This is *great*. It's wonderful to learn something new—something new every day, if you can, as my ninety-five-year-old Grandma Robson tells me. But the trouble our species, or our culture, seems to have with knowledge is that it seems to bring arrogance, and seems to diminish rather than nurture respect. You'd think the more you understood something, the more you'd respect it, too, but that's just not always the case.

The lasers and all are wonderful—sweller than swell—and I get the impression from the vulcanologists that they have that respect, an acknowledgment of the power and workings of mystery, which certain other scientists and cultures are not always comfortable with—a force that is sometimes ignored or dismissed as myth.

One reason for the vulcanologists' respect could be that it's right before their eyes—that mixture of long-ago myths fitting the truth long before their microscopes ever arrived on the scene, and the knowledge that those myths will continue to fit the truth long after the microscopes are gone.

About twenty miles offshore from the Big Island's east coast—toward the direction we were watching the vaporous spirits of the lava flow drift, floating just above the waters to the horizon—scientists have discovered that a new "sister" island is forming—that Pele is continuing, in both spirit and the physical world, her southeasterly trick of old, trying to find a new place in which to receive her lover; which I think we can safely say is life itself.

Called Loihi Seamount by scientists, the top of the new coming island is still about 3000 feet below the ocean's surface. If Loihi continues to grow at the rate that the Big Island grew (and is growing), it'll be about 60,000 years before Loihi rises from beneath the sea.

Likely as not, an asteroid will have smacked the Earth again during that time, making another ice age: a fine exclamation mark to the greenhouse warming we're currently aiding and abetting. Likely as not, we'll be gone, and the survivors—bacteria, ferns, and perhaps a few multicelled ocean organisms—will have to start all over again.

The planet desires life; even at its very molten core, there is a seething, a *desire,* for life.

Perhaps Loihi will be up and about, by then. Likely as not, this is what that new world will look like, then. Lichens. *Kipakus.*

It is impossible to be arrogant.

In the morning, before leaving, I drive up the tiny winding road to the 9000-foot trailhead that leads to Red Hill, toward the summit of Mauna Loa. I return the lava rock I had stashed in my car to the base of Mauna Loa—back to its source—and know, in a way that I rarely get to feel anymore, that I have done something correct and right.

$\mathcal{B}$ECOMING

$\mathcal{W}$ATER

Susan Zwinger

$\mathcal{T}$he Apprenticeship.

Lie on a large log at the high-tide line by the ocean an hour before the highest high tide of the month. The waves will boom below human hearing. Take on the power of the incoming ocean in your bones.

Take notes from the great cacophony of gulls, terns, cormorants, crows, eagles, and ducks as they spiral around thousands of haystacks out from shore. The ferocious pounding that brings you fear, grants them safety, feeds the richest bird rookeries of the globe on islands off the coast of Alaska and British Columbia and Washington and Baja California. The ultimate movable feast pours down the fjords, channels, rivers, to run south along the Kuroshiwo, endless conveyor belts of organic debris.

The wave energy absorbed through a 5.5-foot-diameter Sitka spruce log polished to marble from winters of storm will pulse into your bones. Choose a log too heavy to move, whose shallow root system splays outward 9 feet in all directions, writhing like Medusa's head. In the farthest reaches of its snake-roots should hang macabre seaweeds, bits of rope, mangled ships, snarled deck chairs, all limp as dead bodies of sailors.

On top lie with your eyes closed. The impact of that first wave will make the log sigh. The next, shudder. Well past high tide, the water may still rise and rise, punched shoreward by a storm somewhere at sea. Make sure the upper end of the log has been grounded since last winter. But keep some danger.

Water will churn under your log into pockets and holes underneath; waves will slam dance and gulp unpleasantly. Water may keep rising farther than the high-water line. Make sure of escape. Your universe will be made wholly of sensation. Into you will come the rhythms of Earth: of asteroids hitting, of their explosions, of the periodic wipeouts of life, of the punctuated equilibrium of evolution. Finally, the Big Bang.

A Great Beast Wave will strike. It will shower you with spray. It will condense under your log which will move slightly on its angry back. You will flip on your stomach and grasp two large roots. You will watch the power knit and unfurl.

Prone, you will ride with John Muir on top of his conifer whipping in a Yosemite thunderstorm. You will sail with Joseph Conrad through angry seas. You may drown with Captain Ahab midst the slash of the great white tail. If you are fortunate, you will find yourself about to go down with Amelia. . . .

Step Two:

Go to the downtown library; pull huge maps of your bioregion from the drawer. Carefully trace all the edges of water, all the lakes, all the rivers onto large paper. Do not include cities or artificial borders. Move your pencil slowly, sensuously, knowing that each crook and curve is intimately known by someone who loves it.

Step back. View the waterways of the Earth as dendritic veins. Imagine the humps and lumps implied underneath as those of a muscular lover.

Apprenticeship over, work begins.

Become one giant Earth wave, with a wave length of half the planet, pulled by moon and sun, dragged by friction and gravity. Pile up on one side of the globe, then shudder to a pause and change direction. Swell up under fishermen off Vietnam, caress skin divers in the Caribbean, strand a cruise vessel in Glacier Bay.

Become fascinatingly deadly. Travel farther north toward the poles, go to extremes. In mesotidal Puget Sound, vary only 16 feet. At Anchorage on Turnagain Arm gape 33 feet. Rush in on the south and out on the north side of the deep glacial channel creating standing waves, bore tides, walls of vertical churning water 4 feet high. Make tourists screech to a halt in their cars. Remain totally uncanny.

Try this—

Be born of a woman. Try floating around in a liquid for nine months. Or be a woman and surround liquids and cycles of liquids with an intricate nautilus of flesh. This will be hard for some of you.

Drink eight to ten glasses of water a day.

Wear down entire mountain ranges and dump them in layers. Slice whole mountains in half, leaving chains of faceted spurs up U-shaped valleys like pinking shears. Gouge long grooves in stone like horizontal fluted columns, all the way from Alaska to New Mexico. Carve whole mountains into half domes, then fill the valley with concessioners and tourists, solo free climbers, bumper to bumper traffic, then wipe the whole mess out again.

Or, gently surround Zostra marina sea grass twice a day. Protect and feed hundreds of thousands of salmonoids, Dungeness crabs, ducks, geese, and the myriad of tiny organisms that form the basis of life. Allow yourself to be named by the Coastal Salish, then by the Danish settlers, then by the Orion Company developers, and then as Padilla Bay . . . but know that none of them count.

Spread over the wings and back of the great white trumpeters who, like Lazarus, have returned from the dead, from near extinction (only 69) in the 1930s, to a healthy recovery. Then glint like diamonds as the giant birds toss you off. Or drip off the wings of cormorants stretching in great black crosses against the bright scintillation of wind across your surface. Feed thousands of brant geese and other waterfowl for whom you are a vital link.

Or, try this—

Pile up in a huge mound 200 feet high and destroy all of Valdez, Alaska, and half of Anchorage. Toss train cars across town in Seward, Alaska. Crush cities in South America and Asia simultaneously.

Or rise gracefully under surfers and kayakers, carry them along, speaking all the time to their muscles, challenge them, let them know a slight shift in weight or twitch of hips changes direction. Make them mad with desire to be out on you.

Fill human eyes with warm salt brine at least once a month. Let them weep for themselves or their dog or a child. Let them weep for all of the losses on this unusual planet.

Make captaining a ship a religion, not a profession.

Flow in and out of a million tidal pools twice a day, gently surrounding the caves and crannies crammed with delicate hydroids and isopods and nudibranchs. The Sistine Chapels of pendulant chartreuse anemones, purple sea stars, and crimson dorises. Create a biological soup as the basis of all marine life. Fill up thousands of sleek fat salmon and follow them hundreds of miles into the interior of continents. Then disgorge your detritus as they litter the land with the nutrients from sea.

Or try this—

Fill camp cook pots with small trickles of yourself seeping out from the cliffs, slipping through the mudstone and shale, flickering through ferns, coating grass blades like icicles, propelling off rock lips in white tongues of foam. Become miniature waterfalls. End up as rust-colored tannin, a forest sampler of detritus: a forest smoothie.

Steep each different part of yourself in a different plant. Make one trickle licorice flavored, sweet, having absorbed in deep leafy woods the *Abrus precatorius*. Indian licorice.

Sweet and clear, flow out from the subterranean labyrinths of Mount Olympus's glaciers. Melt with rain's hot blade cut down through the ogives and mill holes, siphoning melted glacier into your underground reasoning. Carry within you microscopic blades of sheered rock called "glacier flour," turn yourself opaque turquoise blue. Flow through the rainforest, filtered by western red cedar and western hemlock seven feet in diameter. Take into you the communion of leaves, insects, lettuce leaf lichens, ground-up birds, essence du marmot, and whatever else it offers. With this soupy-brew nourish estuaries, marshes, and bays.

Liquefy ancient forest and send it swirling far out on the Japanese current curving sharply toward the Far East with the Coriolis effect of Earth turning. Send it out on the Kuroshiwo, translated "Black Tide," toward Asia in a giant flush. Feel two-mile drift nets scraping the life from you to feed an exponentially expanding human biomass.

In your crashing waves, snap together organic particles from yourself and nuggets from the ancient forest like Lego blocks. Scavenge dissolved organic material from the rainforest, glue them into fibrils of colloidal (gelatinous) proteins. Loop these fibrils into bacterial clumps. Create with this bacteria the very algae which feeds the entire food chain.

Benthic metabolism.

Try this—

Have poets write about you as if you are alive. Scientifically, it is absolutely true, you are alive. You have a pulse, the waves, and a metabolism, your food chain. A personality, a character, a consciousness, and a sense of purpose. Not just poetically speaking, but within the perfection of the trophic food-chain spiral, the balances of life forms, and your tremendous drive toward more and more complexity and away from Chaos.

In that explosion of foam, build the bulk of whales on a molecular level.

Try this—

Turn into spray, spin rainbows. Mist down granite boulders over mosses, lichen, and a myriad of tiny yellow columbine, foam flowers, and deep pink shooting stars.

Or swallow the bodies of sailors, drunken yachters, drug smugglers, expatriates, unwatched toddlers, cement-footed mobsters, disowned spouses, humans who no longer wish to live. Dissolve them all into lovely detritus and blend them back into life. Bless them, recycle them.

Or drill deep into granite and rip it apart with your bare hands.

And be sure to delight each new child, and each human being. Follow them down streambeds. Patiently receive into you all the rocks and sticks they throw in. Do not swallow every smooth flat stone they throw at you obliquely: let one or two bounce. Humor them. Let them know in their veins that you both are connected everywhere. Enchant them. And through enchanting, change them forever.

Where the Suwannee Meets the Sea

Jeff Ripple

March weather in northwest Florida is an unruly child, unpredictable and mischievous. One day might be breathless and warm and sunny, and the next morning a chill gale buffets the Gulf of Mexico, raising whitecaps and making travel by small boat—kayak in my case—miserable and sometimes dangerous. By evening, the wind may drop, and the Gulf becomes a perfect mirror reflecting the ebbing hues of the dying light. But I have learned to never count on this.

This morning I'm lucky as I launch my kayak from Shell Mound at the Lower Suwannee National Wildlife Refuge a few miles north of Cedar Key, drawing the last of an incoming tide, a balmy air temperature of 62°F, and a light but steady breeze out of the east. The morning sun is diffused by high overcast, and a low, dense bank of clouds crouches over the western horizon. White pelicans orbit a thermal, rising in slow circles as if climbing an invisible spiral staircase. Western sandpipers and ring-billed gulls watch with bright eyes from a mud flat as I paddle past, angling northwest on a course that will take me past Hog Island, Buck Island, and the Long Cabbage Keys before crossing the wide firth of Clark Creek to Deer Island, my first stop. From there, I'll aim for a long line of trees, hazy with distance, that marks where the wide, forked tongue of the Suwannee River finally tastes the sea. Two miles beyond that will find me riding the sinuous back of the river itself.

The Lower Suwannee National Wildlife Refuge claims twenty-six miles of a borderland to the Gulf of Mexico known by official state decree as the Nature Coast (formerly the Big Bend), where the peninsula of Florida arcs toward the north and west to join the Panhandle. It is a "low-energy" coastline, one where the wind rarely blows onshore with any consistency, as it does on the east coast and Panhandle, and so is characterized by salt marshes cleaved by numerous tidal creeks, shallow bays, a few coastal islands, and thousands of jagged, winding skeins of oyster bars. Mostly it is a vast estuary, a place where salt water from the Gulf mingles with fresh water from mainland swamps and rivers, including the Homosassa, Crystal, Withlacoochee, Waccasassa, and Steinhatchee rivers, as well as the broad Suwannee. Much is protected state or federal land within three national wildlife refuges and one state preserve.

After forty-five minutes of paddling, I approach Deer Island, having glimpsed a bald eagle soaring overhead while paddling across Clark Creek. A dolphin gave me a cursory inspection on its way out to the Gulf. Deer Island is one of several private—but completely undeveloped—islands within the refuge. About a mile long, it bristles with gnarled live oaks, red cedar, cabbage palms, saw palmetto and slash pine—typical of the coastal islands in this area. Its higher portions are connected by fecund swaths of low-lying salt marsh dominated by cordgrass and black needlerush. I beach my kayak and throw myself on the sandy shore. The tea-colored water is calm here in the lee of the island with the easterly breeze. The sun has become bright and hot, and I shed the spray pants I had pulled over shorts to keep my legs warm and slather on sun block instead.

Deer Island is remarkable for the long, crescent-shaped, white sand beach on its western edge, a feature many islands in this area lack. While some visitors may perceive the scarcity of good beaches in this region as a geological deficiency, I must admit I'm grateful. This circumstance alone has probably discouraged the building of wall-to-wall beach front condos on the Nature Coast and slowed the onslaught of new coastal residents. The decided minority of folks who enjoy vast stretches of undeveloped hinterland, abundant wildlife, and quiet shorelines where encounters with their fellow humans are rare consider the area an undiscovered gem, a piece of relict "Old Florida." They are all too happy to direct beachgoers south to St. Petersburg or northwest to Panama City and Destin. I believe the residents of the Nature Coast, mostly commercial crabbers and aquaculturists, prefer it this way, too.

After a few leisurely stretches, I push off from Deer Island and paddle northwest toward a gap in the treeline on the horizon, which marks the mouth of East Pass. Once away from the lee of Deer Island, I raise my sail and skid over the chop until the wind slackens halfway across the bay, forcing me to drop the sail and paddle the remaining mile and a half to East Pass. To the west, I hear waves breaking on Halfmoon Reef, a long oyster shoal. The tide is falling.

In an estuary, tide dictates the movements of both humans and wildlife. Boating of any kind becomes increasingly difficult as the tide ebbs, exposing vast muddy flats that extend seaward from the marshes. On days when the wind howls from the northeast, even the scant few inches of water that normally lie at low tide in natural channels through the flats vanish. Fiddler crabs gather to feed en masse, sweeping over shorelines in such numbers that it is as if the land itself has picked up and clickity-clicked away. Flocks of shorebirds follow and gorge on this mobile smorgasbord. As water flows out of marshes into creeks that widen into bays, it sweeps many small animals toward the Gulf, where hungry mouths wait for them in eddies or deeper channels.

This process is reversed when the tide begins to rise and flood the oyster bars and salt marshes. Predators move in with the water to feed. From the kayak, on a high tide, I often watch stupendous fish moving through shallow water above oyster bars, their broad tails flapping the air. These are usually black drum and red fish (red drum), which frequently grow to more than fifty pounds. The fish love crabs, at times literally standing on their noses as they energetically search for the reclusive crustaceans among crevices and holes in an oyster bar. Sheepshead—flat, vertically striped, heavy-scaled fish that remotely resemble freshwater sunfish—also target crabs at high tide, ghosting along the edge of a bar in slightly deeper water to take advantage of the bold and the foolish.

Estuaries have been called the cradles of the sea because so many marine creatures spend their early lives there. Through these protected nurseries tidal water ebbs and advances—the sea's pulse, slow and rhythmic. To walk a mud flat as the tide boils around your feet is to shuffle through the pounding blood of the planet. On both tides, nutrients and organisms pass between the salt marsh and surrounding nearshore waters in an unrelenting cycle of nourishment and death.

The Suwannee meets the Gulf of Mexico like a snake with its mouth full. Born in the Okefenokee Swamp of southern Georgia, the river has distended and coiled its way through northern Florida for more than two hundred miles before gaping at the Gulf, grasping Hog Island (not the same Hog Island I passed near Shell Mound) in its maw. The river swirls around the island—shaped rather like a monstrous, tailless stingray—splintering into several passes, of which East Pass and Alligator Pass are the largest. Hog Island is a massive clot of river swamp, marsh, and brackish creeks that on my USGS map look like spider veins spreading across white paper flesh.

As I follow East Pass upstream, itself several hundred feet wide, Hog Island squats to my left. I paddle until Dan May Creek wriggles away to my right about a half mile from where East Pass empties into the Gulf and then dip a finger into the inky water and taste. No hint of salt. Even without sampling, I know I'm in fresh water by looking at the plant communities bordering the pass. Where at the mouth I had kayaked beside black needlerush and cordgrass—prominent salt marsh species—I now am flanked by sharp-toothed embankments of saw grass, a freshwater sedge, intermixed with needlerush at the shoreline.

Another half mile puts me past the marsh and into river swamp. This part of East Pass resembles the Suwannee of legend. Majestic bald cypress, tupelo, and red maple line the muddy bank. I spot in this stretch more ospreys and their nests in close proximity to one another than I have seen anywhere else along the coast. There are at least a dozen individual birds, possibly more that I don't see. Two have nests no more than fifty yards apart. The ospreys' ringing chirps echo between the forested banks of the pass and shadow me for the remaining distance to the river. Sturgeon roll, drawing the dark Suwannee over their backs like greatcoats, and less than a mile from the river, I watch two manatees frolic near shore, either mating or in play. The manatees disappear as a powerboat races too fast around a bend. Perhaps they know firsthand the impact of a boat hull or its slashing propeller. The whine of the engine drowns out the ospreys, and as the boat passes from sight around the next bend, its wake rolls under me and into the swamp, slapping noisily against tree trunks.

Even within a refuge, it's almost impossible to find measureless sanctuary. Nearly all federal lands—parks, wildlife refuges, forests, preserves, monuments—are mandated to accommodate a variety of personal and commercial human uses, some incredibly intrusive, including jet skis, powerboats and airboats, snowmobiles, mining, logging, and military flyovers—which in my mind discourage attempts for more personal, spiritual explorations, such as hiking, canoeing, wildlife observation, or ethical hunting and fishing. Worse still, the welfare of the land and its wild inhabitants—the underlying reason for the purchase of federal conservation lands—is often compromised as a result.

Clouds obscure the sun again, and the western sky has darkened to the color of a manatee's skin. I'm running out of time. I reach the Suwannee, tie my kayak to a tupelo, and eat a late lunch among a nest of roots. The tapestry of cypress and tupelo, alligators and sturgeon, even the bright, hot fury of the ospreys dim in the gathering gloom. The Suwannee shoves its obsidian bulk through the trees, strong and fluid, toward the sea. I turn my kayak and flow with it, pointed home.

$\mathcal{S}$ PINDRIFT

Jennifer Ackerman

$\mathcal{T}$he sea has gone the color of pewter. A sharp, clean wind blows scuds of foam along the beach and forces my gaze downward; fine sand stings my legs. It is spring, a day or two after a violent storm. Near the waterline are scarps two feet high, miniature cliffs where the charged-up surf has gnawed its way into the continent. I have come down to the shore with my father, who is visiting for a day or two. We have brought binoculars in the hopes of spotting a storm waif, a petrel, perhaps, or a shearwater—some birds will fly for days before a storm at sea, then drop as soon as the storm hits land—but we see only Bible black grackles fighting the wind and a knot of three gulls hunkered down on the sand like clenched fists. The storm has resculpted the contours of the beach, scoured it of all familiar form. The beach grass is scribing arcs in the sand like dark circles under tired eyes.

The storm was born when a cold front moving in from the northwest collided with a mass of hot, muggy air from the south, prompting a line of violent thunderclouds. At the ferry dock, on the fishing piers, people dropped what they were doing, stood and watched the huge black curtain move across the water. Soon they were standing in freakish noon darkness as complete as a total eclipse of the sun, and in stillness, save for the steady tick and creak of boats on their moorings and the tide slip-slapping beneath the piers. The moment had that dreamlike quality of a luminist painting where time rolls forward. When the storm finally struck, rain lashed down, pelting the sand like buckshot. Winds gusting to eighty miles per hour fueled ten-foot seas that took the beach apart.

Our footsteps break the crust of the upper beach with the good crunch of dry sand, but as we head down toward the water, we slog along in the softer sediment, and my dad's breathing grows heavy. He has recently recovered from an allergic reaction that nearly killed him. During a routine diagnostic test, so small a wrench as iodine—an element in seawater, rocks, and soil, and in small amounts essential to our own well-being—produced an ana-phylactic attack that unhinged his whole system, swelled his throat, shut his airways, made his heart stop cold. My father is an energetic man with a keen intellect, a good sense of humor, and passion for his work. He is careful in his habits and attentive to his health. But here was something utterly beyond control, a case of mistaken identity by his immune system, a small blunder that nearly cost his life.

When my stepmother, Gail, called in a shaken voice, I thought: *No. Not him. Not now.* By the time I reached the hospital, his heart had stabilized and the threat of death had passed. Gail and I stood by his bed in the critical care unit waiting for some sign of consciousness. Between us hung the deep unspoken fear of mental diminishment. When he finally stirred, he said in a voice muffled through tubes and masks, "My first sick day in twenty years."

As we round the cape, my father's chest is tense and heaving. For rest, we find a log thrown up by the sea and sit looking down at the little wrecks beaten by the surf: legless shells of lady crabs, mermaid purses torn from their moorings, the busted-up helmets of horseshoe crabs.

The last hurricane-force storm to hit this region was a giant northeaster that struck hard on Ash Wednesday, 1962. The U.S. Weather Bureau called it an extratropical cyclone, "unusual in com-position and behavior." It was a saucer-shaped affair, a strong cir-cular low-pressure system reaching up to 40,000 feet that moved out of the Midwest the first weekend in March, crossed the Appalachians, dumping three feet of snow in Virginia, and then traveled east toward the coast. Monday night it joined another, uncharted storm developing in the Atlantic, forming a giant trough of low-pressure air from Cape Hatteras to Cape Cod, six hundred miles long and three hundred miles wide. Winds blowing down the long fetch of that trough whipped up twenty- and thirty-foot waves that crashed down on the coast.

All day Tuesday, the rain fell and the waves came closer and closer upon each other, slamming into the shore every six or seven seconds. With the new moon of Ash Wednesday came heavy tides, five to ten feet above normal, which sent the sea sliding far up into the bay, into salt creeks and marshes. In Lewes, the swollen bay cut straight through the beach and moved in to meet the canal, carrying with it porches, roofs, and trailers. Up the coast at Bower's Beach, the high tide pushed houses off their foundations and ferried them a mile or more back into the marshland. Downcoast, the sea dredged new channels through the barrier beaches and reduced boardwalks, houses, and hotels to rubble.

At daybreak on Thursday, people emerged from shelters to survey the damage. They moved about numbly in the dull, sodden morning, stopping and standing before front doors banked by mountains of sand, cars submerged in seawater, boats torn loose from their moorings and spattered against pilings. In Bethany, Rehoboth, and Ocean City, five or six feet of sand packed Route 1 and some of the lower streets, topped by chairs, cocktail tables, books, kitchen utensils, and hotel beds still perfectly made. Off Lewes Beach an eight-room house unfamiliar to townspeople rose and fell in the surf. At final count, the storm left sixteen hundred people injured and twenty-five people dead. It was the storm of the century, the sort that drives home the foolhardiness of getting mixed up with the coast on anything like a permanent basis.

I pick up a tiny seastar on my finger, an apparent casualty of the recent storm, but it soon curls one arm, and I set it down in the damp sand near the surf. A grackle straddles an overturned horseshoe crab, cocking its head upside down to get at the meat. Another one plucks a rolling mole crab from a retreating wave; there's a quick flash of orange innards before the bird swallows. The day my father left the hospital he found that everything he touched and smelled gave him intense pleasure, even simple things, like the smell of the earth before rain. The experience had the effect of a kind of scouring, a sloughing off of layers. It made him look at things he had been running past for years, made him rethink life and vow to savor what remains. That meant focusing less on what is considered productive in the narrow sense and more on the ordinary, the everydayness of life. It meant more time with Gail, more bird-watching, and more Bach. Also, more loving-ness.

This wind could drive a straw into a tree. My dad's hat blows off and skips toward the surf. I run after it, miss it on the first grab, and plunge into tile waves to retrieve it, soaking my sneakers. It took me a long time to forgive my father's leaving; it is only in recent years that I have come to know him well. The love I felt for my mother was a kind of blurring of boundaries; her death came close to self-erasure. Looking up at my father over the chiseled beach, I realize that I love him not only as a child loves a parent, but as a good companion in this shifting world. I want to see him finish out his odyssey, see the wisdom of his later years. He stands to take the water-soaked hat, still breathing heavily. He hugs me tight, and I feel like leaping in a frenzy of feeling, of urgent love. Instead I lean in and together we set our shoulders against the wind and go the short way home.

When my husband and I came to Lewes three years ago, it was with the hope of having a child and giving it an early dose of salt air and warm sand. But nature at first didn't cooperate. Now it's time to leave here, move inland to the mountains, knowing that the first outdoor smells of this baby finally growing inside me will not be the sweet stink of mud flats but some waft of woodsy soil or meadow clover, the smells I grew up on.

This place has taught me: If there is some design in this world, it is composed equally of accident and order, of error and deep cre-ativity, which is what makes life at once so splendid and so strange. I have been able to see this more easily along the littoral, where the meetings and transitions are everywhere apparent.

"It gives one a feeling of confidence to see nature still busy with experiments, still dynamic, and not through or satisfied because a Devonian fish managed to end as a two-legged character with a straw hat," Loren Eiseley once wrote. "There are other things brewing and growing in the oceanic vat . . . things down there still coming ashore." I learned recently that marine biologists exploring the continental slope a few miles off Cape Henlopen and Cape May made an astonishing discovery. In the cold, the dark, the density at the bottom of the sea, a zone once thought utterly lifeless, they found an amazing array of creatures. From an area of soft ooze roughly the size of two tennis courts, they pulled 90,677 animals (not counting the little things, the nematodes, copepods, ostracods, and other meiofauna). In the group were representatives of 171 families and 14 different phyla (land has only 11 phyla). Each of the more than two hundred samples brought up something different: jellyfish, anemones, corals, snails, clams, peanut worms, ribbon worms, beard worms, and lamp shells—bivalved creatures that look like mollusks but are in fact brachiopods, animals of deep antiquity. Of the 798 species, 460 had never been seen before.

It seems that the life of the deep sea has diversified by distributing itself over countless little environments, many of them created by the animals themselves: mounds of sediments, depressions, empty worm burrows, patches of seaweed, glass sponges rising on graceful stems. Food drifts down to these seafloor habitats in erratic pulses—a decaying fishhead or the carcass of a seal—creating tiny local communities different from those just a few meters away. Scientists estimate that they've surveyed less than a tenth of one percent of the deep sea. Given the area of the seafloor, something like three hundred million square kilometers, this vast domain might hold a reservoir of ten million undescribed species. And not all of them small. Some giants lurking in the deep sea pastures have recently surfaced in human awareness: tube worms ten feet long with furry blood-red tentacles living around deep-sea vents, the giant squid *Architeuthis,* big as a city bus, which has never been seen but has yielded up a monstrous tentacle or two. News came this spring of the first new species of whale to be discovered in nearly three decades, an elusive beaked creature with a tiny cranium, a long jaw, few teeth, and an appetite for squid.

Imagine inventing water—two hydrogen atoms and a single oxygen atom in a V-shaped molecule with an odd electrical asymmetry that makes one molecule bond with another and thus holds the ocean together, along with salt and all the other earthly elements in seawater—and then on top of it a hammerhead shark, sixty-foot squid, this whole rich broth of life!

That I should be surprised by the sea's diversity is a sign of deep land bias. After all, life was born in the sea, and evolution's big bang, that explosive radiation of animal forms in which nearly all the major groups now on earth first appeared, took place in primordial waters. Of these groups only a small number evolved the basic trick of living outside the ocean. Movement to land was the exception, not the rule.

The sea has a habit of upsetting expectations. Among my favorite new findings is one that has stood on its head the traditional view of ocean life as a linear or pyramidal food chain, in which plankton are eaten by tiny crustaceans such as copepods, which feed the larger animals, and so forth, in an uninterrupted line from smallest algae to largest whale. The idea goes back a long way. Peter Brueghel the Elder drew the first picture of it in 1556, a nightmarish image of an enormous glassy-eyed fish beached on a river bank, its gaping mouth regurgitating a cornucopia of smaller fish, which are in turn regurgitating even smaller fish. Some early species of marine pathologist is slicing open the belly of the big fish with an oversized bread knife, while his unfortunate partner stumbles away, half man, half fish, his piscine appetite apparently having gotten the better of him.

This pyramidal view held for centuries until those marine ecologists charged with the duty of finding ever smaller particles in the sea discovered picoplankton, bacteria less than two microns in size—hundreds of millions in every liter of seawater. These marine bacteria are too small to be eaten by the tiny crustaceans that are the major food source for much of the marine web. The bacteria feed on waste produced by algae and protozoa, and are, in turn, eaten by some of the same organisms.

Then came the discovery that in a single teaspoon of seawater there are more than seventy-five million viruses, those tiny particles composed of gene and protein that exist somewhere between the living and the dead. Viruses do not eat, move, or reproduce on their own. When they invade a living cell, they commandeer its genetic machinery and reproduce. The cell dies and its membrane bursts, releasing a flood of new virus particles, which go off by the thousands. (We are swimming in a sea of DNA.) The chief aim of these marine viruses, it turns out, is to infect their larger microbial brethren, the bacteria, and also phytoplankton. In so doing, they may determine the mix and abundance of those organisms that feed so much of marine life. Since a virus can destroy a whale as well as a bacterium, it's not at all clear what sits at the bottom of the pyramid or the top. In fact, the only certainty is that the marine food web is no pyramid at all, but an immense tangle of biological activity from surface to floor.

Among those hordes of viruses floating in the sea today are perhaps the descendants of some that moved into the earliest cells, carrying bits of foreign genetic information, wayward genes that eventually led to the whole multifarious tumult of life, including our own odd species, with its tendency to find more meaning in life on the other side of stopped breath.

Edward O. Wilson has said that the human mind does not have an instant capacity to grasp reality in its full chaotic richness, the accidents and quirks, the unruly elements, the organisms imperfect and emergent. The world abounds in phenomena that are still mysterious and unpredictable. What happens to a person in anaphylactic shock is well understood, but not the question of why the same allergen will produce body-wracking in one individual and no response in another. That is still a puzzle having to do with the question of genetic individuality. We have only a ghost of an idea of what triggers the differentiation of cells into a photosynthesizing cell in a strand of marsh grass, the sperm of an osprey, or the cell of a human heart. The full spectrum of life—its subtle relationships, strange couplings, chains of dependence, as evident on a mud flat as in a rain forest—remains unplumbed.

Weather, too, is a conundrum. We can restart a man's heart but we can't forecast the landfall of a hurricane. Some climate experts say that weather is simply a seamless web of abnormalities, affected by each gust of wind, each flap of a butterfly. And now it's apparent that things could be even more iffy than they are. Scientists studying the planets of our solar system have found that they tend to tilt chaotically on their axes. The accumulation of small gravitational tugs from neighboring planets, coupled with each planet's own wobbly rotations, set up resonances, which change the shape of the planet's orbit and the tilt of its axis. A planet's tilt angle determines the seasons. Mars may undergo chaotic variations in its tilt angle up to 85 degrees, causing wild extremes of climate. Fortunately for us, the moon, so big and so close, exerts enough gravitational pull not only to heave the oceans twice daily, but to keep Earth's tilt from varying more than a degree or two. So in a sense, the moon is our climate regulator, stabilizing us enough to permit our own familiar brand of chaotic weather and evolution of life.

Given all the confusion and complexity in the world, so much at sixes and sevens, so much wild change and variety—given all this, the wonder is that there is order or structure at all, likenesses or rules, universals on a giant scale.

I never fully understood my father's love for mathematics until I read about pi, that transcendental number with its digits marching to infinity in a pattern as yet unfathomable. "Pi is obvious in the disks of the moon and the sun," writes Richard Preston. "The double helix of DNA revolves around pi. Pi hides in the rainbow, and sits in the pupil of the eye, and when a raindrop falls into water pi emerges in the spreading rings. Pi can be found in waves and ripples and spectra of all kinds, and therefore pi occurs in colors and music. Nature seems to know mathematics."

The shore has taught me this, too. Out on the tip of the cape one morning, cloudy gray but gleaming, I saw things the way physicists say they are, when a dense cloud of shorebirds appeared, then vanished, then appeared again like a flash of mercury, their swerves and dips and semaphore twists so unified they seemed a single wave rolling from light to dark to light again.

The evolutionary reason for flocking is defense; hawks seem confounded by the unity of the flock and are unable to concentrate their hunger on any one individual. A flock may rush an attacking raptor, bursting apart in its face. The phenomenon has been noted in fish, too. Minnows zip into a compact quiver when alarmed by the rising shadow of a predator, and perform complex maneuvers in the face of attack, splaying apart like a fountain, or exploding outward radially like a bursting bomb. The fish rely on their sense of distant touch, the lateral line, to "know" where their neighbors are. No collisions have ever been observed.

Flocking birds and schooling fish seem to have entered a dimension in which signals are superfluous. A zoologist who filmed a flock of thousands of dunlins discovered that the swerves and turns spread through a flock from bird to neighboring bird in a seventieth of a second. That's about three times faster than the speed at which a single bird can react to the movement of its neighbor. The high-speed patterns of motion in flocks and schools are so fluid, precise, and well coordinated that they have suggested to some scientists ideas of thought transference and electromagnetic communication. But the patterns more likely result from individual birds and fish following a few simple behavioral rules: Avoid predators, match the speed of your neighbors, and don't collide with them. The patterns unfold on their own, from the bottom up. Beautiful they are and yet, presumably, they depend upon no puppeteer, no "higher intelligence" at all.

Little examples abound of disorderly systems crystallizing into neat mathematical order. When waves encounter some random variation on the shoreline, even something so diminutive as a child's sandcastle, the water will reshape the anomaly by depositing sand or carrying it away until it has sculpted evenly spaced scallops along the beach. Drizzle sandgrains on a pile in a steady trickle, and the pile will grow into a cone-shaped mound with a characteristic slope or angle, the angle of repose, a convex version of the ant lion's pit. The pile will reach this state all by itself, without any hand shaping it. Add one more speck of sand to the pile, and it may cause just a tiny shift in a few grains or, if one collision leads to another in a chain reaction, a catastrophic landslide. Scientists note that little shifts are common; big ones, rare. The law dictating the frequency and size of the avalanches is ubiquitous in nature. It's seen in the flow of water through a river, the pattern of energy release during earthquakes and forest fires, the ebb and flow of sunspot activity, even the evolution of species.

It seems to me that the mind is peculiarly well equipped to find beauty in the unity among vastly different things, to take pleasure in the discovery that we are 70 percent water, like the planet, that the chemical composition of our blood is strangely similar to that of seawater. The more unlikely the likeness, the more beautiful.

Take chaos, the amplifying of small uncertainties in dynamic systems like water and weather and the oscillations of the heart, which results in behavior that cannot be predicted in the long term, but follows mathematical laws nonetheless. Chaos is everywhere in the natural world. When blue mussels bunch together higgledy-piggledy in chaotic fashion on the sea bottom, the bumpy, irregular surface of the thicket causes turbulence in the water flow, a maelstrom of eddies and whorls still not fully understood. (There's so much going on in turbulent water flow that not even the world's fastest supercomputers can track a cubic centimeter of water for more than a few seconds.) It turns out that the chaotic flow draws phytoplankton from the surface down to the bottom dwellers, enhancing the mussels' food supply. So a mollusk finds chaos a part of its essential everyday equipment.

The same may be true for us. Some scientists are convinced that our minds spend much of their time in a state of chaos directly analogous to that of the weather or the turbulent flow of water over a bumpy bed of mussels, that it is the very property of the brain that makes perception possible. In response to the smallest of inputs, vast collections of neurons shift their pattern of activity, allowing the brain to respond flexibly to the outside world. As Wallace Stevens says: "The law of chaos is the law of ideas, of improvisations and seasons of belief."

When I return to the cape a week or so after the storm, the scarps are mostly gone, dissolved again into the beach face, but the ocean is still roiling with several days of wind and rain. On the way here, I saw two male summer tanagers razzing each other, staking out their spring territory, and a collection of kingbirds on the phone wires above the beach plum, which has erupted in full white bloom.

A light breeze is blowing as I head out along the ocean side toward the tip of the cape. Bits of spindrift blowing across the sand lodge and pass into iridescent bubbles. Last night I read about a new theory linking bubbles with the origin of life. It says that the simple chemicals present on early Earth—hydrogen, nitrogen, carbon—gave birth to such big complicated molecules as RNA, DNA, and proteins with the help of bubbles on the surface of primordial seas. The theory is the boldest kind of guesswork, but is rooted in some solid facts. Bubbles are just whiffs of gas enclosed in a skin of water, born of the action of wind and waves, the splash of raindrops and snowflakes, the belch of undersea volcanoes. At any given moment, they cover three or four percent of the ocean surface, an area roughly the size of North America. As a bubble travels through the atmosphere and ocean, it scavenges organic materials, minerals, metals, and clay particles, then concentrates them within its skin. Here they grow in size and complexity in response to changing temperatures and pressures. When the bubble pops, a rich little brew of chemicals is spit into the air and carried aloft by winds. The theory goes that sometime during Earth's first 700 million years, atmospheric chemistry triggered by lightning and ultraviolet light from the sun worked its alchemy on these chemical dollops, and the molecules grew even more complex, fell to sea as rain or snow, and were once again sucked into a bubble. The cycle was repeated again and again in the early seas, until some lucky collection of concentrated chemicals vaulted into being as a nucleic acid, parent of us all.

Sand has been moving during the night, riding currents from the south to feed the cape. My progress around the hook is slow. There's new ground here. It's low tide. And every few feet I stoop to scrutinize the wrack line, the beards of seaweed and smashed clam shells. I'm moving slowly these days, anyway, feeling heavier and more than a little morning sick. Pregnancy has made me first and foremost my physical self, a warm thumping habitat of bone and blood. I should be at home packing, not dawdling over sea grass and bubbles. But it's good to be out: schools of little whitecaps, cries of the sanderling and the osprey, light sea wind like a child's breath.

$\mathcal{O}$RION $\mathcal{R}$ISES ON THE $\mathcal{D}$UNES

Henry Beston

$\mathcal{S}$o came August to its close, ending its last day with a night so luminous and still that a mood came over me to sleep out on the open beach under the stars. There are nights in summer when darkness and ebbing tide quiet the universal wind, and this August night was full of that quiet of absence, and the sky was clear. South of my house, between the bold fan of a dune and the wall of a plateau, a sheltered hollow opens seaward, and to this nook I went, shouldering my blankets sailorwise. In the star-shine the hollow was darker than the immense and solitary beach, and its floor was still pleasantly warm with the overflow of day.

I fell asleep uneasily, and woke again as one wakes out-of-doors. The vague walls about me breathed a pleasant smell of sand, there was no sound, and the broken circle of grass above was as motionless as something in a house. Waking again, hours afterward, I felt the air grown colder and heard a little advancing noise of waves. It was still night. Sleep gone and past recapture, I drew on my clothes and went to the beach. In the luminous east, two great stars aslant were rising clear of the exhalations of darkness gathered at the rim of night and ocean—Betelgeuse and Bellatrix, the shoulders of Orion. Autumn had come, and the Giant stood again at the horizon of day and the ebbing year, his belt still hidden in the bank of cloud, his feet in the deeps of space and the far surges of the sea.

My year upon the beach had come full circle; it was time to close my door. Seeing the great suns, I thought of the last time I marked them in the spring, in the April west above the moors, dying into the light and sinking. I saw them of old above the iron waves of black December, sparkling afar. Now, once again, the Hunter rose to drive summer south before him, once again autumn followed on his steps. I had seen the ritual of the sun; I had shared the elemental world. Wraiths of memories began to take shape. I saw the sleet of the great storm slanting down again into the grass under the thin seepage of moon, the blue-white spill of an immense billow on the outer bar, the swans in the high October sky, the sunset madness and splendour of the year's terns over the dunes, the clouds of beach birds arriving, the eagle solitary in the blue. And because I had known this outer and secret world, and been able to live as I had lived, reverence and gratitude greater and deeper than ever possessed me, sweeping every emotion else aside, and space and silence an instant closed together over life. Then time gathered again like a cloud, and presently the stars began to pale over an ocean still dark with remembered night.

During the months that have passed since that September morning some have asked me what understanding of Nature one shapes from so strange a year? I would answer that one's first appreciation is a sense that the creation is still going on, that the creative forces are as great and as active to-day as they have ever been, and that to-morrow's morning will be as heroic as any of the world. *Creation is here and now.* So near is man to the creative pageant, so much a part is he of the endless and incredible experiment, that any glimpse he may have will be but the revelation of a moment, a solitary note heard in a symphony thundering through debatable existences of time. Poetry is as necessary to comprehension as science. It is as impossible to live without reverence as it is without joy.

And what of Nature itself, you say—that callous and cruel engine, red in tooth and fang? Well, it is not so much of an engine as you think. As for "red in tooth and fang," whenever I hear the phrase or its intellectual echoes I know that some passer-by has been getting life from books. It is true that there are grim arrangements. Beware of judging them by whatever human values are in style. As well expect Nature to answer to your human values as to come into your house and sit in a chair. The economy of nature, its checks and balances, its measurements of competing life—all this is its great marvel and has an ethic of its own. Live in Nature, and you will soon see that for all its non-human rhythm, it is no cave of pain. As I write I think of my beloved birds of the great beach, and of their beauty and their zest of living. And if there are fears, know also that Nature has its unexpected and unappreciated mercies.

Whatever attitude to human existence you fashion for yourself, know that it is valid only if it be the shadow of an attitude to Nature. A human life, so often likened to a spectacle upon a stage, is more justly a ritual. The ancient values of dignity, beauty, and poetry which sustain it are of Nature's inspiration; they are born of the mystery and beauty of the world. Do no dishonour to the earth lest you dishonour the spirit of man. Hold your hands out over the earth as over a flame. To all who love her, who open to her the doors of their veins, she gives of her strength, sustaining them with her own measureless tremor of dark life. Touch the earth, love the earth, honour the earth, her plains, her valleys, her hills, and her seas; rest your spirit in her solitary places. For the gifts of life are the earth's and they are given to all, and they are the songs of birds at daybreak, Orion and the Bear, and dawn seen over ocean from the beach.

$\mathcal{W}$HO $\mathcal{O}$WNS THE $\mathcal{B}$EACH?

John Hay

$\mathcal{I}$n the "off" and empty season, after the tides had erased all signs of a hundred thousand human feet, it was hard to believe that the beach could be owned or claimed by anyone. It took on the air's cold or warmth, receiving, passing things on, from one day and seasonal mood to another, not as on the land with its plant and animal reactions and obstructions, the hiding; shadowing; coming forth intermittently; but in bold and naked sight, reducing weather to its single qualities.

One day the Cape would be sunny and comparatively warm, and on the next in would come the authentic northern wind, the polar air, roaring and sweeping around with fierce abandon, riotously hard and cold, freezing the ground, cutting at a man, diving on him with an icy weight. The winter wind is so definite when it comes, overwhelming a fairly moderate climate, where roses often bloom late into the fall and hollies grow, as to make you think of icebergs, sliding down from the north unexpectedly to stand hundreds of feet overhead. The sky, threatening snow, writhes and purls up with gray clouds spreading fanwise like auroras, and in the evening the sun goes down with a coppery band on the horizon overhung by a bank of steely-blue clouds as menacing as a shark.

And the great beach received what came to it, retaining its primal right to a deeper breath and regularity, a harsh "poverty-stricken" environment where man has no lease worth the paper. It did seem utterly deserted, although the herring gulls and blackbacks flew up steeply over the wind-buffeted waves, then banked and glided away, and draggers occasionally moved parallel to the beach bucking the choppy seas, their lines out astern. The wind threw stinging clouds of sand ahead of it. Except for the fishermen and the gulls, it was an abandoned world, glistening wide and cold, lost to importance and sense so far as human society was concerned. For many there is no force quite so inclusive as his own.

Since the beach is comparatively empty and isolated during fall and winter, the sight of life on its sands may seem as rare as a rider approaching you across the desert. I remember what an extraordinary thing it seemed one afternoon to see a tiny red crab moving very slowly along, high-legged over the bare slopes of the beach. I identified it later as a species of spider crab. Green crabs, rock crabs, calico crabs, and others are common along the protected shores of the Cape, but out on this stretch of beach they are rarities. This baby with its beak, antennae, and eyes backed and covered by a knobbed and spiky shell, seemed like an exotic from another world, which in fact it was, having been flung in by the surf from rocks and seaweed forests in the waters beyond it. It not only added to the beach, but to me, since it made me realize that these sands were only shelving off into further dimensions. The beach is a repository of freight, wreckage, and lives from foreign lands.

This also happens occasionally on land. We all know that the sea is out there, that the wind swirls over us, and the storms carry more traffic than planes, but strangers sometimes appear as if to prove that no place is what it seems to be. One spring a vermillion flycatcher suddenly appeared in the neighborhood. I saw it in its exciting tropical gaiety as it flew down next to a shining patch of spring rain on an asphalt road. It is a native of Texas and New Mexico. Black or turkey buzzards ride the great airs of spring and sometimes fly northward, wheeling unexpectedly overhead. In November of 1962 I saw a black stork, *Ciconia nigra,* which had somehow managed to make it all the way across the Atlantic Ocean, perhaps managing to stop for rests in such areas as Greenland and Newfoundland. It landed near the Coast Guard Station, now National Seashore Park headquarters, at Eastham, in an exhausted state, to be picked up by the Audubon Society and later transported to the warmer climate of Florida.

The black stork breeds from Central Europe to Korea and China, and it winters in Africa after a long round of migratory journeys. Its advent was greeted with a certain amount of mild curiosity and even some jokes in the local paper; one of which had to do with its liking for Cape Cod scallops on its arrival. What better reason for coming here! (The truth is that like other newly captured birds, it had to be force-fed.) In any case it was a rare event, joining Cape Cod with Africa, and to see it was equivalent to seeing an antelope on Route 6. With large strong wings, attenuated red legs, a long, stout pinkish bill, red around the eyes, it waited in captivity with what seemed to be an air of great sadness, transplanted as it was, taken in to a gray cold land without any sound but engines, human voices, and the wind, without any greenery but the thin-needled pines; and it roosted silently, twitching occasionally in its inactive unused state, an unwilling, unwitting Marco Polo in New England.

This is a narrow place, restricted by nature and by men, but foreign lives still fly to it like sparks in the air, and the sea beyond it takes things on their way with more room than analogy is yet aware of. What the sea sends in, like a dead skate, a starfish, horse mussel, or finger sponge, seems perfectly familiar as fish, marine, background animals, but they are also genuine primitives, remote not only from human physiology and complete understanding but from that part of the earth's surface that we inhabit. In fact many of the hints of marine life that are either brought up along the beach, or that appear in offshore waters, like a whale or a dolphin, having a theatricality, an off-stage hint of a wealth of other acts, tricks, and forms still to be seen. The simple, primal watery element has embodiments of use which are comprehensible and have been studied for a long time, but these are endowed with physical natures and captivity that might make an air-breathing, earth-bound human quite envious.

During a violent coast storm, with winds up to seventy and eighty miles an hour, an exhausted harbor porpoise was cast up on a bay beach recently and there it died. I confess I had never seen one out of water or even close to me before. For all the pictures I had seen, and all I had read, nothing prepared me for such perfection. Its round body, four to five feet long, was butt-ended at its head, in which there were small eyes, and small teeth in the jaws. It had just as much of the quality of flow as a raindrop, and at the same time was a solid packing of energy. Its skin graded down from the jet black of its back and upper sides through streaks of gray like rain along the sea down to a white belly, and without scales, it had a thick, smooth satiny polish like ebony or horn, perhaps reminiscent of synthetic rubber or plastic but of an organic texture which neither of those products could equal. The porpoise had a single fin on its back and a tail that could strike vertically for power and thrust. Its body was fairly heavy, weighing about a hundred pounds, but everything of speed and liquidity and dashing, leaping strength was reflected there. It lay on the upper part of the beach, conspicuous among the long piles of storm litter, the logs, pieces of broken dories, and thick seaweed, spectacular in its simplicity, a black and white that made me think of breaking waves in the night sea. I saw it curve over the surfaces of the water with consummate grace, slide away, and disappear.

"Where did you ever see more of nothing?" I was once asked as I looked out over endless dry Texas plains billowing like waves. Nothing or everything. Who knows? Who knows what the emptiness leads to or contains? The beach lies open. Its sands and rattling stones lead back through ages of weathering and change and are at the same time part of the wide give and take of the present.

The tiny spider crab, though isolated on the beach, was also a link with a teeming offshore existence, which hid in shadowy worlds of kelp and rockweed, or floated and roamed by with a free energy that was in complete denial of our tightening fall and winter world. Backed by a cliff, walking on sands shadowed and cold, faced by the churning waves, it is hard to believe in a life so rich. There are no rocky shores revealed at low tide and streaming with weed to prove the temperate fertility of the sea. The beach is a transition zone between one environment and another, but except in those areas where the cliffs are reduced to low sand hills, protecting a marsh or estuary behind them, the transition is a sharp one, the sands dipping from the inconstant sky to the constancy of salt water.

Along those stretches of beach where the sea has taken stones and boulders and deposited them offshore, storms sometimes bring in fairly large quantities of seaweed, which need beds of stone for their attachment. The fucus or rockweed, the laminaria or kelp, and some of the "red" algae like Irish moss which are among the more common kinds found along the beach, have no roots, since the plants take all their nourishment from the sea water that surrounds them, but are anchored by holdfasts, stubby structures which in the laminaria may look like the exposed, above-ground roots of some tropical trees, and in the fucus a round expansion of the tissues at its base, which is strongly and tightly sealed to the surface of rocks and stones.

Everything about these weeds, with divided, narrow, or tapering fronds to resist being torn by the waves, with bladders serving as floats, with gelatinous surfaces, with hollow stems, are eloquent of the nature of salt water, its ebb and flow, its depths, its capacious circulation. The seaweeds found on the beach, black, thin, dried out, or fresh and slippery, olive green, brown, or red, having been torn loose by a storm, start growing beyond the violent action of the surf and grow for the most part to a depth of some forty or fifty feet. Different varieties like different depths, but since they are not free floating unless torn loose they are not found beyond the point where rays of sunlight, necessary for manufacturing food, cannot reach them.

Over and beyond them, in surface waters where the light penetrates before being absorbed, is a vegetation, varying in abundance according to place and season, but of incredible numbers over all, the one-celled microscopic organisms that are the basic food of all the seas. The seaweeds are simple and primitive in structure compared with much of the plant life on land, the more hazardous, contrary environment, and the members of the phytoplankton (the planktonic plants), even more so, although the diatoms, which form a large part of it, show a variety of outer form. Each diatom has a skeleton, made largely of silica, an outer shell hard enough to resist easy dissolution when the plant dies. It is formed like a pillbox, or a casket, or it is shaped like a quill, a ribbon, or rod, or it is joined with others in beads and chains. Each is minute, an etched, crystalline perfection, and each is lost in other billions, which we might only see on occasion as a green or greenish-brown stain across the water.

The shells of dead diatoms rain down through the water and form thick deposits on the floor of the sea. The cliffs above the beach are full of them. Cities have been built on their fossilized shells. In their number the diatoms balance the magnitude of the sea. In size they are basic to the existence of the minuscule animals of the zooplankton that feed upon them, and are eaten by large animals in turn. A diatom's delicacy and sparkling beauty as it reflects the light could indicate that universal productivity must start with a jewel, and perhaps end with it too.

That which is minute, like the diatoms, or cells, which are the basic structure of life, is a clue to the significance of things, leading from the simple to the complex and multifarious, but finally rounding us back to where we started. A man himself is the unique single cell with its own nature. Each life has its irreducible quality. I have been told that if you look at a diatom through an electronic microscope, from one increased magnification to another, you can see all its protuberances and layers disappear, and finally a sparkling crystalline form is revealed, like a cosmic surprise.

I suppose it is part of my fate as a large and clumsy animal of the mammalian order, crashing through the underbrush, knocking down trees, and displacing earth's other inhabitants, to miss a great deal, at least with my unassisted eyes. To learn about some new form of life which I may have been passing by for years is often something of a redemption. I can then say that we have not yet been so run down by our own traffic that we have lost the capacity to see.

Not long ago a colony of bryozoans was pointed out to me, at least the gelatinous crusts of the compartments in which they lived, like little tufts and fringes attached to the fronds of seaweed cast up on the beach. They are tiny colonial animals that make cups and compartments joined together in branching stems, from which they send out little crowns of delicate, filamentous tentacles waving in the water. There are three thousand marine species of them, growing in different forms, and having different surfaces for their attachment. I had thought previously that the little pale-colored, branched tufts were a part of the seaweed. Now another small marvel had appeared on my horizon.

The beach was empty where I walked, except for bird tracks, tidal wrack, driftwood, bits of shell, or a finger sponge in evidence of the life alongside it, and depending on the warmth and receptivity to life that the season held, excepting also whatever microscopic animals might be crawling over wet surfaces around the sand grains. Again, emptiness, or poverty, is always qualified. After all the copepods, the nematodes or thread worms, and other groups unseen or unknown to me might be underfoot in vast numbers; and as I continued on there was no counting the number of little holes in the sand made by beach fleas or sand hoppers. As the autumn deepened I supposed they were unoccupied and deserted, since these beach dwellers, as I had heard it, should have been tucked away in their burrows by this time, with the door shut above their heads, waiting for March and April to bring a warm sun which could tease them out of dormancy. But one bright morning in the middle of November I saw a great many of them hard at work.

At first I noticed thousands of little mounds on the surface of the sand in a strip some six to fifteen feet wide along the upper part of the beach, following in general the outlines of the previous high tide. Where a log or shelving bank was in the way, these mounds, and the many holes accompanying them, about knitting-needle size, were concentrated on the seaward side. I noticed that shore birds had attempted to pluck the occupants from their holes and had reached down two to three inches. I scooped out the sand where a hole was, spread it around, and revealed a little animal not over a half inch long, with two large eyes covering the sides of its narrow head. The eyes were not only conspicuous, they were also startlingly white; and the sand-hopper's body flattened on both sides, was a mother-of-pearl, somewhat translucent. This odd creature, one of a family in the order of amphipods is called *Talorchestia megalophthalma,* a title that gives special credit to its eyes.

I put my pale-moon animal back in its hole, but to be held and thrust against its own volition apparently immobilized it, so I let it go free down the sands. After a second or two it made a few big and seemingly crazy hops—on sidelong springs like a toy—down a line of mounds and holes, popped into a hole and promptly disappeared.

I noticed that little spouts and bursts of sand were coming from many of these holes and with a little patience I could see some of the hoppers coming up as if to look around, as is customary with gophers and chipmunks, and then turning around and going back down again. What they were doing of course was a major job of digging, passing the sand up from one pair of legs to another and throwing it out the hole with a jerk. There was hardly time or inclination to pause and look around the far horizon. It was work that had to be done unceasingly, between tides and between seasons. Perhaps, if tomorrow brought consistently freezing temperatures, they might not appear again in any great numbers until spring; but their usual daily round meant frenzied feeding at low tide and after dark when no winged predators were around, followed by another return to the upper beach and another furiously energetic period of digging homes for themselves. Terrestrial animals, which might drown after a period of immersion, and yet bound on this strip of sand to the tides, they had a more legitimate claim to the beach than most of us.

Looking down at them, or in on their busyness, I had an extraordinary Gulliverlike feeling of encroaching on a world to which I did not belong. It was one kind of an eye looking at another without any sense of whether it was seen in turn or not, in a dichotomy of function, race, size, and place. It took the beach out of my possession. This was a place of other-world connections at which I could hardly guess. Do we need to wait for the men from Mars?

These are extravagant animals, with their grandiose if relatively blind eyes, with their feats of digging, their hunger dance. In a sense they have a very narrow range, between upper and lower tide, between one season and the next, between feeding and digging on their strip of sand, between hiding and emerging, and their life span is short; but what a use they make of it!

Talorchestia megalophthalma is now on my life list, as the "birders" put it, a pearly prodigy of moon leaps that may, for all I know, be the beach's foremost citizen.

I also caught a glimpse of another little animal as I turned over a piece of driftwood. It had numerous legs (seven pairs in all, I have learned), and a flattened body, though slightly rounded on top, and oval in shape, reminding me of a pill bug or sow bug, one of my most familiar landed neighbors, which can be found under almost any boulder or log that provides shade and moisture. The marine, or beached member of the family I met, was grayish white in color, and apparently had the same preference for moisture—if not too much, since it evidently lived at the high-tide line, and was "terrestrial" like the sand hoppers. Some of these isopods swim in the open sea, others live in shallow water, or at the low-tide line, and most are scavengers, feeding on dead animal matter.

All these and countless others are symptomatic of a tidal range, an ebb and flow that extends between sea and land in terms of millions of years of emergence and adaptation. In them the two worlds find their division and also their meeting and intercommunication. Their characteristic areas, their "life zones," from the tropics to the poles, all require extremes of risk and of the struggle to survive it. In one place or another they dance to the inexorable measure of things, limited in what they do but exceptional in their way of doing it.

On this beach, so unique, so well defined, and at the same time so widely involved, every upward surge of the waves and every bubbling retreat sinking through the sand, every range of tide, from the new moon to the old, every storm, every change in the season, every day and every night, is embodied in existence.

I would think it presumptuous of me to claim any more on behalf of a bug or myself than we could in our honest natures fulfill, but faced by the shining tides of life, I am sure we have great things to do.

My translations are on this beach. I am still a part of its measure, and when I forget those overwhelming controls that human power insists on, and all the artificiality men use to overcome their natural limitations, I begin to partake of this miraculous context. It is a cold beach, a bitter sea. Covered with cold, the sands impersonally receive the shadows moving over them tall and wide, gradually shifting and easing over slopes and shoulders toward the surf with its continual lunge, its pull and push, displacing the pale light that stands over the beach and gives it a hard winter brightness. The waves pour and foam and bubble up the beach and recede with a rainlike glistening and seething that sinks in, leaving dark stains behind. The middle part of the beach shows long thin lines like scars where the last tides came, part of the never ending drawing and erasing on this tablet of the sea's art. It is all clean, and naked, defined, and at the same time rhythmically boundless, providing everything that comes to it with an inexhaustible dimension. It needs another language, and at the same time no language could really encompass it. In this bold breath and silence moving up, scene shifting, always starting again, there are decisions of sun and waves, of wind and light, that leave me with a true silence, a great room to fill, though it is in my blood and veins, the roots of me to feel, and any companion whom I meet must be in an ancient earth sense completely new, with a freshness made of a million years.

The Hawaiian Coast

Mark Twain

At four o'clock in the afternoon we were winding down a mountain of dreary and desolate lava to the sea, and closing our pleasant land journey. This lava is the accumulation of ages; one torrent of fire after another has rolled down here in old times, and built up the island structure higher and higher. Underneath, it is honeycombed with caves; it would be of no use to dig wells in such a place; they would not hold water—you would not find any for them to hold, for that matter. Consequently, the planters depend upon cisterns.

The last lava flow occurred here so long ago that there are none now living who witnessed it. In one place it enclosed and burned down a grove of coconut trees, and the holes in the lava where the trunks stood are still visible; their sides retain the impression of the bark; the trees fell upon the burning river, and becoming partly submerged, left in it the perfect counterpart of every knot and branch and leaf, and even nut, for curiosity seekers of a long distant day to gaze upon and wonder at.

There were doubtless plenty of Kanaka sentinels on guard hereabouts at that time, but they did not leave casts of their figures in the lava as the Roman sentinels at Herculaneum and Pompeii did. It is a pity it is so, because such things are so interesting; but so it is. They probably went away. They went away early, perhaps. However, they had their merits; the Romans exhibited the higher pluck, but the Kanakas showed the sounder judgment.

Shortly we came in sight of that spot whose history is so familiar to every schoolboy in the wide world—Kealakekua Bay—the place where Captain Cook, the great circumnavigator, was killed by the natives, nearly a hundred years ago. The setting sun was flaming upon it, a summer shower was falling, and it was spanned by two magnificent rainbows. Two men who were in advance of us rode through one of these and for a moment their garments shone with a more than regal splendor. Why did not Captain Cook have taste enough to call his great discovery the Rainbow Islands? These charming spectacles are present to you at every turn; they are common in all the islands; they are visible every day, and frequently at night also—not the silvery bow we see once in an age in the States, by moonlight, but barred with all bright and beautiful colors, like the children of the sun and rain. I saw one of them a few nights ago. What the sailors call "rain dogs"—little patches of rainbow—are often seen drifting about the heavens in these latitudes, like stained cathedral windows.

Kealakekua Bay is a little curve like the last kink of a snail shell, winding deep into the land, seemingly not more than a mile wide from shore to shore. It is bounded on one side—where the murder was done—by a little flat plain, on which stands a coconut grove and some ruined houses; a steep wall of lava, a thousand feet high at the upper end and three or four hundred at the lower, comes down from the mountain and bounds the inner extremity of it. From this wall the place takes its name, *Kealakekua,* which in the native tongue signifies "the Pathway of the Gods." They say (and still believe, in spite of their liberal education in Christianity) that the great god Lono, who used to live upon the hillside, always traveled that causeway when urgent business connected with heavenly affairs called him down to the seashore in a hurry.

As the red sun looked across the placid ocean through the tall, clean stems of the coconut trees, like a blooming whiskey bloat through the bars of a city prison, I went and stood in the edge of the water on the flat rock pressed by Captain Cook's feet when the blow was dealt which took away his life, and tried to picture in my mind the doomed man struggling in the midst of the multitude of exasperated savages—the men in the ship crowding to the vessel's side and gazing in anxious dismay toward the shore—the—but I discovered that I could not do it.

It was growing dark, the rain began to fall, we could see that the distant *Boomerang* was helplessly becalmed at sea, and so I adjourned to the cheerless little box of a warehouse and sat down to smoke and think, and wish the ship would make the land—for we had not eaten much for ten hours and were viciously hungry.

Plain unvarnished history takes the romance out of Captain Cook's assassination, and renders a deliberate verdict of justifiable homicide. Wherever he went among the islands, he was cordially received and welcomed by the inhabitants, and his ships lavishly supplied with all manner of food. He returned these kindnesses with insult and ill treatment. Perceiving that the people took him for the long-vanished and lamented god Lono, he encouraged them in the delusion for the sake of the limitless power it gave him; but during the famous disturbance at this spot, and while he and his comrades were surrounded by fifteen thousand maddened savages, he received a hurt and betrayed his earthly origin with a groan. It was his death warrant. Instantly a shout went up: "He groans!—he is not a god!" So they closed in upon him and dispatched him.

His flesh was stripped from the bones and burned (except nine pounds of it which were sent on board the ships). The heart was hung up in a native hut, where it was found and eaten by three children, who mistook it for the heart of a dog. One of these children grew to be a very old man, and died in Honolulu a few years ago. Some of Cook's bones were recovered and consigned to the deep by the officers of the ships.

Small blame should attach to the natives for the killing of Cook. They treated him well. In return, he abused them. He and his men inflicted bodily injury upon many of them at different times, and killed at least three of them before they offered any proportionate retaliation.

Near the shore we found "Cook's Monument"—only a coconut stump, four feet high and about a foot in diameter at the butt. It had lava boulders piled around its base to hold it up and keep it in its place, and it was entirely sheathed over, from top to bottom, with rough, discolored sheets of copper, such as ships' bottoms are coppered with. Each sheet had a rude inscription scratched upon it—with a nail, apparently—and in every case the execution was wretched. Most of these merely recorded the visits of British naval commanders to the spot, but one of them bore this legend:

Near this spot fell
CAPTAIN JAMES COOK,
The Distinguished Circumnavigator,
who Discovered these Islands A.D. 1778

After Cook's murder, his second in command, on board the ship, opened fire upon the swarms of natives on the beach, and one of his cannon balls cut this coconut tree short off and left this monumental stump standing. It looked sad and lonely enough to us, out there in the rainy twilight. But there is no other monument to Captain Cook. True, up on the mountainside we had passed by a large enclosure like an ample hog-pen, built of lava blocks, which marks the spot where Cook's flesh was stripped from his bones and burned; but this is not properly a monument, since it was erected by the natives themselves, and less to do honor to the circumnavigator than for the sake of convenience in roasting him. A thing like a guideboard was elevated above this pen on a tall pole, and formerly there was an inscription upon it describing the memorable occurrence that had there taken place; but the sun and the wind have long ago so defaced it as to render it illegible.

Toward midnight a fine breeze sprang up and the schooner soon worked herself into the bay and cast anchor. The boat came ashore for us, and in a little while the clouds and the rain were all gone. The moon was beaming tranquilly down on land and sea, and we two were stretched upon the deck sleeping the refreshing sleep and dreaming the happy dreams that are only vouchsafed to the weary and the innocent.

In the breezy morning we went ashore and visited the ruined temple of the last god Lono. The high chief cook of this temple—the priest who presided over it and roasted the human sacrifices—was uncle to Obookia, and at one time that youth was an apprentice priest under him. Obookia was a young native of fine mind, who, together with three other native boys, was taken to New England by the captain of a whaleship during the reign of Kamehameha I, and they were the means of attracting the attention of the religious world to their country. This resulted in the sending of missionaries there. And this Obookia was the very same sensitive savage who sat down on the church steps and wept because his people did not have the Bible. That incident has been very elaborately painted in many a charming Sunday-school book—aye, and told so plaintively and so tenderly that I have cried over it in Sunday school myself, on general principles, although at a time when I did not know much and could not understand why the people of the Sandwich Islands needed to worry so much about it as long as they did not know there was a Bible at all.

Obookia was converted and educated, and was to have returned to his native land with the first missionaries, had he lived. The other native youths made the voyage, and two of them did good service, but the third, William Kanui, fell from grace afterward, for a time, and when the gold excitement broke out in California he journeyed thither and went to mining, although he was fifty years old. He succeeded pretty well, but the failure of Page, Bacon & Co. relieved him of six thousand dollars, and then, to all intents and purposes, he was a bankrupt in his old age and he resumed service in the pulpit again. He died in Honolulu in 1864.

Quite a broad tract of land near the temple, extending from the sea to the mountaintop, was sacred to the god Lono in olden times—so sacred that if a common native set his sacrilegious foot upon it it was judicious for him to make his will, because his time had come. He might go around it by water, but he could not cross it. It was well sprinkled with pagan temples and stocked with awkward, homely idols carved out of logs of wood. There was a temple devoted to prayers for rain—and with fine sagacity it was placed at a point so well up on the mountainside that if you prayed there twenty-four times a day for rain you would be likely to get it every time. You would seldom get to your Amen before you would have to hoist your umbrella.

And there was a large temple near at hand which was built in a single night, in the midst of storm and thunder and rain, by the ghastly hands of dead men! Tradition says that by the weird glare of the lightning a noiseless multitude of phantoms were seen at their strange labor far up the mountainside at dead of night—flitting hither and thither and bearing great lava blocks clasped in their nerveless fingers—appearing and disappearing as the pallid luster fell upon their forms and faded away again. Even to this day, it is said, the natives hold this dread structure in awe and reverence, and will not pass by it in the night.

At noon I observed a bevy of nude native young ladies bathing in the sea, and went and sat down on their clothes to keep them from being stolen. I begged them to come out, for the sea was rising and I was satisfied that they were running some risk. But they were not afraid, and presently went on with their sport. They were finished swimmers and divers, and enjoyed themselves to the last degree. They swam races, splashed and ducked and tumbled each other about, and filled the air with their laughter. It is said that the first thing an Islander learns is how to swim; learning to walk, being a matter of smaller consequence, comes afterward. One hears tales of native men and women swimming ashore from vessels many miles at sea—more miles, indeed, than I dare vouch for or even mention. And they tell of a native diver who went down in thirty- or forty-foot waters and brought up an anvil! I think he swallowed the anvil afterward, if my memory serves me. However, I will not urge this point.

I have spoken, several times, of the god Lono—I may as well furnish two or three sentences concerning him.

The idol the natives worshiped for him was a slender, unornamented staff twelve feet long. Tradition says he was a favorite god on the island of Hawaii—a great king who had been deified for meritorious services—just our own fashion of rewarding heroes, with the difference that we would have made him a postmaster instead of a god, no doubt. In an angry moment he slew his wife, a goddess named Kaikilani Aiii. Remorse of conscience drove him mad, and tradition presents us the singular spectacle of a god traveling "on the shoulder"; for in his gnawing grief he wandered about from place to place boxing and wrestling with all whom he met. Of course this pastime soon lost its novelty, inasmuch as it must necessarily have been the case that when so powerful a deity sent a frail human opponent "to grass" he never came back any more. Therefore, he instituted games called *makahiki,* and ordered that they should be held in his honor, and then sailed for foreign lands on a three-cornered raft, stating that he would return someday—and that was the last of Lono. He was never seen any more; his raft got swamped, perhaps. But the people always expected his return, and thus they were easily led to accept Captain Cook as the restored god.

Some of the old natives believed Cook was Lono to the day of their death; but many did not, for they could not understand how he could die if he was a god.

Only a mile or so from Kealakekua Bay is a spot of historic interest—the place where the last battle was fought for idolatry. Of course we visited it, and came away as wise as most people do who go and gaze upon such mementos of the past when in an unreflective mood.

While the first missionaries were on their way around the Horn the idolatrous customs which had obtained in the island, as far back as tradition reached, were suddenly broken up. Old Kamehameha I was dead, and his son, Liholiho, the new king, was a free liver, a roistering, dissolute fellow, and hated the restraints of the ancient *tabu*. His assistant in the government, Kaahumanu, the queen dowager, was proud and high-spirited, and hated the *tabu* because it restricted the privileges of her sex and degraded all women very nearly to the level of brutes. So the case stood. Liholiho had half a mind to put his foot down, Kaahumanu had a whole mind to badger him into doing it, and whiskey did the rest. It was probably the rest. It was probably the first time whiskey ever prominently figured as an aid to civilization. Liholiho came up to Kailua as drunk as a piper and attended a great feast; the determined queen spurred his drunken courage up to a reckless pitch, and then, while all the multitude stared in black dismay, he moved deliberately forward and sat down with the women! They saw him eat from the same vessel with them, and were appalled! Terrible moments drifted slowly by, and still the king ate, still he lived, still the lightnings of the insulted gods were withheld! Then conviction came like a revelation—the superstitions of a hundred generations passed from before the people like a cloud, and a shout went up, "The *tabu* is broken! The *tabu* is broken!"

Thus did King Liholiho and his dreadful whiskey preach the first sermon and prepare the way for the new gospel that was speeding southward over the waves of the Atlantic.

The *tabu* broken and destruction failing to follow the awful sacrilege, the people, with that childlike precipitancy which has always characterized them, jumped to the conclusion that their gods were a weak and wretched swindle, just as they formerly jumped to the conclusion that Captain Cook was no god, merely because he groaned, and promptly killed him without stopping to inquire whether a god might not groan as well as a man if it suited his convenience to do it; and satisfied that the idols were powerless to protect themselves, they went to work at once and pulled them

233

down—hacked them to pieces—applied the torch—annihilated them!

The pagan priests were furious. And well they might be; they had held the fattest offices in the land, and now they were beggared; they had been great—they had stood above the chiefs—and now they were vagabonds. They raised a revolt; they scared a number of people into joining their standard, and Bekuokalani, an ambitious offshoot of royalty, was easily persuaded to become their leader.

In the first skirmish the idolaters triumphed over the royal army sent against them, and full of confidence they resolved to march upon Kailua. The king sent an envoy to try and conciliate them, and came very near being an envoy short by the operation; the savages not only refused to listen to him, but wanted to kill him. So the king sent his men forth under Major General Kalaimoku and the two hosts met at Kuamoo. The battle was long and fierce—men and women fighting side by side, as was the custom—and when the day was done the rebels were flying in every direction in hopeless panic, and idolatry and the *tabu* were dead in the land!

The royalists marched gaily home to Kailua glorifying the new dispensation. "There is no power in the gods," said they; "they are a vanity and a lie. The army with idols was weak; the army without idols was strong and victorious!"

The nation was without a religion.

The missionary ship arrived in safety shortly afterward, timed by providential exactness to meet the emergency, and the Gospel was planted as in a virgin soil.

At noon, we hired a Kanaka to take us down to the ancient ruins at Honaunau in his canoe—price two dollars—reasonable enough, for a sea voyage of eight miles, counting both ways.

The native canoe is an irresponsible-looking contrivance. I cannot think of anything to liken it to but a boy's sled runner hollowed out, and that does not quite convey the correct idea. It is about fifteen feet long, high and pointed at both ends, is a foot and a half or two feet deep, and so narrow that if you wedged a fat man into it you might not get him out again. It sits on top of the water like a duck, but it has an outrigger and does not upset easily, if you keep still. This outrigger is formed of two long bent sticks like plow handles, which project from one side, and to their outer ends is bound a curved beam composed of an extremely light wood, which skims along the surface of the water and thus saves you from an upset on that side, while the outrigger's weight is not so easily lifted as to make an upset on the other side a thing to be greatly feared. Still, until one gets used to sitting perched upon this knifeblade, he is apt to reason within himself that it would be more comfortable if there were just an outrigger or so on the other side also.

I had the bow seat, and Billings sat amidships and faced the Kanaka, who occupied the stern of the craft and did the paddling. With the first stroke the trim shell of a thing shot out from the shore like an arrow. There was not much to see. While we were on the shallow water of the reef, it was pastime to look down into the limpid depths at the large bunches of branching coral—the unique shrubbery of the sea. We lost that, though, when we got out into the dead blue water of the deep. But we had the picture of the surf, then, dashing angrily against the crag-bound shore and sending a foaming spray high into the air. There was interest in this beetling border, too, for it was honeycombed with quaint caves and arches and tunnels, and had a rude semblance of the dilapidated architecture of ruined keeps and castles rising out of the restless sea. When this novelty ceased to be a novelty, we turned our eyes shoreward and gazed at the long mountain with its rich green forests stretching up into the curtaining clouds, and at the specks of houses in the rearward distance and the diminished schooner riding sleepily at anchor. And when these grew tiresome we dashed boldly into the midst of a school of huge, beastly porpoises engaged at their eternal game of arching over a wave and disappearing, and then doing it over again and keeping it up—always circling over, in that way, like so many well-submerged wheels. But the porpoises wheeled themselves away, and then we were thrown upon our own resources. It did not take many minutes to discover that the sun was blazing like a bonfire and that the weather was of a melting temperature. It had a drowsing effect, too.

In one place we came upon a large company of naked natives, of both sexes and all ages, amusing themselves with the national pastime of surf bathing. Each heathen would paddle three or four hundred yards out to sea (taking a short board with him), then face the shore and wait for a particularly prodigious billow to come along; at the right moment he would fling his board upon its foamy crest and himself upon the board, and here he would come whizzing by like a bombshell! It did not seem that a lightning express train could shoot along at a more hair-lifting speed. I tried surf bathing once, subsequently, but made a failure of it. I got the board placed right, and at the right moment, too; but missed the connection myself. The board struck the shore in three-quarters of a second, without any cargo, and I struck the bottom about the same time, with a couple of barrels of water in me. None but natives ever master the art of surf bathing thoroughly.

At the end of an hour, we had made the four miles, and landed on a level point of land, upon which was a wide extent of old ruins, with many a tall coconut tree growing among them. Here was the ancient City of Refuge—a vast enclosure, whose stone walls were twenty feet thick at the base and fifteen feet high; an oblong square, a thousand and forty feet one way and a fraction under seven hundred the other. Within this enclosure, in early times, had been three rude temples; each two hundred and ten feet long by one hundred wide, and thirteen high.

In those days, if a man killed another anywhere on the island the relatives were privileged to take the murderer's life; and then a chase for life and liberty began—the outlawed criminal flying through pathless forests and over mountain and plain, with his hopes fixed upon the protecting walls of the City of Refuge, and the avenger of blood following hotly after him! Sometimes the race was kept up to the very gates of the temple, and the panting pair sped through long files of excited natives, who watched the contest with flashing eye and dilated nostril, encouraging the hunted refugee with sharp, inspiriting ejaculations, and sending up a ringing shout of exultation when the saving gates closed upon him and the cheated pursuer sank exhausted at the threshold. But sometimes the flying criminal fell under the hand of the avenger at the very door, when one more brave stride, one more brief second of time would have brought his feet upon the sacred ground and barred him against all harm. Where did these isolated pagans get this idea of a City of Refuge—this ancient Oriental custom?

This old sanctuary was sacred to all—even to rebels in arms and invading armies. Once within its walls, and confession made to the priest and absolution obtained, the wretch with a price upon his head could go forth without fear and without danger—he was *tabu*, and to harm him was death. The routed rebels in the lost battle for idolatry fled to this place to claim sanctuary, and many were thus saved.

Close to the corner of the great enclosure is a round structure of stone, some six or eight feet high, with a level top about ten or twelve in diameter. This was the place of execution. A high palisade of coconut piles shut out the cruel scenes from the vulgar multitude. Here criminals were killed, the flesh stripped from the bones and burned, and the bones secreted in holes in the body of the structure. If the man had been guilty of a high crime, the entire corpse was burned.

The walls of the temple are a study. The same food for speculation that is offered the visitor to the Pyramids of Egypt he will find here—the mystery of how they were constructed by a people unacquainted with science and mechanics. The natives have no invention of their own for hoisting heavy weights, they had no beasts of burden, and they have never even shown any knowledge of the properties of the lever. Yet some of the lava blocks quarried out, brought over rough, broken ground, and built into this wall, six or seven feet from the ground, are of prodigious size and would weigh tons. How did they transport and how raise them?

Both the inner and outer surfaces of the walls present a smooth front and are very creditable specimens of masonry. The blocks are of all manner of shapes and sizes, but yet are fitted together with the neatest exactness. The gradual narrowing of the wall from the base upward is accurately preserved.

No cement was used, but the edifice is firm and compact and is capable of resisting storm and decay for centuries. Who built this temple, and how was it built, and when, are the mysteries that may never be unraveled.

Outside of these ancient walls lies a sort of coffin-shaped stone eleven feet four inches long and three feet square at the small end (it would weigh a few thousand pounds), which the high chief who held sway over this district many centuries ago brought thither on his shoulder one day to use as a lounge! This circumstance is established by the most reliable traditions. He used to lie down on it, in his indolent way, and keep an eye on his subjects at work for him and see that there was no "soldiering" done. And no doubt there was not any done to speak of, because he was a man of that sort of build that incites to attention to business on the part of an employee. He was fourteen or fifteen feet high. When he stretched himself at full length on his lounge, his legs hung down over the end, and when he snored he woke the dead. These facts are all attested by irrefragable tradition.

On the other side of the temple is a monstrous seven-ton rock, eleven feet long, seven feet wide, and three feet thick. It is raised a foot or a foot and a half above the ground, and nests upon half a dozen little stony pedestals. The same old fourteen-footer brought it down from the mountain, merely for fun (he had his own notions about fun), and propped it up as we find it now and as others may find it a century hence, for it would take a score of horses to budge it from its position. They say that fifty or sixty years ago the proud Queen Kaahumanu used to fly to this rock for safety, whenever she had been making trouble with her fierce husband, and hide under it until his wrath was appeased. But these Kanakas will lie, and this statement is one of their ablest efforts—for Kaahumanu was six feet high—she was bulky—she was built like an ox—and she could no more have squeezed herself under that rock than she could have passed between the cylinders of a sugar mill. What could she gain by it, even if she succeeded? To be chased and abused by a savage husband could not be otherwise than humiliating to her high spirit, yet it could never make her feel so flat as an hour's repose under that rock would.

We walked a mile over a raised macadamized road of uniform width; a road paved with flat stones and exhibiting in its every detail a considerable degree of engineering skill. Some say that wise old pagan, Kamahameha I, planned and built it, but others say it was built so long before his time that the knowledge of who constructed it has passed out of the traditions. In either case, however, as the handiwork of an untaught and degraded race it is a thing of pleasing interest. The stones are worn and smooth, and pushed apart in places, so that the road has the exact appearance of those ancient paved highways leading out of Rome which one sees in pictures.

The object of our tramp was to visit a great natural curiosity at the base of the foothills—a congealed cascade of lava. Some old forgotten volcanic eruption sent its broad river of fire down the mountainside here, and it poured down in a great torrent from an overhanging bluff some fifty feet high to the ground below. The flaming torrent cooled in the winds from the sea, and remains there today, all seamed, and frothed and rippled, a petrified Niagara. It is all very picturesque, and withal so natural that one might almost imagine it still flowed. A smaller stream trickled over the cliff and built up an isolated pyramid about thirty feet high, which has the semblance of a mass of large gnarled and knotted vines and roots and stems intricately twisted and woven together.

We passed in behind the cascade and the pyramid, and found the bluff pierced by several cavernous tunnels, whose crooked courses we followed a long distance.

Two of these winding tunnels stand as proof of Nature's mining abilities. Their floors are level, they are seven feet wide, and their roofs are gently arched. Their height is not uniform, however. We passed through one a hundred feet long, which leads through a spur of the hill and opens out well up in the sheer wall of a precipice whose foot rests in the waves of the sea. It is a commodious tunnel, except that there are occasional places in it where one must stoop to pass under. The roof is lava, of course, and is thickly studded with little lava-pointed icicles an inch long, which hardened as they dripped. They project as closely together as the iron teeth of a corn sheller, and if one will stand up straight and walk any distance there, he can get his hair combed free of charge.

We got back to the schooner in good time and then sailed down to Kau, where we disembarked and took final leave of the vessel. Next day we bought horses and bent our way over the summer-clad mountain terraces, toward the great volcano of Kilauea (Ke-low-way-ah). We made nearly a two days' journey of it, but that was on account of laziness. Toward sunset on the second day, we reached an elevation of some four thousand feet above sea level, and as we picked our careful way through billowy wastes of lava long generations ago stricken dead and cold in the climax of its tossing fury, we began to come upon signs of the near presence of the volcano—signs in the nature of ragged fissures that discharged jets of sulfurous vapor into the air, hot from the molten ocean down in the bowels of the mountain. Shortly the crater came into view. I have seen Vesuvius since, but it was a mere toy, a child's volcano, a soup kettle, compared to this. Mount Vesuvius is a shapely cone thirty-six hundred feet high; its crater an inverted cone only three hundred feet deep, but not more than a thousand feet in diameter, if as much as that; its fires meager, modest, and docile. But here was a vast, perpendicular, walled cellar, nine hundred feet deep in some places, thirteen hundred in others, level-floored, and *ten miles in circumference!* Here was a yawning pit upon whose floor the armies of Russia could camp, and have room to spare.

Perched upon the edge of the crater, at the opposite end from where we stood, was a small lookout house—say three miles away. It assisted us, by comparison, to comprehend and appreciate the great depth of the basin—it looked like a tiny martin box clinging at the eaves of a cathedral. After some little time spent in resting and looking and ciphering, we hurried on to the hotel.

By the path it is half a mile from the Volcano House to the lookout house. After a hearty supper we waited until it was thoroughly dark and then started to the crater. The first glance in that direction revealed a scene of wild beauty. There was a heavy fog over the crater, and it was splendidly illuminated by the glare from the fires below. The illumination was two miles wide and a mile high, perhaps; and if you ever, on a dark night and at a distance, beheld the light from thirty or forty blocks of distant buildings all on fire at once, reflected strongly against overhanging clouds, you can form a fair idea of what this looked like.

A colossal column of cloud towered to a great height in the air immediately above the crater, and the outer swell of every one of its vast folds was dyed with a rich crimson luster, which was subdued to a pale rose tint in the depressions between. It glowed like a muffled torch and stretched upward to a dizzy height toward the zenith. I thought it just possible that its like had not been seen since the children of Israel wandered on their long march through the desert so many centuries ago over a path illuminated by the mysterious "pillar of fire." And I was sure that I now had a vivid conception of what the majestic "pillar of fire" was like, which almost amounted to a revelation.

$\mathcal{T}$HE $\mathcal{W}$ORLD OF $\mathcal{R}$EEF $\mathcal{F}$LATS

Rachel Carson

$\mathcal{T}$he world of reef flats is inhabited by echinoderms of every sort: starfishes, brittle stars, sea urchins, sand dollars, and holothurians all are at home on the coral rock, in the shifting coral sands, among the gorgonian sea gardens and the grass-carpeted bottoms. All are important in the economy of the marine world—as links in the living chains by which materials are taken from the sea, passed from one to another, returned to the sea, borrowed again. Some are important also in the geologic processes of earth building and earth destruction—the processes by which rock is worn away and ground to sand, by which the sediments that carpet the sea floor are accumulated, shifted, sorted, and distributed. And at death their hard skeletons contribute calcium for the needs of other animals or for the building of the reefs.

Out on the reefs the long-spined black sea urchin excavates cavities along the base of the coral wall; each sinks into its depression and turns its spines outward, so that a swimmer moving along the reef sees forests of black quills. This urchin also wanders in over the reef flats, where it nestles close to the base of a loggerhead sponge, or sometimes, apparently finding no need of concealment, rests in open, sand-floored areas.

A full-grown black urchin may have a body or test nearly 4 inches in diameter, with spines 12 to 15 inches long. This is one of the comparatively few shore animals that are poisonous to the touch, and the effect of contact with one of the slender, hollow spines is said to be like that of a hornet sting, or may even be more serious for a child or an especially susceptible adult. Apparently the mucous coating of the spines bears the irritant or poison.

This urchin is extraordinary in the degree of its awareness of the surroundings. A hand extended over it will cause all the spines to swivel about on their mountings, pointing menacingly at the intruding object. If the hand is moved from side to side the spines swing about, following it. According to Professor Norman Millott of the University College of the West Indies, nerve receptors scattered widely over the body receive the message conveyed by a change in the intensity of light, responding most sharply to suddenly decreased light as a shadowy portent of danger. To this extent, then, the urchin may actually "see" moving objects passing nearby.

Linked in some mysterious way with one of the great rhythms of nature, this sea urchin spawns at the time of the full moon. The eggs and sperm are shed into water once in each lunar month during the summer season, on the nights of the strongest moonlight. Whatever the stimulus to which all the individuals of the species respond, it assures that prodigal and simultaneous release of reproductive cells that nature often demands for the perpetuation of a species.

Off some of the Keys, in shallow water, lives the so-called slate-pencil urchin, named for its short stout spines. This is an urchin of solitary habit, single individuals sheltering under or among the reef rocks near the low-tide level. It seems a sluggish creature of dull perceptions, unaware of the presence of an intruder, making no effort to cling by means of its tube feet when it is picked up. It belongs to the only family of modern echinoderms that also existed in Paleozoic time; the recent members of the group show little change from the form of ancestors that lived hundreds of millions of years ago.

Another urchin with short and slender spines and color variations ranging from deep violet to green, rose, or white, sometimes occurs abundantly on sandy bottoms carpeted with turtle grass, camouflaging itself with bits of grass and shell and coral fragments held in its tube feet. Like many other urchins, it performs a geologic function. Nibbling away at shells and coral rock with its white teeth, it chips off fragments that are then passed through the grinding mill of its digestive tract; these organic fragments, trimmed, ground, and polished within the urchins, contribute to the sands of tropical beaches.

And the tribes of the starfish and the brittle stars are everywhere represented on these coral flats. The great sea star, Oreaster, stout and powerful of body, perhaps lives more abundantly a little offshore, where whole constellations of them gather on the white sand. But solitary specimens wander inshore, seeking especially the grassy areas.

A small reddish-brown starfish, Linkia, has the strange habit of breaking off an arm, which then grows a cluster of four new arms that are temporarily in a "comet" form. Sometimes the animal breaks across the central disc; regeneration may result in six- or seven-rayed animals. These divisions seem to be a method of reproduction practised by the young, for adult animals cease to fragment and produce eggs.

About the bases of gorgonians, under and inside of sponges, under movable rocks and down in little, eroded caverns in the coral rock live the brittle stars. With their long and flexible arms, each composed of a series of "vertebrae" shaped like hourglasses, they are capable of sinuous and graceful motion. Sometimes they stand on the tips of two arms and sway in the motion of the water currents, bending the other arms in movements as graceful as those of a ballet dancer. They creep over the substratum by throwing two of their arms forward and pulling up the body or disc and the remaining arms. The brittle stars feed on minute mollusks and worms and other small animals. In turn, they are eaten by many fish and other predators, and sometimes fall victim to certain parasites. A small green alga may live in the skin of the brittle star; there it dissolves the calcareous plates, so that the arms may break apart. Or a curious little degenerate copepod may live as a parasite within the gonads, destroying them and rendering the animal sterile.

My first meeting with a live West Indian basket star was something I shall never forget. I was wading off Ohio Key in water little more than knee deep when I found it among some seaweeds, gently drifting on the tide. Its upper surface was the color of a young fawn, with lighter shades beneath. The searching, exploring, testing branchlets at the tips of the arms reminded me of the delicate tendrils by which a growing vine seeks out places to which it may attach itself. For many minutes I stood beside it, lost to all but its extraordinary and somehow fragile beauty. I had no wish to "collect" it; to disturb such a being would have seemed a desecration. Finally the rising tide and the need to visit other parts of the flat before they become too deeply flooded drove me on, and when I returned the basket star had disappeared.

The basket starfish or basket fish is related to the brittle stars and serpent stars but displays remarkable differences of structure: each of the five arms diverges into branching V's, which branch again, and then again and again until a maze of curling tendrils forms the periphery of the animal. Indulging their taste for the dramatic, early naturalists named the basket stars for those monsters of Greek mythology, the Gorgons, who wore snakes in place of hair and whose hideous aspect was supposed to turn men to stone; so the family comprising these bizarre echinoderms is known as the Gorgonocephalidae. To some imaginations their appearance may be "snaky-locked," but the effect is one of beauty, grace, and elegance.

All the way from the Arctic to the West Indies basket stars of one species or another live in coastal waters, and many go down to lightless sea bottoms nearly a mile beneath the surface. They may walk about over the ocean floor, moving delicately on the tips of their arms. As Alexander Agassiz long ago described it, the animal stands "as it were on tiptoe, so that the ramifications of the arms form a kind of trellis-work all around it, reaching to the ground, while the disk forms a roof." Or again they may cling to gorgonians or other fixed sea growths and reach out into the water. The branching arms serve as a fine-meshed net to ensnare small sea creatures. On some grounds the basket stars are not only abundant but associate in herds of many individuals as though for a common purpose. Then the arms of neighboring animals become entwined in a continuous living net to capture all the small fry of the sea who venture, or are helplessly carried, within reach of the millions of grasping tendrils.

FROM *Season at the Point*

Jack Connor

"*Hey*, the starlings have something," says Jeff Bouton, lifting his binoculars to his eyes. "See them balling up? *Harrier!* Going left, just right of the round-topped pine."

Two dozen starlings swoop down in a tight flock, not quite making contact with the hawk below. The harrier tilts, flaps once, flaps again, then wobbles left, low over the tree line. The starlings regroup and swoop once more. The hawk keeps on coming—wobble, flap-flap, wobble. The undersides of the wings flash cinnamon.

"Immature female," says Bouton.

As she reaches a pair of tall cedar trees, the starlings let her go. She crosses in front of the water tower, flaps past the lighthouse, veers left past the silo behind the lighthouse, and finally disappears over the red-shingled roof of St. Mary's-by-the-Sea, a retreat house for nuns that is the southernmost building in New Jersey. The hawk is heading west-southwest, across the fourteen miles of salt water at the mouth of the Delaware Bay.

"Now we're cooking with Crisco," says Bouton, lowering his binoculars. "That's raptor number one."

He is standing on a raised deck that is the hawkwatch platform at Cape May Point State Park. The houses and hotels of Cape May City, two miles to the east, shimmer in hazy silhouette under the rising sun. Dragonflies hover above the pond in front of the platform. Above them, martins and swallows loop through the air, squeaking and chirping. Laughing gulls *ho-hah* from the beach to Bouton's right; a wren sings from the woods to his left. Cars pull into the parking lot behind him steadily, and doors and trunk lids bang as beachgoers unload. "Have you got the sunscreen?" *"Jennifer*, wait for your mother!"

"Kestrel," Bouton announces. "Over the round-topped pine, going left. Probable female . . . Definite female. Hold it—there's another. Two A.K.s coming, both females."

The two falcons follow the same route as the harrier, but they are smaller birds, pumping harder, flying more swiftly. The starlings do not pursue.

Bouton is barefoot, tan, and twenty-one years old. He wears a tight-chested T-shirt, baggy black shorts, a wristband of braided rope, and the tab from a pop-top soda can on a silver chain around his neck. The peak of his baseball cap is folded upward, like a bicycle racer's. His sunglasses hang from a red cord. "A punk birder," he calls himself.

His equipment is modest: a spiral notebook, a thirty-cent pen, a palm-sized VHS weather radio, a pair of 8.5 × 44 Swift binoculars, and a battered Bushnell spotting scope strapped loosely to an old gun stock by strips of fraying duct tape.

It is August 17 and the first hour of the first day of the thirteenth year of the Cape May Bird Observatory's Autumn Hawk Watch. Bouton will stand here scanning the skies from dawn to dusk seven days a week for the next three and a half months. Depending on weather, winds, the nesting success of the raptors that have bred to the north, and his own attention to the task, he expects to count between fifty thousand and eighty thousand hawks passing his position—more hawks in one season than most people, even most birdwatchers, will see in a lifetime.

The Point's census has averaged 66,000 hawks a season for the last twelve fall seasons, more than eighty hawks for each hour of observation time. No place in the Eastern United States can match these numbers. Hawk Mountain, Pennsylvania, the lookout with the next highest count, averages a third as many. For variety, no lookout in all of North America and few places in the Western Hemisphere compare with Cape May. Twenty-four species of hawks have been recorded at the Point, and seventeen of them are annual migrants, including two eagle species, three falcons, five buteos (red-tailed, broad-winged, red-shouldered, rough-legged, and Swainson's), and three accipiters. The two most cosmopolitan hawks, the osprey and the peregrine falcon, both of which occur on all continents but

Antarctica, are seen in greater numbers in Cape May than anywhere else in the world. And hawks are only one part of the migration pageant on the Cape May peninsula. Eight owl species, seventeen sparrows, thirty-six warblers, and forty species of shorebirds are annual visitors. Western kingbirds and clay-colored sparrows from the West, black rails and purple gallinules from the South, lapland longspurs and white-winged crossbills from the North, Eurasian wigeons and Eurasian green-winged teals from Iceland and farther east—all are virtually expected birds in Cape May, though they are rarely seen elsewhere in New Jersey or in any other mid-Atlantic state. The list of "accidentals" recorded at the Point includes black-browed albatross, South Polar skua, Eskimo curlew, magnificent frigatebird, sooty tern, white-winged tern, chestnut-collared longspur, and dozens of other exotic species. When Bouton and two companions spotted a long-billed curlew flying over the hawkwatch platform on October 9 last year, the list of all bird species recorded in Cape May County reached 410, a total higher than the lists for most states in the U.S. and equal to the list for all of mainland Alaska, an area more than a thousand times as large.

"The curlew came right out of the gap," says Bouton, pointing, "calling all the way. Best nonraptor I saw all fall." "The gap" is a low row of phragmites and buttonbush beyond the pond in front of the platform that leads to a line of taller oaks, poplars, and tupelos bordering the South Cape May Meadows half a mile east. Right, or south, of the gap are two red-and-white radio towers and "the merlin sticks"—a cluster of dead trees where merlins often perch, sometimes feeding on songbirds and shorebirds they have caught. Farther right and south stands a powder-blue water tower and then the jumble of rooftops and steeples of downtown Cape May. The line of buildings ends at the Second Avenue jetty, which is hidden behind the grassy dunes that run around the inlet and up the beach back to the platform. The most prominent landmark on Bouton's right is a concrete bunker two hundred yards from the platform. It was three hundred yards from the water when it was built in 1942, equipped with four 155-millimeter artillery guns, and covered with sod. The Point's beach has been eroding for decades, however, and the sod and land around the bunker are long gone. Today a dozen fishermen are standing on the bunker's roof, their lines leading to the surf breaking against the bunker's wooden pilings, which were once forty feet underground.

"Falcons tend to come up the flight paths between the gap and the bunker," says Bouton. "The ones we get to see, at least. I'm sure we miss a lot of merlins and peregrines that fly down along the ocean paralleling Second Avenue and never turn this way. When they get to the jetty, they jump off right there, heading straight south. 'Delaware, here we come.' I've seen a few peregrines do it—on really clear days when I just happened to be scanning that way with the scope. But most days they're too fast and that's too far away."

Most other hawks—eagles, buteos, and accipiters—are first seen cresting the horizon north, or left, of the gap. Bouton's landmarks in this direction are a red-and-white radio tower; three prominent trees he calls "the round-topped pine," "the round-topped oak," and "the flat-topped oak"; a line of cedars; and finally the most useful directional guide on the platform's scene—a hundred-foot wooden tower eighty yards from the platform. It was a radio tower during World War II, part of the Coast Guard station at the Point, and each of its three guy wires still holds five insulator caps spaced at regular intervals. "They must have known back then there'd be a hawkwatch here someday," says Bouton, "so they never took it down. That tower is about the best thing that ever happened to hawkwatchers in New Jersey. You tell folks there's an eagle out beyond the bottom two insulators on the left-hand guy wire, and everybody's on it in a second."

Why Cape May sees so many birds is largely a mystery, although two obvious factors are its peninsular geography and its rich mix of natural habitats. Hawks tend to follow "leading lines" on their migration paths—mountain ridges, river valleys, and lake, bay, or ocean shores that both direct and restrict their flights. Cape May stands at the meeting point of two such leading lines, the Delaware Bayshore on the west and the Atlantic Coast on the east. Southbound hawks following either coast are funneled to the Point, where they find themselves facing the fourteen-mile overwater flight to Delaware. Depending on their species and the winds of the day, they may depart directly, backtrack up the Bayshore, swirl up high over the Point to gather altitude for a long glide out, or put down for the night in the woods at Higbee's Beach, Pond Creek, or elsewhere around the peninsula. Hawks can still find food and protection in these woods. Cape May County's human population has nearly doubled in the last twenty years, and local conservationists despair about the future, but at the moment much of the county remains relatively undeveloped. Swamps, creeks, forests, orchards, pastures, and saltwater meadows and marshes form a patchwork refuge for migrating birds of all kinds.

But explaining the Point's hawk numbers by noting that the South Jersey peninsula is a funnel and refuge does not do justice to Cape May's special attractiveness to birds of prey, nor does it touch on the puzzles behind the magnitude of the phenomenon. It is like explaining that Henry Aaron holds the major-league record for home runs because he was a well-conditioned athlete with quick reflexes, or that Napoleon conquered Europe because he was an experienced military man with a lot of ambition. "Funnel" and "refuge" are part of every explanation of the Cape May hawk migration because they are the most identifiable components of the phenomenon. We know there must be other causes for the magnitude of the Cape May flight; we just don't know what they are. Really, Cape May's hawk migration has never been fully explained. At our present level of knowledge, it *cannot* be fully explained.

Run your eye down a map of eastern North America and you will note that a couple of dozen peninsulas along the Atlantic coast are oriented more or less in a southerly direction. All of them are migration funnels; many are green and undeveloped; all of them are good places to look for birds on an autumn day. Not a single one of them sees the number of hawks Cape May sees. Some can be dismissed as unworthy rivals, of course. Baccaro Point in Nova Scotia is obviously too far north; the majority of hawks nest south (or west) of the Maritime Provinces. Cape Sable at the tip of the Everglades is too far south; most hawks winter north of the Florida peninsula. Connecticut's Hammonasset Point and South Carolina's Cape Romain are both located on peninsulas which are apparently not large enough for a hawk flight to build—their funnels are too short. The peninsula that leads to North Carolina's Oregon Inlet is too thin, more straw than funnel. (Cape Hatteras, Cape Lookout, and Cape Fear, all farther south on the Carolina coast, are on islands, not peninsulas. Since the majority of hawks do not cross water unless forced to do so, island-based hawkwatches generally record only ospreys and falcons, the most seaworthy raptors.)

But other places make better, more intriguing comparisons. Why, for example, is Cape May's flight so much larger than the hawk flight at Point Lookout in southern Maryland? Point Lookout stands at the junction of the Potomac River and the Chesapeake Bay, both of which seem to qualify as potential leading lines. The St. Marys County peninsula is green and undeveloped, very similar in size to the Cape May peninsula, and at a latitude only one degree different from Cape May's. No one bothers to count hawks at Point Lookout, however. In fact, the hawk flight is so meager that (according to the records of the Hawk Migration Association of North America) no one has ever bothered to conduct a season-long count there. The Potomac is slightly smaller than the Delaware, and the Chesapeake is not the Atlantic. Does that make all the difference? Or could the shapes of the two peninsulas be a crucial factor? Most hawks coming south from Canada and New England are heading toward the Carolinas, Georgia, and the Gulf Coast—on a track that runs roughly southwestward, paralleling the Appalachian Mountains. The St. Marys County peninsula bends eastward against this track; the Cape May peninsula bends with it. Is that southwestward bend one of the reasons so many hawks are led to Cape May Point? Are they tricked by the promise of this right-handed turn—fooled into coming down onto the peninsula because it seems that it will carry them where they want to go? Would the Cape May flight be less spectacular if the peninsula were a mirror image of itself and Cape May Point, like Point Lookout, stood on the easternmost extension of the land? We don't know the answers to these questions. Do hawks have an internal compass that helps them orient during migration? Can they distinguish a southwestern bend from a southeastern one? We don't know. Are the hawks that reach Cape May there by choice, or are they lost and trapped? We don't know.

South Jersey's nearest match among Atlantic Coast peninsulas is the Delmarva Peninsula, and the resemblance is very close. Look at the map with your glasses off and they seem to be twin images of the same body of land. The belly of the Delmarva leads to the southwest-bound appendix of Cape Charles just as the belly of South Jersey leads to the southwest-bound appendix of Cape May. Cape Charles has a hawk count, too, at Kiptopeke, its southernmost tip. It is one of the higher counts in the East, averaging 15,000 to 20,000 hawks a year, but it has never come close to matching Cape May's 50,000 to 80,000 hawks, and those who claim to understand hawk migration have a particularly difficult time explaining Cape

May's superiority to Kiptopeke. If "funnel" and "refuge" were all that made the Cape May flight what it is, Kiptopeke, not Cape May Point, would be the primary hawk-migration stop on the East Coast. Kiptopeke's east-side leading line is the same Atlantic Ocean coastline that directs hawks to Cape May; its west-side leading line is the Chesapeake Bay; and Cape Charles and the rest of the Delmarva Peninsula offer even more natural habitat than Cape May and South Jersey. Finally, Kiptopeke is directly southwest of Cape May Point! Shouldn't we see at Kiptopeke a number of hawks that have come south from Delaware, eastern Pennsylvania, and areas farther west (migrants that never reach New Jersey) *and* the hawks that departed from Cape May? Where else can all those Cape May hawks be going? Any hawk crossing Delaware Bay on a southward or southwestward track must next encounter the Chesapeake. If the funnel effect is what brings hawks to Cape May because they hesitate to cross the Delaware River, shouldn't it have an even stronger influence on the Cape Charles peninsula as the bird encounters the wider Chesapeake? And, finally, if the funnel effect is not what is primarily responsible for the Cape May hawk flight, what is?

Cape May was celebrated among birders as a migration trap long before the Cape May Bird Observatory came into existence and regular hawk counts began in 1976. Raptor researcher Bill Clark and the various teams of banders he has organized have been capturing and banding hawks at the Point since 1966; the amateur ornithologist Ernest Choate studied hawk flights here throughout the 1950s and 1960s and coordinated two season-long hawk counts in 1965 and 1970; Roger Tory Peterson, Robert Allen, James Tanner, and others conducted six season-long hawk counts at the Point in the 1930s. Witmer Stone, curator of birds at the Academy of Natural Sciences in Philadelphia, studied the birds of Cape May and South Jersey for half a century (1890–1939) and lived at the Point for the last twenty years of his life. In 1937 Stone published his two-volume classic, *Bird Studies at Old Cape May,* in which he sketched the bird life of the county, presented his theories on habitat needs and migration, and traced the records of bird observations in Cape May County back to the early 1800s when John James Audubon, George Ord, and Alexander Wilson visited. "If birds are good judges of excellent climate," Alexander Wilson wrote in about 1810, after one of his six trips to southern New Jersey, "Cape May has the finest climate in the United States, for it has the greatest variety of birds."

In fact, the history of birdwatching at Cape May goes back to at least 1633, when David Pieterson de Vries, one of the first Europeans to set foot on the peninsula, reported that the flocks of "pigeons" there (possibly passenger pigeons, now extinct) were so numerous they darkened the sky.

Nevertheless, when in the fall of 1976 an unknown young birder named Pete Dunne completed the first continuous daily count at the Point and reported a total of 48,621 hawks for the season, a widespread response among the birding community was simple disbelief. Forty-eight thousand hawks was nearly twenty thousand more hawks than Hawk Mountain had seen in its best year ever, and the conventional theory at the time was that the majority of hawks migrated along the inland ridges that led to Hawk Mountain. Migrant raptors seen along the coast were thought to be primarily straying birds that had been pushed off the main route by strong winds and had lost their way. Dunne's total was also 30,000 more hawks than the Point's own banders had predicted the count would be, and twelve times the 3,900 hawks counted by Choate in his 1965 hawk count at the Point. It even eclipsed Choate's 1970 count of 41,021—a count that had included a freakish, single-day flight of twenty-five thousand kestrels on October 16, 1970, which had been disbelieved itself.

In 1977 Dunne sat in a lifeguard chair borrowed from the state park beach patrol, and growing crowds of hawkwatchers gathered at his feet. "Birdwatchers I'd been reading about my whole life showed up," he said later. "It was all I could do to keep from climbing down and genuflecting." Some, openly skeptical of his 1976 total, came to scrutinize his identification and record-keeping skills; others wondered if the 1976 total had been an aberration—a consequence of unusually frequent northwest winds that would not be repeated. Northwest winds were even more common in 1977, however, and the count went off the scale. Dunne's final total was 81,145 hawks—an average of 146 per hour, nearly five every two minutes. "Superlatives fail under these conditions," wrote the editors of *American Birds,* the journal with the last word on such matters. "Cape May Point must now be considered the Raptor Capital of North America."

The state park built the hawkwatch platform in 1980, with room for fifty or sixty observers, and the parking lot lanes nearest it were regularly filled with the cars of birders, some of whom had driven from as far away as Kansas, Louisiana, Ontario, and New Brunswick to see the flight. In 1981 a team of three counters, sharing the season-long watch, broke Dunne's 1977 record with a count of 88,937 hawks. The next year the platform had to be doubled in size to serve the growing crowds. The deck is now thirty strides long and five across, approximately the size of two railroad cars, and should probably be doubled again. On days of northwest winds in late September and early October, when the raptor migration reaches its peak, more than a hundred observers pack together here. The platform is sometimes so crowded with visitors elbow to elbow, banging their binoculars and telescopes into each other, that the counter must retreat down the ramp to the grass below to have room to scan the sky.

The flights are still not well understood, however, and skepticism lingers about the Point's numbers. Most observers now grant that the old theory about the primacy of the inland ridge routes underestimated the importance of the coastal route, but some still believe the totals reported from the Point are too high. Visiting hawkwatchers from the inland sites tend to be especially skeptical. Counting migrants on the ridges is much simpler than it is at Cape May. To migrants heading south on the inland route, any rocky outcrop is pretty much like all the rest. They have few reasons to stop at Hawk Mountain or Raccoon Ridge or any other ridge lookout, and fewer reasons still to backtrack. You can spend a couple of days at Hawk Mountain and not see a single raptor put down in a tree; you can spend a week there and not see one reverse course. Counting along the ridges could hardly be easier: here comes a merlin; there it goes; add one to your total.

Counting at Cape May Point, on the other hand, could hardly be more difficult. The Point is very different from anything a migrant raptor has encountered before (unless he has passed through in other years), and it forces each bird to make a choice: go, delay, or stay? The ocean presses in from the left; Delaware Bay opens wide on the right; the woods and meadows below promise food and refuge; and the Delaware landscape appears low on the southwestern horizon, just close enough to offer hope for a successful crossing, just far enough to spell danger. Each hawk's decision to cross or backtrack or put down in a tree reflects a number of variables, including how far he has already flown that day, when he has last fed, how strong and from which direction the wind is coming, and what other hawks of his species are doing. As the hawks test the winds and study the other birds over the Point, their milling, circling, and reversing creates an endless series of puzzles for Cape May's census-taker. The falcons and ospreys passing on the right over the bunker and dunes, on the ocean side of the platform, sometimes swing out to sea and circle around to pass again. The broad-wings and other buteos that usually first appear to the northeast, behind the tower, often soar close to the platform and then turn back north toward the Beanery or follow Sunset Boulevard westward to drop from sight in the woods along the Bayshore. Harriers come from all sides, pumping hard and low over the wavetops on the right, gliding high at the limit of vision directly overhead, wobbling in and out of sight over the woods behind the tower. Sharpies sometimes come in overhead and fly directly out to sea, other times they join the broad-wings soaring west along Sunset Boulevard, and sometimes they stop to rest in the trees around the pond. A merlin which has been perching on the tallest tree in the merlin sticks drops from sight—chasing prey, you assume—and five minutes later a merlin pumps by on your left carrying a songbird in its talons. You didn't see it cross the pond, but merlins are stealthy and quick, so you decide it is the same bird—until you look back right and see a merlin perched in the tallest tree in the sticks again. A kettle of twenty-two broad-wings crests the horizon behind the tower, circling over the Beanery, and slowly drifts westward to drop from sight in the direction of Higbee's Beach. Half an hour later, a kettle of eighteen broad-wings appears over the Beanery, and following the same route as the earlier group, drops from sight over Higbee's. Half an hour after that, a kettle of twenty-six broad-wings executes the same maneuver. How many individual broad-wings have you seen? Were there three separate groups, sixty-six different birds? Or was it the same kettle, losing and gaining members as it circled the Point? And, what should you make of the situation on the sticks now? The tallest tree is empty, but one merlin stands on a shorter tree twenty yards to the left and another perches fifty yards to the right. What's your merlin total so far? Two, three, or four? Did you turn to watch that one with the songbird go out to sea? Or could it have swung around you and returned while you were counting the broad-wings? And, over the bunker, here comes a peregrine with a missing tail feather.

Didn't you see a peregrine the day before yesterday missing that same feather? And don't some of the hawk banders believe peregrines fly out to sea for miles, then return to feed again on the shorebirds in the Meadows? And look, here's the biggest kettle of broad-wings today—fifty-five birds, low on the horizon over the Beanery. Has there been time enough for that earlier kettle to have circled all the way back from Higbee's, or are these birds an entirely different group?

First-time visitors to the Point, especially those who have learned hawkwatching on the ridges, often find the Cape May flight a disorienting experience, and they regularly question the official counter's methodology, sometimes to his face ("How do you know you didn't count that one already?"), more often behind his back ("He's double and triple counting the same birds"). More troublesome are the questions and criticisms from the local birders and platform veterans, all of whom seem to have their own pet ideas about which birds should be added to the totals and which not. Each new counter finds himself in the center of a controversy that has continued for years.

Jeff Bouton knew all this before he arrived last year. He was brought here because of the controversy that surrounded his predecessor, Frank Nicoletti. Nicoletti was finally told to quit his post, after three seasons—although he is universally regarded as the best hawkwatcher the Point has ever seen.

No one who stood with him on the platform doubted Nicoletti's ability to identify individual birds. Hawkwatching is a sport of long distances and subtle details, and Nicoletti, a burly, bearded man in his mid-twenties, saw farther and more sharply than anyone else. "He operates way out beyond me," said Pete Dunne, an extraordinary birder himself. "I think he was born with ten-power eyes. Nicoletti's dedication was also extraordinary. No single observer before him had spent 700 hours on the platform during the season, and not even the teams of observers, dividing the observation time, had totaled 1,000 hours. Nicoletti spent more than 1,000 hours each of his three seasons, and he did it alone. He arrived so often before dawn and stayed so long after dark that he began a count of migrating owls. During the day he refused to leave the platform for longer than the three or four minutes it took to get back and forth to the Park's rest room. When it rained and other birders went home, Nicoletti sat in his truck in the parking lot with the engine running and wipers going, on the off-chance that a hawk might fly by. Two months after the fall count ended in December, he began another count, a February-to-June census of northbound hawks at Braddock Bay, New York, on the shore of Lake Ontario. When the Braddock count finished, he worked as a short-order cook for a few weeks in July, then reported back to the Point on August 1 to start again. "The Iron Man," he was called, and by late October his eyes were so red from scanning the sky they glowed like a pair of brake lights.

But all of Cape May's census-takers before Nicoletti had used mechanical hand counters to keep track of their totals. On days of big flights most had used three hand counters simultaneously—one for sharp-shins, one for kestrels, and the third for whatever species happened to be the next most common hawk of the day. Nicoletti refused to use hand counters at all, insisting he could keep all counts in his head. He also refused to total the birds at regular intervals. Even on slow days census-takers are supposed to note totals every hour on the hour—along with wind, temperature, and cloud-cover data. Nicoletti often seemed to let several hours pass before he picked up his clipboard to pencil in his numbers, and the daily totals board hanging from the platform seemed always to be at least three or four days out of date.

Nicoletti's counts for merlin and peregrine falcon were especially high. For the eight years of counts before Nicoletti's tenure, the average merlin total was about 1,000 birds a season; for Nicoletti's three years the average was more than 2,500. In his first year on the platform, Nicoletti's count for peregrine was 518, two hundred more than had ever been seen there in a single season. In his third season he reported 615 peregrines, a number higher than most estimates for the entire eastern North American population of the species. Were the populations of merlin and peregrine exploding? Or were Nicoletti's totals careless guesstimates?

At least as troublesome for the Cape May Bird Observatory (CMBO) as questions about these numbers was Nicoletti's demeanor on the platform. He seemed aloof and rarely spoke to any visitors except a handful of platform regulars. Other counters had thrived as the natural center of attention, using the position as a chance to interest visitors, most of whom are novices, in hawks and hawkwatching. Nicoletti preferred to stand silently in the least crowded corner of the platform, sweeping his binoculars back and forth across the sky.

His defenders argued that Nicoletti's style was a consequence of his intensity—"Frank wants to identify every hawk first"—and that his counts were higher than those before him because he saw farther and paid more careful attention than other observers.

Two years ago, when CMBO was looking for a counter for the spring hawkwatch it sponsors in Sandy Hook, on the north shore of New Jersey, Nicoletti recommended Jeff Bouton, a young birder he'd met at Braddock Bay, and Bouton took the job.

In a three-month census at "The Hook," Bouton proved to be a skilled observer who was careful about keeping his data sheets complete and up-to-date and talked with anyone who happened by. Late that summer CMBO called him again. Frank Nicoletti would not be allowed to continue as CMBO's official counter in the fall. Would Bouton like to replace him?

The offer put Bouton in an awkward position. "How could anyone who loves raptors turn down a chance to be the counter at Cape May Point?" Bouton remembers thinking at the time. "But I figured I had to say no. Frank was my mentor. Then he called me up. He'd heard I'd been offered the job, and he told me to take it. He said he was pissed about getting pushed out, but he'd be even more pissed if someone he didn't know took his place."

Bouton counted until December 6 last year, and his totals for the season, written in grease pencil eight months ago, remain on the totals board nailed to the side of the platform.

It was a mediocre year by the Point's standards, except for the osprey and Cooper's hawk counts, both all-time records, and the counts for the two species whose totals had seemed most out of line during Nicoletti's years, the merlin and the peregrine. There were no complaints about Bouton's censusing techniques, but his merlin count was right at Nicoletti's average, and his peregrine count was seventy birds *higher* than Nicoletti's highest count.

For the low counts on the other birds, Bouton wonders if he is partially to blame. "I'm sure I missed some Swainson's hawks," says Bouton. "The first one I saw Frank had to show me. He came walking over one day, not even wearing binoculars, and pointed up in the sky. 'Hey, there's a Swainson's!'

"I think I might have been too conservative counting eagles, too. I don't like to count them until I see them fly over the horizon and out of here, but I wonder if I undercounted them. Everybody warned me the first season would be a learning process, and they were right.

"One day I turned around and there was a beautiful blond sitting on that bench right there. Really dynamite. Best looking woman up here all season. The platform was crowded, and I tried to play it cool—making my way toward her real slow, identifying birds for people along the way. But I stopped to show someone an osprey, and next thing I looked up and she was getting into her car out in the parking lot. *Alone.*" He shakes his head, "That was the worst mistake I made all year. Young female birdwatchers are extremely rare."

$\mathcal{I}$SLAND IN THE $\mathcal{S}$TREAM

John A. Murray

The vessel in which I was to embark for East Florida, being now ready to pursue her voyage, we set sail with a fair wind and tide. Our course was south, through the sound, betwixt a chain of sea-coast-islands, and the main. In the evening we came to, at the south end of St. Simon's Island . . . Next morning early we again got under way, running by Jekyl and Cumberland Islands, large, beautiful, and fertile, yet thinly inhabited, and consequently excellent haunts for deer, bear, and other game.

—William Bartram, Travels, 1791

$\mathcal{C}$umberland Island is a barrier island along the southern coast of Georgia. Eighteen miles long, two to three miles wide, with fifty feet of vertical relief, the island has few human inhabitants. It is warmed by the Gulf Stream and enjoys a climate best described as perpetual spring. Three major ecosystems are found on the island—salt marsh, maritime forest, and beach. Wildlife ranges from alligators to white-tailed deer. East of the island is Gray's Reef, the largest live-bottom reef north of the Florida Keys and a designated National Marine Sanctuary. Since 1972 Cumberland Island has been a national seashore, but it is a unique national park in that the number of visitors is strictly limited. Currently that number is three hundred per day. In this respect, Cumberland presents a vision of our larger national parks—Yosemite, Grand Canyon, Yellowstone—in the future, when such restrictions become more widespread.

Naturally I had to visit the place, and see how the system works, for one day we will have it in the West.

Eighty miles south of Atlanta, en route to Cumberland Island, traffic on Interstate 75 came to a halt. What was pouring from the sky was not rain. It was a biblical effusion, a drenching bottomless deluge, a thundering waterfall that would if unchecked soon flood iniquity from that province of the world. Somewhere in the atmosphere above a black anvil cloud was climbing toward outer space. Down the center of that column poured the heavens. Never in North America had I seen such a violent monsoon. And, of course, a few people continued to drive. Everyone else was pulled over on the shoulder. Eventually the dark colossus rolled east toward the sea. In its wake, the road under water in low places, traffic cautiously crawled forward. A half mile ahead, a red sports car with bald tires and Florida plates was wrapped around a white oak tree. A state trooper had just pulled over and was about to earn his pay.

That did it. I had no idea where I was, but I was getting off. I exited at the next interchange. The Georgia highway map told me the road was U.S. 341. It was headed in generally the right direction—south and east toward Cumberland Island—and the slow pace of the fugitive byway was agreeable. It was classic Southern farm country. Cultivated fields of soybean and tobacco, planted sections of corn and peanuts, neatly aligned groves of peach and pecan trees. And everywhere woodlots overgrown with kudzu and wild grape vines.

Gone were the Carolina parakeets and ivory-billed woodpeckers.

Gone forever.

As the miles added up, the cotton fields became more abundant, the cotton bolls several sizes larger than those in Mississippi and Alabama. About every third or fourth crop had been harvested, the loose cotton piled in enormous white stacks. The stacks were approximately the size of a city bus. From this raw field cotton would come flags and funeral shrouds, dress shirts and pleated skirts, beach towels and bed sheets, tablecloths and wedding dresses, hospital linen and baby diapers.

By the time I'd driven through Pulaski County and Dodge County and passed through the villages of Jaybird Springs, McRae, Scotland, and Lumber City (founded 1837), I was no longer in the

Georgia Midlands. The country was flatter, with black tupelo swamps spreading wherever the land was low. Mud turtles rested on half-sunken logs and wood ducks patrolled and bull frogs chanted. Stout papyruslike cane grew to heights of ten and twelve feet wherever the mud had gathered and started to form land. The air was hot and sticky and I was reminded that Cumberland Island is at the same latitude as Cairo, Egypt.

Water, water everywhere, and the faint odor of decay.

Okefenokee Swamp an hour to the south.

And the flora was changing. Around the houses, and in just the space of a few miles, there were suddenly banana trees, pomegranate trees, orange trees, and palm trees. I had crossed a border and was now in the subtropics. Nearly every home had its own giant live oak tree, a venerable behemoth with a trunk as massive as a corn silo. On the recumbent branches grew fertile gardens of resurrection fern, green moss, and trailing wisteria, and over the entire tree were draped hundreds of yards of Spanish moss, the long gray strands forever waving like ghosts reluctant to leave the place.

The overall impression was of strength and grace, of a tree that was not just a tree but a self-sufficient ecosystem.

The homes along U.S. 341 were of two varieties: unpainted wooden shanties that appeared to be held together with nightly prayers and rambling white-columned affairs of the sort that inspired Margaret Mitchell's epic tale of Tara. The former outnumbered the latter by a factor of about one hundred to one, a ratio that brought to mind ancient Mayan society prior to the mysterious collapse.

At a little town called Hazelhurst, county seat of Jefferson Davis County, I got some gas and turned south on U.S. 23.

Tired of solitude, I turned on the radio.

On a fading FM rock station from Macon there was a live interview with Georgia native Chuck Leavell, former keyboardist for Macon's own Allman Brothers Band and now playing for the Rolling Stones on the Voodoo Lounge tour. The Stones would perform in Atlanta later that week. In a thick southern accent, Chuck told picaresque tales of touring with the band. Mick Jagger loved Atlanta, Leavell chuckled, for two reasons: the blues clubs and the strip clubs. "What are you most proud of in your career?" inquired the interviewer. Leavell's answer was surprising. Not playing with slide guitar genius Duane Allman, or providing backup on Eric Clapton's *Unplugged* album, or touring with Keith Richards and company. He was most proud of having been voted the 1994 Georgia Tree Farmer of the Year. Leavell, it seemed, owned a 1,200-acre tree farm in the country south of Macon.

Georgia has more planted trees than any state in the union, and tree farming was big business in U.S. 23 country. Everywhere there were cultivated stands of loblolly pine, known locally as Rosemary pine because of the sweet-smelling resin. Some of the stands were young and not yet thinned out. Others were mature and cleared and soon to be converted into houses and paper. Others were past their prime—perhaps a benevolent owner was letting them change slowly to hardwood forest.

By the time I reached Folkston and turned east on State Route 40, cypress trees were growing thickly in the swamps on either side of the road. Cypresses are strange, ancient trees dating back to the age of dinosaurs. The way they evolved—a tall straight trunk and then a weirdly shaped flat crown with branches sharply angled— suggests that at one time they were heavily browsed by long-necked animals. The brontosaurus is gone, but the cypress remains. All you need is a little imagination to picture those immense vege-tarians splashing ponderously among the cypress. The only relict of the dinosaur age remaining in the swamps today is the alligator, a tenacious egg-layer that somehow outlasted tyrannosaurus and the rest of that cold-blooded bestiary.

Fifteen miles from the coastal village of St. Mary's, where I would spend the night, I smelled the ocean for the first time. Actu-ally I smelled the salt marshes. The odor was sulfurous, reminiscent of the valley of the Firehole River in Yellowstone. It is a smell that conjures up memories. Every drop of our blood contains the same percentage of salt as sea water. In the womb, along about the fifth or sixth week, we carry facial gills, our breathing apparatus from ages ago. Women's monthly periods are timed to the lunar tides in which our predecessors once lived and procreated and died.

Coming back to the sea, as they say, is coming back home.

Just this side of St. Mary's I passed the entrance to the King's Bay Naval Submarine Base, home of the Atlantic fleet of Trident nuclear submarines. A marine guard was busily saluting all the incoming cars with blue officers' decals, and I pitied him that piece of duty, four hours on, eight hours off for days on end. A little far-

ther on was the Gilman Paper Company pulp mill. It was an imposing structure, though one not designed by Frank Lloyd Wright or
any architect who has ever been seriously influenced by Wright.
On the other side of St. Mary's was the waterfront of saltwater bars
and seafood restaurants, and the fishermen's dock where I would
catch the ferry. The ranger at the Cumberland Island visitor's center had good news and bad news. The good news was that my
reservations for the ferry and campground were duly registered in
the logbook. The bad news was that the mosquitoes and sand fleas
were at a five-year high, a result of the recent drenching rains. The
other bad news was that a local teenage gang was breaking out the
windows of cars in the visitor's overnight parking lot and stealing
everything they could get their hands on.

My first stop was the local police station, just down the street.
Looking for advice, but no one was there. It was Sunday, and the
sign said if you had a problem to call 911.

Next stop was the Goodbread House, a yellow-painted Victorian home that had been converted into a bed-and-breakfast. I was
greeted there by Betty and George Kraus, sitting on the porch with
their nine or ten cats. She was a retired junior high school teacher and
he was a retired forester for the state of Georgia. They were friendly
as Georgians are, and she seemed to like me because we had both
worked as teachers. Within minutes the situation was resolved. I
would spend the night in their restored 1885 home, and they would
watch the car for the three nights I'd be on Cumberland Island.

That night after Betty's poached flounder and candied yams I
went upstairs and stacked the pillows and read the book I had
brought: William Bartram's *Travels Through North and South Carolina, Georgia, East and West Florida,* which was originally published
during George Washington's first term. William Bartram was the son
of John Bartram, the colonial botanist, and undertook some of the
earliest surveys of southeastern flora for his father. I read through the
first two chapters, as the naturalist arrived in Savannah, Georgia, and
traveled south by horse, and fell asleep shortly after he reached St.
Mary's, which was at that time "the utmost frontier" (his words) of
settlement. The Okefenokee Swamp, the source of the St. Mary's
River, Bartram spelled phonetically as "Ouqquaphenogaw," which
suggests the pronunciation may have changed over time. The
swamp, he wrote, was an "enchanted land" where "the daughters of
the sun lived."

At breakfast I was introduced to Lauren and Paul Saxton, who had arrived late and would be going to the island with me on the morning ferry. Lauren was about fifty, with short gray hair and a sharp nose and a serious, intense quality about her. Paul was physically her opposite, about the same age but full-fleshed and fat around the waist. He was bald, wore a beard not yet fully gray, and had an edge to him. The first thing he said after shaking hands was, "This is the first time in a month I haven't felt like killing someone."

Lauren asked me what I did and I told them. Then it was their turn. They were from Plainfield, New Jersey, Lauren a family practice attorney, and Paul a former corporate executive who now owned his own computer consulting company, which in these days is the accepted way of describing a state of professional unemployment.

After wolfing down his cheese omelet and rasher of bacon and homemade biscuits Paul sighed sadly and said he always forgot to bring something and this time he had forgotten to bring his folding knife.

I always carry two on camping trips, and so I gave him one. He opened the blade and saw the blood stains and asked about them. I told him that I had last used the knife in August to skin a caribou in northern Alaska. A look of horror passed over his face.

"You hunt?"

I nodded.

"With a gun?"

After I affirmed that yes, I indeed hunted, they excused themselves and ran upstairs to pack their bags.

We met again at the dock.

The place was swarming with people. There were two groups: a mob of eleven- or twelve-year-old children, attended to by a pair of frantic teachers who had lost control of both themselves and their class, and a boisterous crew of river rafters from "French Broad River Outfitters" in western North Carolina.

Paul had a slightly panicked look on his face.

"We've been coming here for twenty years and I've never seen anything like this before. It's like a carnival. Where do these freaks come from?"

"Calm down, honey," his long-suffering wife implored.

"But Sea Camp will be a zoo. Look at this. Cases of beer. Banjos. Guitars. They've even got CD players for Christ's sake."

"Just relax."

He actually looked as though he might have a fit, and she glanced at me for help, and so I set my backpack and cooler down beside their four duffel bags.

After a brief orientation by a ranger we were herded onto the boat. I found myself sitting between Paul and Lauren on the starboard side, facing the tangled green bank of Florida, three or four hundred yards distant. Every time the wind died the air vibrated with the music of mosquitoes and sand fleas. I mentioned something about the musical quality of the insects and Paul launched into a lecture on atonal music. It went on and on, with references to obscure European composers you and I have never heard of.

With a grinding of gears and a belching of diesel smoke, the *Cumberland Queen* got under way. We were at last headed down the tannin-colored St. Mary's River toward Cumberland Sound and beyond that Cumberland Island. The tide was coming in and the captain announced the trip would take a bit longer than usual.

Paul was still rambling on about atonal music. I was watching one of the members of the French Broad River group as she pulled her T-shirt up, wondering what she was doing. Someone handed her a baby and she began to feed it.

"You two ever catch a Springsteen concert?" I asked, hoping to get Paul to shut up about atonal music.

They looked at me as if I'd just spoken Greek.

"You know, from Asbury Park, New Jersey?"

"We know who he is," said Paul. "We just don't consider what he does to be music."

It was going to be one of those trips.

It being late November, the cordgrass salt marshes had lost their summer green and turned a rich golden color. There were long-legged birds, herons and cranes, stalking in the golden marshes. Even as I watched a crane stabbed a silver fish, a mullet probably, in its beak and then flew off to feed at the top of a sabal palm.

Midway down the St. Mary's River one of the North Carolinians, who had been drinking a can of beer, exclaimed, "I think I'm going hurl," and then fulfilled the prophecy.

"I'd like to hurl him is what I'd like to do," exclaimed Paul, loud enough so everyone at our end of the boat could hear.

"Paul," whispered his embarrassed wife.

"I don't care. I may have to use some of my New Jersey rudeness before this trip is over."

Toward the end, after we turned into the blue waters of Cumberland Sound, a pair of dolphins appeared and followed the boat. You saw their triangular dorsal fins and their gray backs and then suddenly their rounded contoured heads, and then they would dive under the waves and resurface somewhere else.

One of the deck hands, a darkly tanned man made of solid muscle, stepped from the cabin to watch the dolphins. After a moment he pointed to a distant pair of enormous concrete bunkers to the north.

"That's where they keep the warheads."

I asked him about a sizable naval vessel a mile up the Sound, surrounded by floating docks.

"That's the *Canopus*. A submarine tender. That's one Clinton decommissioned."

"I voted for Clinton," said Paul defensively.

The deck hand indicated that he had served on the *Canopus* before the budget cuts.

"What's the fishing like around here?" I asked.

"Sea trout are moving up the rivers to spawn. I caught a couple of them last night on the bridge."

The captain called and the man stepped back into the cabin. We were nearing the dock at the Dungeness Ruins on Cumberland Island. The 200-year-old ruins were not visible from the dock. All you could see was the dock and the jungle. There was no one waiting at the dock, and so we continued on to the Sea Camp visitor's center, which was a large cypress cabin set among enormous live oaks and a thick brush of sawtooth palmettos. Cypress is the ideal wood for cabins because it is naturally oily and resistant to rot.

Paul and Lauren were among the first off the boat. The first people off, Paul had confided, got one of the pushcarts. The pushcarts made it easier to move gear to the Sea Camp campground, half a mile distant. They sat near their pushcarts, pretending not to guard them. No one was permitted to leave until after the orientation lecture by the ranger.

One of the children, a boy with thick Buddy Holly glasses, a lad who reminded me of myself at that age, was solemnly informing a group of girls that they were now in Jurassic Park and that there were dinosaurs everywhere. Just then a red-haired ranger in shorts walked by. His freckled white skin, peeling and burned, seemed not to like the light of the subtropics.

"Is that true, mister?" asked one of the girls.

"What?"

"That there are dinosaurs on Cumberland Island?"

"Well, there are alligators."

"Are they big?"

"Some are. There's a female on Raccoon Key over ten feet."

The little boy beamed.

After a while I walked over to the visitor's center. On the porch was a small outdoor museum. Under glass were fossilized shark teeth, the strange extraterrestrial-looking skull of a loggerhead sea turtle, the big-domed skull of a dolphin, various seashells, a pair of white-tailed deer antlers, miscellaneous mammal vertebrae, shed snake skins, pressed beach wildflowers, bird feathers, a scorpion in a bottle, a baby alligator hide, a stuffed screech owl, and other novelties. It was a sort of pre-Linnean *wunderkammern,* or cabinet of curiosities, and the informality was refreshing. Something was lost, as well as gained, when we began to precisely catalogue and organize nature.

The orientation was held outside because of the size of the group. We were warned about ticks (one young man on the Willow Pond Trail came in with 500 on his person), tick fever, chiggers, Lyme disease, scorpions, centipedes, fire ants, poison ivy, poison oak, standing pond water, amoebic dysentery, malaria, rabies, brown bats, rattlesnakes, water moccasins, alligators, barracudas, sharks, sting rays, sea urchins, wild horses, wild pigs, changing tides, sunburn, sun stroke, and so on. The only time the crowd took serious note was when the ranger gave directions to the clothing optional beach. When it was over we were assigned camping spots.

Paul and Lauren led the way. The hard sand trail was lovely, winding through a green tunnel formed by the overhanging branches of ancient live oak trees, all draped with Spanish moss.

When we reached our campsites on the far side of the oak forest—the sound of the surf coming from over the dunes—Paul

267

and Lauren dropped everything and ran off to the beach. I stayed and set up my tent. When I was done I placed my cooler and food inside a chicken-wire box mounted on a wooden post. Before leaving for the beach I stopped to study the world's largest spider web, occupied by a golden orb spider as big as my hand. Trapped in the web was the partly consumed red carcass of what had recently been a green chameleon.

There was a boardwalk over the dune field to the beach. Reaching the steps at the top of the dunes I saw it was a magnificent wild beach running north and south into the hazy distance, the sand as white as field cotton, the cloudless sky one shade less blue than the sea. Once off the hot planks the sand was smooth and firm and warm underfoot. There were already a few people in the water and a few others were having lunch on the beach. Out beyond the breakers the sea was calm and blue, sparkling under the sun. You could see several boats, small fishing rigs and shrimpers and long container ships, sprinkled at random to the horizon. Although the tide was going out, there were a few lazy waves coming in. They came in toward the long beach slowly, gathering weight, and then broke over smoothly in the shallow water. I walked in the water and it was pretty much what you'd expect in November. A cool breeze was blowing steadily from the sea. Otherwise the beach would have been very hot.

As I said, the beach was all I'd hoped for. The cool breeze and warmth and open spaces and friendly people were a natural balm, a soothing medicine, the perfect antidote for urban civilization. Some people have therapists, medication regimes, behaviorists, weekly groups, and twelve-step programs. Others have places like Cumberland.

I walked north, to where the island curved to a point, with no other object than to find a place to lie down and spend the rest of the day doing as little as possible. I spent the afternoon among the dunes sunbathing, reading Bartram on the amazing crystal springs of Florida (the passage that inspired Coleridge's poem "Xanadu"), swimming whenever I became hot, and studying the changing colors of the sea and the way the shadows moved beneath the clouds drifting over the sea.

Lauren and Paul met me late in the afternoon on the beach and invited me to their place for dinner. Paul was a changed man, thoroughly sedated by a few hours on the beach, and I accepted. We cannot always choose our companions, but we can always make the best of it.

Sitting around the campfire that night, our faces more red from the afternoon sun than the fire, scratching our stomachs from a gourmet chicken teriyaki meal prepared by Paul, drinking beer from my cooler, we kept the conversation as casual as possible, saving the serious topics—the existence of UFOs, life after death, poltergeists, the future of the human race—for the next night.

Off in the distance someone with a guitar was singing old Grateful Dead songs.

After an hour of small talk it began to rain, at first gently and then not so gently, and so I retired to my camp. Several minutes after extinguishing the candle, a family of raccoons, a mother and her brood, began scratching insistently around the tent. This went on for a while, and so I finally offered them an apple, and they dragged it off into the night, clucking in religious ecstasy, and did not disturb me again.

As I drifted off into sleep a part of me wanted to run off into the night with them, climb the trees, explore the clearings, and wander the beach under the stars. Animals love the night in ways we humans have forgotten. But with the rain pouring down and the Jovian thunder and lightning I was just as glad to be sleeping peacefully in my nice dry tent.

Islands. No man is an island. The universe is an island. An island is a universe. There are islands on the sun, and the sun is part of an island called the Milky Way. The earth is an island. There are islands where there was once sea, and beneath the sea there are sunken reefs that once were islands. Australia is an island. A desert oasis is an island. An iceberg is an island. A mountaintop is an island. Manhattanites live on an island. There are islands in the middle of crowded cities. You see them in the vacant eyes of people living without love, without faith, without opportunity, estranged from nature and themselves. According to William Blake every grain of sand is an island. Inside a microscopic cell there are islands. The isles of the pancreas produce insulin. Some historians refer to medieval Byzantium as an island. To a carpenter ant, your desktop is an island. When I think of my life, I think of times that were like islands, some like Cyclops and others like Calypso.

Ulysses knew about islands. Excalibur rests at the bottom of a lake with an island called Avalon, and that lake is found on the island of England, and near that lake is said to be a stone that reads *Hic iacet Arthurus, rex quondam, rexque futurus* ("Here lies Arthur, who was once king and king will be again"). Shakespeare's last major play was about a shipwreck on an island and is based on what happened to Sir George Somers and his friends at Bermuda. Napoleon was banished to an island south of France. The ship that took men to the moon was launched from an island. Our national parks are islands. Some of our islands are national parks.

I was thinking about all this the next morning, lying on my back in the darkness, waiting for first light. It would be a busy day and I was planning it out carefully. A day well planned is a day well lived.

When the birds began to sing I ate my breakfast of Fig Newtons and put on my daypack and set out for the south end of the island, where I would spend the day exploring. I had the beach to myself and it was the sort of brilliant red Homeric sunrise one might recall ages hence, sitting in a nursing home, reflecting on the high points of the journey.

All across the beach were scattered shells. Some were as small as your fingernail, others as big as your head. There were knobbed whelks, dogwinkles, periwinkles, augers, sundials, olives, limpets, scallops, cockles, coquinas, angel wings, and the less exotic clams and mussels. My favorite was the miniature half-inch auger, which resembled the detached horn of a three-inch rhinoceros. From the aperture each shell swirled in a tight logarithmic spiral from right to left in ever-narrowing circles to a sharp point. They were camouflage-colored either lemon yellow or light sandy brown. The soft, dead inhabitants had formerly made their living drilling into the shells of other gastropods and devouring the contents, or feasting on defenseless sea worms. Scattered among the treasury of shells were the remnants of hermit crabs, ghost crabs, fiddler crabs, horseshoe crabs, starfish, squid, sea cucumbers, sponges, sea fans, whip and star corals, sundry fish, and, in one case, a deceased seagull. After an hour at the high-tide wrack, my pack was a bit heavier and smelled of the sea.

The sun was well up from the sea now and I was sweating freely under the T-shirt I soon pulled off.

Two miles down the beach there was a trail to the west, and I followed it toward the largest dunes on the island. There were tracks everywhere: the sharply cloven tracks of white-tailed deer, sunken in soft places to the dew claws; the massive imprints of slow-plodding wild horses; the delicate humanlike hands of raccoons. Everything left its autograph here.

The dunes were covered with live oaks and cabbage palms, and some of the palms were surprisingly tall. The live oaks had all been shaped and sculpted by the sea winds, much like trees at timberline. Facing the sea, the branches were shortened, but on the inland side the branches extended normally. The elevation of the dunes provided a nice view of the distant sea, extending blue and flat beyond the green of the brush forest, and the cool breeze coming in from the sea grounded the bugs I knew would be a problem on the other side of the dunes.

Back on the trail I soon caught sight of Cumberland's most famous historical site.

The Dungeness Mansion, built by General Nathaniel Greene in 1783, was like something from a William Faulkner novel. It was a ruined four-story mansion of brick and mortar, a once busy country residence that now consisted of partially collapsed walls, woodless floors, empty windows, and bat-infested chimneys. The shingled roof had been blown off long ago by a hurricane. It was the sort of ruined place elegiac poets of the Thomas Gray school love. I tried to picture it in former days—the great parties with whale oil lanterns out on the lawn and linen-covered tables laid with venison and wild boar and sea bass, the silver platters of cheeses and fruits and cakes, the jugs of Madeira wine and kegs of Carolina beer. There were dances at Dungeness, and weddings, and horse races with fine stock whose descendants now live like the Snopses in the swamps. I pictured General Greene sitting outside in a hammock reading just-delivered, month-old letters from his friends Washington and Jefferson up north in Virginia, or perhaps the latest book on the vast unknown interior of Africa by Mungo Park or James Bruce, and I marveled at how much the world has changed in two centuries.

Out back of the mansion was a graveyard with antique faded headstones covered with green moss and fallen oak leaves and the glistening paths of garden snails. The inscriptions told of a loving wife, a Revolutionary war hero, a young daughter taken by God too soon, and others forgotten by time. I thought of John Muir sleeping in the graveyard up the coast at Savannah on his thousand-mile walk to the Gulf. The cemetery was, Muir wrote, the "ideal place" for the "penniless wanderer" to sleep, for naturalists, unlike the rest of the human race, are not afraid of ghosts.

As I left Dungeness Ruins there were wild turkeys strutting about the grounds, and it made a romantic picture—the gutted shell of the once great colonial house, the overgrown vegetable and flower gardens, the brick patios and promenades, the stately planted magnolias with bright green leaves, the royal palms imported from the Caribbean, the Spanish moss hanging from everything.

It was, someone said back at Sea Camp, an excellent place for a picnic.

Beyond Dungeness were the Indian middens, each pile of accumulated oyster shells representing centuries of Indian feasts. Here the first Americans had shelled oysters for 3,000 years. I tried to imagine what life was like on Cumberland before the Spanish and French and British, before the slave ships and the Dust Bowl days and the Trinity site. I thought about what Mark Twain said: "It was wonderful to discover America, but it would have been more wonderful to miss it."

Farther back was the salt marsh and a deer trail out to the far southwestern point of the island, where I spent two hours waving off mosquitoes and digging among the old dredge spoils for fossilized shark teeth, ray plates, sea drum teeth, and turtle plates. Most of the dredged fossils, according to the ranger at the orientation talk, were of Pliocene age, from 1.8 to 5 million years old. I had absolutely no luck at all, and could only marvel at the hundreds of fiddler crabs scurrying around the place in vast comical herds.

It was now afternoon, and so I returned to the eastern beach and sat down on the edge of an extensive marshland for lunch. There was a mosquito hatch ongoing in the marshes, but the sea breeze kept them from me, and the view of perhaps ten thousand swallows diving and feeding among the swarm was truly amazing. I took several photographs here, because I knew no one would believe me when I later reported there were ten thousand swallows. Throughout the lunch hour I was serenaded by dozens of frogs, but saw only one.

The southeastern tip of the island, with its view across the mouth of the St. Mary's River into Florida, proved an irresistible attraction, and among its jetties and dunes I spent the rest of the day. Here, on the protected side of the jetty I shed my clothes and swam in the clear warm lagoon as egrets and herons fished in the shallows. I probed among the rocks of the jetty for a time, examining trapped squid, crabs, starfish, shrimp, jellyfish, sea cucumbers, fish fry, and other fauna, and left after I saw what appeared to be a scorpion fish hiding with its venomous barbs in a pool where I'd almost stepped.

Following dinner that night, Lauren, Paul, and I sat around the campfire and solved all the riddles, mysteries, and lingering questions of human existence. Something about a campfire inspires the human spirit to such endeavors. Lauren believed the chief obstacle to human progress was the manner in which we treat children. So long as they are considered property, she insisted, the blights of the human condition would persist. In her practice she had dealt with this issue for twenty years, and spoke with the voice of experience. I asked her about Plato's suggestion in *The Republic* that children be raised by professionally trained people, rather than by whatever parents nature provides, and she recalled that this idea had been tried on some kibbutzes in Israel and in the old Soviet Union and hadn't worked very well. On the nature of the revolution we agreed. The details were left for others to work out.

Sometime after midnight the philosophers retired, and a short time later the raccoons, accompanied by curious armadillos, arrived.

The next day I spent walking to the far north end of the island. On the wide empty beach I felt variously like Robinson Crusoe, Gilligan, Prospero, the first man, the last man. The grueling trek at other times brought back memories of Parris Island, twenty years earlier, and the long death marches under the hot southern sun with me carrying the platoon colors. In the Willow Ponds, the Sweetwater Ponds, and Lake Whitney, I saw many birds, especially wading birds, but no alligators, otters, ospreys, wandering Florida panthers, or red wolves. The only excitement came just before lunch, when I snuck up on two white-tailed deer bucks drinking from a pool of stagnant water and startled them at a distance of about twenty feet by saying hello. I turned back at the north end of the island—ahead was an ominous swarm of mosquitoes and sand fleas rising from the waters of Christmas Creek.

After several hours of walking south there was a human form in the distance, and I waved and soon met a ranger on patrol. His name was Brian and he was from Utah, had a pregnant wife and two children back in St. Mary's, and was praying for a transfer to Zion National Park, which he said was the most beautiful place on earth. I asked him about local wildlife, and he said the most interesting animals were the Caribbean manatees that had taken up residence in the waters near the Gilman Paper Company, attracted by the warm water from the discharge pumps. They now lived around Cumberland year-round, and the company was working closely with federal biologists to ensure their safety. He said it was a good example of private–public cooperation, and I couldn't disagree. I asked him what the biggest management problems were on the island, and he said Greyfield Inn, a private inholding, and what to do with Plum Orchard Mansion, the old Andrew Carnegie place. We shook hands, and I bid him well on the reconnaissance.

As I returned to Sea Camp five miles later there was a small band of wild horses feeding quietly among the seagrasses. There were five of them: a gray stallion, three paint mares that appeared to be related, and a six-month-old gray foal. The stallion was a lean solid animal, always alert, flaring his nostrils into the breeze and turning his ears. On his back and neck were a constellation of white scars and partially healed bite marks.

It is a tough life, that of a stallion.

I got within thirty feet of them, and went no closer. The mares had no wounds and showed considerably more body fat than the stallion. The foal was happy and playful as are all young animals. I studied their feet, having shod my share of horses in my youth, and saw the sort of long-toed, heel-shattered, sand-cracked hooves that are a farrier's nightmare. The essence of a horse's health, and value, are in its feet.

It wasn't long before a dirty white stallion and a second herd of mares came trotting up a deer trail. Even as I watched, the new arrivals caught sight of the smaller band of horses at my side. The dirty white stallion assumed a tense, rigid position and whinnied a challenge. His mares stopped behind him. He was a big powerful animal, with more weight on him than the gray.

From beside me came the response, and at this point I climbed a dune to remove myself from the field of battle.

Indignant snorts and whinnies went back and forth. Much striking of the ground with front hooves and thrashing of heads.

The contest began with a thundering gallop to the water's edge, the dirty white intruder pursuing the gray stallion. When they reached the water the two horses stopped. Gulls and terns and pelicans scattered in every direction. The field of conflict belonged to the stallions. They stood perfectly still for a long moment. The tension steadily built.

Suddenly the fight began, and it was strictly a street brawl, with no rules, no time-outs, no ice packs waiting in the corner.

In the first confrontation the stallions reared up on hind feet and lashed with sharp front hooves. Each landed at least one painful blow in the initial exchange. When the fisticuffs were over the score was roughly even. After that the horses took turns at "finding the jugular." When they tired of that sport, both necks running red with blood, they played "try to castrate your opponent." This dangerous maneuver was attempted with teeth and hooves and involved undertaking defense and offense simultaneously. The heat of the engagement was now intense, both horses covered with blood and sweat. The gray was more nimble than the white and delivered several well-aimed kicks near the groin of the white. Just when it seemed the gray might gain the advantage, the white stallion pivoted on his front feet and landed a devastating blow to the most sensitive area of his opponent. The effect was immediate. The gray walked a few steps and collapsed as if shot. From that position, head down and legs tucked in under the body, the injured gray did not, could not, move.

Through all this the mares steadily fed, showing little interest in the outcome.

The victor walked over and stood beside his vanquished opponent as rigidly as he had in the earlier invitation to battle. The issue of who would keep the harem in question appeared to have been settled.

The little foal watched intently as his father lay defeated, absorbing another lesson in the world of adulthood. He alone among the equine spectators seemed affected by the scene.

The white stallion, snorting victory, then trotted over to claim his prize, the three mares and the bewildered foal, which he briskly escorted over the dunes to his waiting band of mares and foals.

But it was not over, not yet.

The dazed opponent shook the stars from his head. The sight of his mares and foal being led away roused his deepest instincts. He rose to his feet. Overhead the clouds were just then turning the color of watermelon rind. The whole beach was washed in red light. Ignoring evident agony, the gray cantered stiffly toward the white, vocalizing with a sound that could best be described as a roar.

The white stallion turned to face him. He snorted some sort of message to his mares and then trotted back to the open beach where there would be more room to move.

Another battle ensued, this one bloodier than the first but three times slower. It was like a prizefight in the fifteenth round, after the heavyweight boxers are exhausted and trying to remain on their feet until the bell sounds and the score is tallied and read by the judges. Only here there was no bell, no referees, no attending managers, promoters, physicians. This was nature in the raw.

On and on it went, up and down the beach. A run, then a tangle, then another run. Over and over. An irresistible force and an immovable object. A fight, it would seem, to the death.

Twilight descending, the clouds showing the last ruddiness on their bellies.

Suddenly all seven of the mares that had come to the party with the dirty white stallion looked up simultaneously and trotted as if responding to a distant call down the deer trail toward the swamp. The three foals in that group followed. The mares and foal of the gray remained behind in the sea grass pasture, milling about in confusion. To whom did they belong now? The white stallion broke off from savaging the gray in the neck long enough to whinny for his mares to stay. They did not heed his call. He whinnied a second time with the same result. The mares had apparently had enough of the spectacle, and were leaving. He hurried after them.

That, then, was the outcome: each stallion would keep his respective harem.

It seemed such a waste, but aggression is the force that drives nature and evolution, that separates the durable from the decrepit, the decisive from the indecisive, the destined from the doomed.

Suddenly it was nearly dark. The first star twinkled between the pale clouds.

Low tide had reached its ebb. The waves began inching back toward the high-tide wrack of last night.

I looked around and there was no one else on the beach. Everyone was back at Sea Camp preparing for tomorrow. It was just me and the sand and the sea. I sat on the dune, my back to the land, my eyes toward the sea, and chewed on the stem of a sea oat. The sand was warmer than the air, and the sea was warmer than both. I lingered, thinking about nothing, watching the sea under the stars. Eventually a rainstorm drifted slowly out to sea from the north Florida coast and I watched the lightning flash in the hollows of the clouds, illuminating amphitheaters and antechambers of darkness, and every so often the lightning reached down and touched the sea, and I never heard anything from this storm but distant thunder.

Early the next morning I was awakened by the pounding surf. The wind had come up during the night, and the waves were crashing on the beach. With my ear against the sleeping pad I could hear the concussion of each swell. For a long time I lay in the dark listening to the sea. At five o'clock I lit the candle lantern and waited for the tent to warm. After several minutes the space was comfortable, and so I made a pillow of the sweater and read the last chapter of Bartram by candlelight. The chapter was just a few pages long and briefly described Bartram's return to Philadelphia after his expedition to the South. While passing through Savannah he had observed pack horses and wagons loaded with passenger pigeons. The previous night the local residents had taken pine-resin torches into the woods. Blinded and startled by the light, the "multitudinous" wintering flocks had dropped from the branches to the ground, where they had been beaten to death.

A week after Christmas, in deep snow and cold, the son of pioneering botanist John Bartram arrived at his father's house on the banks of the Schuylkill River.

There followed in the book an essay about the Creeks, Chero-kees, and Choctaws of the American Southeast. William Bartram observed that "here the people are all on an equality, as to the pos-session and enjoyments of the common necessaries and conve-niences of life." There was a "venerable senate" or council among each of the tribes, over which a chief presided. The chief was not born into the office, as with King George III of England, but, rather, earned it and was elected to it, as with the democracies of ancient Greece and Rome. Privileged classes were anathema in a society based on hard work and achievement. Among the "aborigines" there was less emphasis placed on private property than among those of European descent, but nevertheless each family was enti-tled to all the crops it had personally grown, while still depositing a portion in the communal area, from which less fortunate families could draw allotments. It was considered a disgrace and bad luck among the Indians not to help the poor.

Item: Bartram reported that the southeastern American tribes had invented a novel game they called "football," which was their "favourite, manly diversion." Football was played on "an extensive level plain" on which the players seized and carried the ball from the opposite party down the field and tried to hurl it "midway between two high pillars, which are the goals."

Item: Marriage was entered into "only for a year's time." Each year the contract between a man and a woman was renewed. Polygamy was permitted, and every man took as many wives as he could support, with the understanding that the first was "queen, and the others her handmaids and associates." After a marriage had been ended by either party, "the father [was] obliged to contribute towards [his children's] maintenance during their minority."

Above all, Bartram emphasized, the frontier southeast of his country was by no means a wilderness, but was the ancient habi-tation of populous nations that had built highways, canals, artificial lakes, pyramids, ceremonial mounds, walled cities, fortresses, ceme-teries, and planted fields and gardens.

So concluded the Quaker Bartram.

At five-thirty I heard an unusual birdsong and put on my jeans and shirt and stepped from the tent. The sand and twigs and leaves were wet under my toes. Everything was wet. The air was heavy with the scents of the forest and the sea. Somewhere the bird twittered again. A local naturalist could name the species for you, perhaps even provide the Latin binomial. I cannot. I can only tell you the lovely melody was composed of seven notes. The lyric quickly dropped three notes and then went down four, but not all at once. It was like a stream that slides down a series of falls, each of slightly different height. Overhead there were still stars between the boughs of the trees. The air was cold and damp and still in the forest, and I walked quickly down the path. My eyes were accustomed to the shadows, and so I did not need the flashlight. No one was up yet. Sea Camp was uniformly still, but for the rumble of the surf.

Out on the wooden boardwalk the chill was suddenly gone and I could feel the warmth of the sea. It was like the warmth of a lover across the bed—a gentle heat that holds you near. The Gulf Stream carries with it a heat from far away.

The sky to the east held the faintest gray. All else remained blackest night: stars, constellations, nebulae, galaxies. To the north was the Big Dipper. To the west my old friend Orion held last watch. The planet Mercury glistened like a spilled drop of plumber's solder on the eastern horizon. A desolate world named for a dead god, forever too close to the sun. Burned on one side and frozen on the other. Similar to Milton's view of the afterlife, or travel brochures for Iceland.

The waves boomed and crashed rhythmically in three- and four-foot swells. A steady wind blew from offshore. If you watched the gray it did not appear to change, but if you looked away for a moment and then looked back you could detect the gray had lightened a shade. It was like watching someone's spirits change very slowly as you try to cheer them up.

As I walked along the dunes a ghost crab darted down its hole. It entered backward, rear end first, claws last. There it would rest. Anything that tried to roust it would be pinched.

Yes, the long night was ending. The great day was beginning.

I walked up the beach into the wind, searching for the tracks of the horses, but they were gone. The sea had washed them away. Because of the wind I walked over a dune topped with sea oats. Out of the wind it was not so bad. When I looked back over the dune a bit later I was treated to a wonderful sight. The eastern horizon was glowing with all the hope that ever attended a birth in this world. The sky was clear except for one small assemblage of clouds, coincidentally floating above the exact point where the sun would rise. Even as I watched, the distant cloud deck caught the first light. The warm colors were like those my son brought with him from the womb.

Out of the birth canal, into the world.

Then the sun, loving mother of nine planets, too bright for any but the blind to look at.

Shortly after the sun cleared the water a flock of sea gulls flew by, searching for treasures left by the tide. Then followed the terns and pelicans.

Lauren and Paul suddenly appeared out of nowhere and asked me to take their picture. I remarked that they both looked ten years younger than when I first met them three days earlier, a statement that had the virtue of being true. They both loved to hear that, and after I took several photographs and wrote their address in my notebook and promised to mail them a nice print, they hurried off to finish packing.

After a while, I followed the boardwalk back toward camp and then at the last minute cut south along the dunes, found a place out of the wind, and lay down. I was not ready to leave the sea just yet. Who ever is? As I stretched out I heard the thump of deer. I never saw them, but I heard them thumping away. They must have been feeding on the lee side of the dune.

I stayed there on the white sand just this side of the dark wind-shaped trees for quite some time, soaking up the sun. If Cumberland Island were a glimpse of the future in parks, I was relieved. Rarely had I had such a fine experience in a park—no annoying cars, a manageable number of park visitors, plenty of solitude. For once people were compelled to leave the roads behind and use their legs and really get to know one small place well, rather than to drive frantically all over the country and actually see very little. For such an experience in Yellowstone or Yosemite I would gladly wait for a permit. When that day inevitably comes to the parks out West—which are islands as much as Cumberland—I will be the first to welcome it.

Finally the ferry boat horn sounded, telling everyone that the boat had arrived and would be departing shortly for the mainland. I left the island that day, but resolved to never leave it behind in my thoughts. In the end Cumberland, like so many of our finest parks, is too large to be folded in a map, captured in a photograph, or compressed into an essay. It is a place where the tides quietly rise into the brackish marshes and nourish the shrimp larvae, where the deer mice gather fallen acorns and the bobcats watch with eyes like polished topaz, where the river otters play in the freshwater lakes and the king snakes climb the mossy live oaks looking for treats, where the peregrine falcons rest on their migrations each September and the loggerhead sea turtles come to lay their eggs every summer. It is a place where the sun will forever rise on wild beaches that will never know the plague of mechanized development. It is a place to carry deep inside and hold close whenever you feel yourself in turmoil, and instantly be at peace.

$\mathscr{N}$OTES ON $\mathscr{C}$ONTRIBUTORS

Jennifer Ackerman • Jennifer Ackerman has written widely on natural history and the sciences. Her articles have appeared in *The New York Times*, *The Nature Conservancy*, and *National Geographic*, where she works as an editor. *Notes from the Shore* is her first published book.

Rick Bass • Rick Bass lives in northwestern Montana with his wife and two children. He is the author of such acclaimed books as *Ninemile Wolves, The Deer Pasture, The Watch,* and *The Sky, the Stars, the Wilderness.* In recent years he has been deeply involved in the effort to save the wildlands of his home valley, the Yaak.

Henry Beston • Henry Beston (1888-1968) purchased fifty acres along the great outer dunes of Cape Cod, after serving as a volunteer in the First World War, and began his solitary year of contemplation and observation of nature recorded in his most famous work, *The Outermost House.* His works include *Herbs and the Earth* (1935), *The St. Lawrence River* (1941), and *Northern Farm: A Chronicle of Maine* (1948).

Kenneth Brower • Ken Brower, son of noted conservationist David Brower, lives in San Francisco with his wife and son. His early books—*Micronesia* and *Earth and the Great Weather*—are now considered classics of the genre. Like his father before him Brower travels widely around the world, writing and speaking out on conservation issues.

Rachel Carson • Rachel Carson, simply put, was one of the most influential nature conservationists of the twentieth century. Together with such figures as Bob Marshall and Aldo Leopold, she helped to create a world in which nature is given formal protection under federal law. In books like *Silent Spring*, which related the environmental effects of pesticides, she exerted an enormous influence on public policy. A marine biologist by training, she also wrote a number of best-selling books about the sea, including *The Edge of the Sea.*

John Cole • John Cole lived for seven years on Long Island's East End and made his living as a saltwater fisherman. His articles have appeared in *The New York Times, Harpers, Country Journal, Esquire, The Atlantic,* and *The Boston Globe.* He is the author of *Fishing Came First* and *Striper: A Story of Fish and Man.*

Jack Connor • Jack Connor is the author of the highly acclaimed *Complete Birder: A Guide to Better Birding.* He has written about birding and other subjects for *Newsweek, Harrowsmith, Country Journal, The Washington Post,* and other publications.

Charles Darwin • One can count on the fingers of one hand the scientists who have truly revolutionized the human condition— Isaac Newton, Charles Darwin, Albert Einstein, James Watson. It was Darwin who first provided a firm theoretical and empirical basis for the theory that life is in a continual state of change and evolution. On the voyage of the HMS *Beagle* (1831–1836) he first began to develop the ideas that would later shock the world. The reverberations of that historic voyage of discovery are still being felt.

Jan DeBlieu • Jan DeBlieu grew up in Wilmington, Delaware, and worked for many years as a reporter for eastern newspapers. Since 1984 she has focused on issues of oceanography, ecology, and endangered species biology. Her books include *Meant to Be Wild*, about endangered species in the Deep South, and *Hatteras Journal*, a collection of essays, arranged seasonally, about life on the Outer Banks of North Carolina.

Daniel Duane • Daniel Duane grew up on the California coast. At an early age, he began surfing with his father, a San Francisco attorney and master surfer. Duane specifically chose the program at the University of California, Santa Cruz, for his graduate study in American Literature, so that he could surf every day. In 1997 he was awarded a doctoral degree. He currently lives in San Francisco. His articles and essays have appeared nationally in such publications as *Rolling Stone* and *The Los Angeles Times*. He is the author of three books, including *Caught Inside*, a surfing memoir, and two novels.

John Hay • John Hay, a recipient of the Burroughs Award, is past president of the Cape Cod Museum of Natural History and former professor of environmental studies at Dartmouth College. He has written *The Run, The Undiscovered Country*, and *The Immortal Wilderness*, among many other works of natural history.

Marybeth Holleman • Marybeth Holleman lives in the hills above Anchorage, Alaska, with her son and her partner Rick, an oceanographer at the University of Alaska. Holleman teaches part-time in the English Department of the University of Alaska. Her work has been published widely in journals and reviews, and she is currently working on a book about Prince William Sound and its recovery from the 1989 *Exxon Valdez* oil spill.

Gilbert Klingel • Gilbert Klingel was a naturalist of the early twentieth century. In 1930 he and a companion wrecked their thirty-eight-foot yawl on the coast of Great Inagua Island in the Bahamas. Nine years later Klingel wrote a memoir of his time on the island entitled *Inagua, An Island Sojourn*. Since its publication it has become a classic in the genre of adventure narratives.

Barry Lopez • Barry Lopez is one of America's most distinguished writers. His books include such celebrated works as *Of Wolves and Men, Arctic Dreams, Crossing Open Crossing*, and *All About This Life*. He has been the recipient of numerous awards and honors, including a Guggenheim Fellowship, the American Book Award, and the John Burroughs medal for nature writing. He lives in Oregon with his wife Sandra, an artist.

Nancy Lord • For the past twenty years, Nancy Lord has made a living fishing for salmon on the west side of Cook Inlet near Homer, Alaska. Lord has during that time also distinguished herself as a writer of prose, both in fiction (*Survival*, a collection of short stories) and in the more recent book of essays *Fishcamp, Life on an Alaskan Shore*.

John Muir • John Muir needs little introduction to lovers of nature and literature. Born in Scotland, Muir grew up in Wisconsin and worked for a time in a factory before leaving civilization behind and devoting himself to studying, protecting, and writing about wilderness. His travels took him across North America, including several expeditions to the coasts of British Columbia and Alaska (as far north as the Bering Sea on the Coast Guard cutter *Corwin*). His writings on Alaska are now considered classics of the genre.

Jeff Ripple • Jeff Ripple, a natural history writer and professional photographer, devotes his time to exploring and documenting his home state of Florida. His books include *Big Cypress Swamps and the Ten Thousand Islands*, *Sea Turtles*, *The Florida Keys*, *Florida: The Natural Wonders*, and *The Southwest Florida's Wetland Wilderness*.

Henry David Thoreau • Henry David Thoreau is generally credited with having created the nature essay as a modern literary form. Born in Concord, Massachusetts, in 1819, he later graduated from Harvard and worked as a village schoolmaster and as a country surveyor. His friends and associates included such luminaries as Ralph Waldo Emerson and Nathaniel Hawthorne. Thoreau published two books in his short lifetime: *A Week on the Concord and Merrimack Rivers* (1849) and *Walden* (1854). His most influential piece of writing was a short essay entitled "Civil Disobedience," which inspired a variety of twentieth-century philosopher-activists, including Mahatma Gandhi, Martin Luther King, Jr., and Nelson Mandela, in their search for political justice.

Mark Twain • Samuel Langhorne Clemens, popularly known as Mark Twain, was born in 1835 and died in 1910. Those seventy-five years spanned a time of unprecedented change in American culture, and Twain's many books provide a detailed and often hilarious history of a nation lurching through its frequently turbulent adolescence. His books include *The Adventures of Tom Sawyer, Huckleberry Finn, The Prince and the Pauper, A Connecticut Yankee at King Arthur's Court, Joan of Arc, Life on the Mississippi,* and *Roughing It.*

William W. Warner • William W. Warner was born in New York City and graduated from Princeton University. After a career in the foreign service and the Peace Corps he joined the Smithsonian Institution in 1964, where he worked for many years. *Beautiful Swimmers* was awarded the Pulitzer Prize in 1977.

Susan Zwinger • Susan Zwinger, daughter of acclaimed artist and writer Ann Zwinger, lives on a small island in Puget Sound near Seattle, Washington. She has written on subjects as diverse as the Mojave Desert, the interior of Alaska, and the new national monument in southern Utah (Grand Staircase-Canyons of the Escalante).

$\mathcal{A}$ CKNOWLEDGMENTS

Jennifer Ackerman: "Spindrift," from *Notes from the Shore*. Copyright 1995 by Viking Penguin. Reprinted with permission of Viking Penguin, a division of Penguin Books USA.

Rick Bass: "Hawaii." Copyright 1995 by Rick Bass. Reprinted with permission of the author.

Henry Beston: "Orion Rises on the Dunes," from *The Outermost House*. Copyright 1928, 1949, 1956 by Henry Beston, 1977 by Elizabeth C. Beston. Reprinted with permission of Henry Holt and Company.

Kenneth Brower: "On the Reef, Darkly." Copyright 1992 by Kenneth Brower. Reprinted with permission of the author.

Rachel Carson: "The World of the Reef Flats," from *The Edge of the Sea* by Rachel Carson, illustrated by Robert W. Hines. Copyright 1955 by Rachel L. Carson. Reprinted with permission of Houghton Mifflin.

John Cole: Excerpt from *Striper*. Copyright 1962 by John Cole. Reprinted with permission of the Lyons Press.

Jack Connor: Excerpt from *Season at the Point*. Copyright 1974 by Jack Connor. Reprinted with permission of Atlantic Monthly Press.

Jan DeBlieu: "April Blow," from *Hatteras Journal*. Copyright 1989 by Jan DeBlieu. Reprinted with permission of the author.

Daniel Duane: "Something Wicked This Way Comes," from *Outside* magazine. Copyright 1998 by Daniel Duane. Reprinted with permission of the author.

John Hay: "Who Owns the Beach?" from *The Great Beach* (University of New England Press, 1997). Copyright 1986 by John Hay. Reprinted with permission of W.W. Norton.

Marybeth Holleman: "In This Light." Copyright 1997 by Marybeth Holleman. Reprinted with permission of the author.

Gilbert Klingel: "The Marvel of a Tide," from *Inagua*. Copyright 1947 by Gilbert Klingel. Reprinted with permission of the Lyons Press.

$\mathcal{A}$BOUT THE $\mathcal{N}$ATURE CONSERVANCY AND THE COASTAL AND $\mathcal{M}$ARINE $\mathcal{P}$ROGRAM

The mission of The Nature Conservancy is to preserve plants, animals, and natural communities that represent the diversity of life on Earth by protecting the lands and waters they need to survive.

Founded in 1951, The Nature Conservancy is a private organization widely recognized as one of the most successful in the field of conservation. Among environmental organizations, we fill a unique niche: preserving habitats and species by protecting the lands and waters their survival requires.

The Nature Conservancy operates the largest private system of nature sanctuaries in the world—more than 1,500 preserves in the United States alone. Some are postage-stamp size, others cover thousands of acres. All of them safeguard imperiled species of plants and animals.

How The Nature Conservancy Identifies Land for Protection

How rare?

How threatened?

We answer these questions in a scientific inventory so we can decide which pieces of land to buy and protect. The inventory indicates the relative rarity of plant and animal species and whether or not they are protected. Once species are identified and ranked, the areas that shelter critically threatened species become the target of Conservancy projects.

How The Nature Conservancy Protects Habitat

The Conservancy works only with willing sellers and donors. We protect land through gifts, exchanges, conservation easements, management agreements, purchases from the Conservancy's revolving Land Preservation Fund, debt-for-nature swaps, and management partnerships. The Conservancy manages the resulting preserves with the most sophisticated ecological techniques available.

Sometimes we restore habitat by prescribed burnings. Another route is removing alien species. Sometimes we use reforestation or fencing—or whatever technique will maintain the preserves and encourage the growth of endangered plants and animals that live there. Most Conservancy preserves are open to the public for hiking, nature study, bird watching, and photography.

The Conservancy's International Program

Operating in the United States for the past forty-eight years, the Conservancy also has launched programs in Latin America, the Caribbean, Asia, and the Pacific.

The Asia-Pacific program, headquartered in Hawaii, is identifying and protecting threatened areas in China, Indonesia, Melanesia, and Micronesia. In Latin America, the Conservancy has joined forces with more than forty-five organizations covering twenty-two countries to provide community development, professional training, and funding for legally protected areas. The Conservancy has pioneered debt-for-nature swaps in Latin America.

The Nature Conservancy Coastal and Marine Program

The mission of The Nature Conservancy's Coastal and Marine Program is to protect and restore natural processes in marine ecosystems and preserve their full complement of biodiversity at select domestic and international sites.

The world's oceans, coastal waters, and estuaries cover 71 percent of the planet's surface and support much of its biodiversity—at least 400,000 organisms. They also help regulate climate, remove carbon dioxide from the atmosphere, and produce much of our oxygen supply. Most of the Earth's major animal groupings—from single-celled protozoa to complex mammals such as the blue whale—make their home in the world's saltwater environments. Moreover, new underwater technology continues to provide startling discoveries, and scientists estimate that as many as ten million yet-undiscovered species may exist in the deep sea alone—a diversity comparable to that of rain forests.

Unfortunately, unsustainable practices are plundering the world's richest and most diverse marine environments, putting at risk essential food supplies and altering entire ecosystems. Overharvesting, destructive fishing practices, habitat destruction, and degraded water quality are among the leading threats.

Many of The Nature Conservancy's marine sites are not exempt from these alarming trends. In response, the Conservancy has made marine conservation an institutional priority with the establishment of an organization-wide Coastal and Marine Program. The program will address the most serious threats to marine biodiversity, from cyanide fishing in the Asia-Pacific region to habitat destruction along the Gulf Coast to nutrification in the Caribbean.

The Conservancy is focusing its efforts on the following sites:

USA
Cobscook Bay, Maine
Peconic Bay, New York
Kachemak Bay, Arkansas
Laguna Madre, Texas and Mexico
Florida Keys, Florida
Apalachicola Bay, Florida
Willapa Bay, Washington
Grand Bay, Alabama
Great Bay, New Hampshire
Palmyra Atoll in the Central Pacific Ocean

Latin America and the Caribbean
Exuma Cays Land and Sea Park, Bahamas
Maya Mountains Marine Area Transect, Belize
Guaraquecaba Environmental Protection Area, Brazil
Sierra Nevada de Santa Maria, Colombia
Corcovado-OSA, Costa Rica
The Talamanca Caribbean Biological Corridor, Costa Rica
Jaragua National Park, Dominican Republic
Parque Nacional del Este, Dominican Republic
Machalilla National Park, Ecuador

Bocas del Polochic, Guatemala
Cerro San Gil/Gulf of Honduras, Guatemala
Rio Platano Biosphere Reserve, Honduras
El Pinacate and Gran Desierto del Altar Biosphere Reserve, Mexico
Isla Espiritu Santo Migratory Bird and Wildlife Refuge, Mexico
La Encrucijada Biosphere Reserve, Mexico
Laguna Madre, Mexico
Loreto Bay National Park, Mexico
Ría Celestún and Ría Lagartos Biosphere Reserves, Mexico
Sian Ka'an Biosphere Reserve, Mexico
Bocas del Toro, Panama
Paracas National Reserve, Peru
Magen's Bay, US Virgin Islands
St. Croix Marine Bioreserve, US Virgin Islands
Salt River Bay, US Virgin Islands
Los Roques Archipelago National Park, Venezuela

Asia and the Pacific
Arnavon Islands, Solomon Islands
Komodo National Park, Indonesia
Kimbe Bay, Papua New Guinea
The Palau Achipelago